ASK THE EXPERTS

Ask the Experts

HOW FORD, ROCKEFELLER, AND THE NEA CHANGED
AMERICAN MUSIC

Michael Sy Uy

OXFORD
UNIVERSITY PRESS

OXFORD
UNIVERSITY PRESS

Oxford University Press is a department of the University of Oxford. It furthers the University's objective of excellence in research, scholarship, and education by publishing worldwide. Oxford is a registered trade mark of Oxford University Press in the UK and certain other countries.

Published in the United States of America by Oxford University Press
198 Madison Avenue, New York, NY 10016, United States of America.

© Oxford University Press 2020

First issued as an Oxford University Press paperback, 2022

Library of Congress Cataloging-in-Publication Data
Names: Uy, Michael Sy, author.
Title: Ask the experts : how Ford, Rockefeller, and the NEA changed American music / Michael Sy Uy.
Description: [1.] | New York : Oxford University Press, 2020. |
Includes bibliographical references and index.
Identifiers: LCCN 2020008327 (print) | LCCN 2020008328 (ebook) |
ISBN 9780197510445 (hardback) | ISBN 9780197510452 (UPDF) |
ISBN 9780197510469 (epub) | ISBN 9780197510476 (Online) |
ISBN 9780197651490 (paperback)
Subjects: LCSH: Music patronage—United States—History—20th century. |
Government aid to music—United States—History—20th century. |
United States—Cultural policy—History—20th century. |
National Endowment for the Arts—History—20th century. |
Rockefeller Foundation—Music patronage—History—20th century. |
Ford Foundation—History—20th century.
Classification: LCC ML3917.U6 U9 2020 (print) |
LCC ML3917.U6 (ebook) | DDC 707.9/73—dc23
LC record available at https://lccn.loc.gov/2020008327
LC ebook record available at https://lccn.loc.gov/2020008328

For Mom, Dad, and Shobe

Contents

Acknowledgments

In writing this book, I've thought a lot about the importance of social networks, personal relationships, and communities. This book would not exist without the influence, support, and encouragement I received from colleagues, friends, and family.

DUNSTER HOUSE, LOWELL HOUSE, AND HARVARD COLLEGE

Over the past decade, two of my most invaluable communities have been Lowell House, where I was a graduate student, and Dunster House, where I now serve as the resident dean. My students serve as a constant source of inspiration, energy, and hope. With Cheryl Chen and Sean Kelly, the faculty deans of Dunster House, I've shared late-night discussions on many topics, sometimes helped with a bottle of wine—always with thoughtfulness and sensitivity, especially for the most difficult situations. I would be completely nonfunctional without Diana Hovsepian, our academic coordinator, whose compassion and judgment are completely unrivaled. I hope I can be as protective of her as she is of me. Thank you to Rachel Barbarisi, who helps keep Dunster running, and to Lucia Baldock, who always finds inspiring ways to turn Dunster from a House to a home. Our resident tutors are finding cures to melanoma and researching black conservative voters, all while being doctors, lawyers, and professional musicians and serving as mentors and advisers to our students. To the students: I'm a person of my word and committed to getting that tattoo, but only if Dunster wins the Strauss Cup.

Thank you to former faculty deans Diana Eck and Dorothy Austin for their loving stewardship of Lowell Love and to resident dean Caitlin Casey and house administrator Beth Terry, who are unsung heroines. A special thank you to Jonathan Bruno and Daria van Tyne (and my godson Albie), Kelly Miller, Allie Feldberg, Monica Bell, Daniel Adler, Jeremiah Wala, and Jess Yarmarkovich. Among the students, thank you especially to Dianisbeth Acquie and John Griffin for their reading eyes and research assistance. Thank you to Katie O'Dair for your friendship and mentorship and to Tiffanie Ting for our Dudley and dim sum dates.

HARVARD MUSIC DEPARTMENT AND MUSICOLOGY COLLEAGUES

At Harvard's Music Department, where I am a lecturer, I have benefited greatly from the wisdom and advice of colleagues and former teachers and mentors. Coteaching a course on social engagement through music with Carol Oja, Kay Shelemay, Matthew Leslie Santana, and Caitlin Schmid has been one of the most personally and intellectually rewarding experiences. The students got a glimpse of what it means to work as a recently immigrated musician, but we perhaps learned more about how pedagogy and scholarly study can have a direct impact on creative practice in our community. Thank you to Carol and Kay for your always thoughtful guidance and support, as well as your generosity in reading many drafts of this manuscript. I proffer my admiration and respect for Braxton Shelley, who is my Saloniki companion, as well as my spiritual inspiration. Kate Pukinskis's mirth, honesty, and baked goods have gotten me through many moments of despair and frustration. I am indebted to Luci Mok, whom I've known since our graduate school adventures—she's gotten me through many trying times with her almond cake and chapchae. I would also like to thank especially Eva Kim, Nancy Shafman, Les Bannatyne, Karen Rynne, Kaye Denny, Kerry Masteller, Anne Shreffler, Tom Kelly, Suzie Clark, and Kate van Orden for all of their support and encouragement. Eva has pushed me through all of life's Power 10s. Luci, Annie Searcy, Monica Hershberger, Caitlin Schmid, Will Robin, and Do Yoon Kim have read drafts of chapters of this book and I thank them for their invaluable feedback and suggestions.

My life would not be the same had it not been for Davitt Moroney's support throughout some very formative years. UBE's performance of Brandenburg 3 is still my favorite. My colleagues in the Hearing Landscape Critically network gave me some of the most exciting of adventures and challenging of conversations: thank you to Jo Hicks, Carina Venter, Dan Grimley, and Stephanus Muller. Jo, you'll always be my favorite AMS roommate. Thank you to Tiffany Kuo, whom I could always vent to while sharing Cajun shrimp at AMS or DTLA, and to Eduardo Herrera, who had the coolest magic tricks.

THE FIELD

The Rockefeller Archive Center provided me two research grants to carry out the largest part of my research on the Ford and Rockefeller Foundations. Thank you to everyone with whom I shared meals and conversations during lunch or on the shuttle. Thank you especially to Lucas Buresch, Bethany Antos, Pat Rosenfeld, and James Allen Smith. While Howard Klein and I may disagree on the interpretation of history, I will always respect and admire his work and dedication to the musical arts.

During the summer of 2014, I interned in the Design Department of the NEA. Thank you to all of my friends and colleagues there, and especially Jason Schupbach, Jen Hughes, Courtney Spearman, Ana Steele, John Clark, Sali Ann Kriegsman, Court Burns, Jennifer Kareliusson, Patricia Loiko, Anya Nykyforiak, Kathy Plowitz-Worden, and Douglas Sonntag. Ana and Sali Ann are treasured DC friends, whom I look forward to seeing every time I'm in town.

BOSTON

As a natural introvert, I relish spending hours alone in archives with materials, or writing in cafés. Thankfully, many of my friends and family have ensured that I have a life outside the library and work. Thank you to Jonathan Fanton, who has always been an inspiring friend and wise sounding board: I'll see you next time at Parsnip's corner table. My rock-climbing crew kept me reaching for higher and higher heights, afterward rewarding ourselves with culinary treats from Jamie Song and Jen Huang's kitchen. My Pandemic team indulged me in my efforts to search for laboratories, even at the risk of permanent scarring. Jen, Ray Di Ciaccio, and Tim Tregubov, you make excellent scientists, researchers, and soldiers—or whatever they're called in the second season. I owe a lifetime's supply of Nespresso to my Baker/Chao friends: Gao Cheng, Gordon Liao, and Do Yoon Kim. I'll miss taking full advantage of the Faculty Commons, discussing credit card perks, and practicing case interviews. Thank you to Sarah Nam and our Iberian adventures. Francisco Lopez, Danielle Qi, Hannah Choi, and Bryan Tseng all deserve numerous Encores, and I always look forward to Sunday crêpes with Francisco and Jérôme Michon. Tieying Yu, Michel Anteby, and Patrick Autreaux make the brightest Lantern Festival companions.

THANKS ABOVE ALL

Thank you to Suzanne Ryan, who saw promise in this book from day one, moving with incredible swiftness and guidance, and to Mary Horn for her help throughout the submission and production process.

Thank you to Norman Hirschy for his continued shepherding, especially with the paperback version of this book.

My family and my friends are my joy in life, even if I don't always emote it. Thank you to Jarrad Aguirre, Julie Bastianutti, Hendrik Coldenstrodt-Ronge, Trang Ho, Matthew Morton, Kuong Ly, Rowland Moseley, Ryan Palapaz, Lillian Tung, Cristiano Amoruso, and Stacey Wallace for years of friendship and memories, and often, places to crash. Nicole Yoneda, Jecy Furlani, and Aaron Rios, I've traveled the world with you, witnessing—and sometimes participating—in your memorable shenanigans. Know that you are my best friends in Vegas, Portland, Boston, Berkeley, Los Angeles, Brussels, and all the universe. Michael Azarian and Anthony Sion, I know of few others who are as generous and thoughtful as you both—I cannot wait for you to be parents to adorable and stylish WeHo babies. Aunt Alex, Uncle Colin, and Claudia, you were and are my English family—the next bottle of Veuve is on me. Shobe, mom, and dad, I love you and am grateful for all of your sacrifices, devotion, and care. I never would have made it this far without your love, free eye drops, bak kut teng, all-you-can-eat sushi, and birthday misua.

INTRODUCTION

NAME. PROJECT DESCRIPTION. Qualifications. Amount Requested. For artists, it's hard to imagine a world without grant applications. Grants-in-aid pay for
specialized study, the cost of equipment, free or reduced-price concerts, and numerous other activities and endeavors. Although asking for financial assistance is not
unique to our time, filling out application forms seems to have achieved a level of
bureaucratic morass that many artists (and academics) can sympathize with. When
exactly did the institutional grant become so ubiquitous—such a normalized means
of funding the arts in the United States? And how are grants evaluated—by which
criteria, by which experts?

One answer comes from public and private arts grantmaking of the 1950s, 1960s,
and 1970s, when the United States experienced a remarkable Big Bang in patronage. After the end of World War II through the U.S. Bicentennial, the National
Endowment for the Arts (NEA), the Rockefeller Foundation, and the Ford
Foundation granted close to $300 million (approximately $2 billion in 2017 dollars) in the field of music alone.[1] Rockefeller's support in music prior to the 1950s
had totaled less than $200,000 over four decades, and Ford had only helped local
music groups near its headquarters in Detroit, Michigan. Apart from a few grants
given by the Carnegie Corporation, no other foundations invested in music or the

Ask the Experts. Michael Sy Uy, Oxford University Press (2020). © Oxford University Press.
DOI: 10.1093/oso/9780197510445.001.0001.

arts. Between the 1950s and 1970s, Ford, Rockefeller, and the NEA served as critical financial patrons for composers, performers, symphony orchestras, opera companies, and university music centers. They sought to increase not only the supply
of music but also the demand for it. Access to professional performances was at the
heart of this postwar cultural ideology, captured in the Ford Foundation's call for
"Millions for Music—Music for Millions."[2]

At the time, educator and historian Ralph Smith characterized the new infra-
structure as a "policymaking complex in cultural and educational affairs . . . shaped
in the Washington bureaucracy and represent[ing] an official's view of the relations
of art, culture, and education."[3] In the words of sociologist Howard Becker, a new
musical "art world" had emerged in the United States.[4] The particularly American
notion of matching grants—where grantees needed to "match" support from other
sources of income—ensured that a mixture of public and private funding dominated
music making in this country. It also guaranteed that the system of arts and music
patronage differed from those of continental Europe and Great Britain.[5]

While this book is titled after three institutions, it's important to remember that
institutions are operated by people. Individuals act as trustees, program officers, and
consultants, and they legitimize their work through "expertise" and "expert consultation." Therefore, the main theoretical framework in this study is a "sociology of
expertise," applied to the arts. Sociologist Robert Evans first explored this area in
2008, with his examination of expert knowledge in modern society, but there has
hitherto been no thorough investigation of how artists and arts funders have functioned as experts in twentieth-century America.[6] Government officials, foundation
leaders, corporate officers, and other members of the "power elite"—to borrow the
term from mid-twentieth-century sociologist C. Wright Mills—valued "expertise"
during an age of scientific and technological progress, bureaucratic management,
and Cold War insecurity.[7] Different kinds and levels of expertise influenced how
individuals approved or rejected grant applications and how they interacted with
each other in the decision-making process. Foundation and government officers
established criteria of excellence and value in the arts that they derived from seemingly objective models of expertise in the sciences.[8] Their system design, however,
also relied on other features.

One of these features was who decided who was an expert. In practice, foundation and Arts Endowment (NEA) staff during this grantmaking period drew upon
a limited set of expertise, primarily from composers at elite institutions, professors
from prestigious northeast universities, and leaders of performing arts service organizations. Among the most influential and widely sought expert-consultants were
Leonard Bernstein, Aaron Copland, Lukas Foss, and Milton Babbitt. The significance was twofold: not only were male, Western high art composers put in charge of

directing large and unprecedented channels of public and private funds, but also, in so doing, they determined and defined what was meant by artistic excellence, deciding the fate of their peers and shaping the direction of music making in this country.

Expertise thus cannot be considered solely an objective or neutral quality, especially in arts grantmaking; rather, it was an exclusionary form of cultural and social capital that only selected members of society were deemed to possess. It was a relational resource and its exercise was a fundamentally social and interactional activity. The system operated under a hierarchy, with some individuals more powerful and influential than others. As sociologist Pierre Bourdieu contends, cultural and social capital were distributed and accumulated in ways greatly influenced by structures of power.[9] Society's trust in experts was rooted in such differences of capital among individuals.

By codifying particular subjectivities and casting them as examples of excellence, this funding model tended to overlook and exclude performers of non-Western music, amateur music makers, folk musicians, and jazz artists. Expertise was exclusionary because its possessors transmitted it through first-degree connections among funders and the consultants they brought into the system. The network of "mutual friends" was tight. Focusing mainly on Western high art traditions, experts provided a service that legitimized government and foundation programs, as well as attached prestige to the decisions these institutions made.

By focusing on the roles of the NEA and the Rockefeller and Ford Foundations, *Ask the Experts* undertakes a sociocultural examination of aesthetic tastes for, and the valorization of, Western art music—avant-garde and classical. The social and moral roles of art music in the United States have long been contested: from the writings of Alexis de Tocqueville, who in the middle of the nineteenth century predicted the democratization of the production and appreciation of art, through Thorstein Veblen, who argued at the beginning of the twentieth century that art works and attendance at arts events had become badges of social standing for the wealthy and leisured classes.[10] A sociocultural approach analyzes how artists and grantmakers distinguished highbrow and lowbrow art in the mid-twentieth century, what little room they allowed for popular and indigenous forms of music, and why they focused on expensive performing arts institutions such as symphony orchestras and opera companies.

The Origins of the Rockefeller Foundation, Ford Foundation, and NEA

Private philanthropy has long played a significant role in arts and music patronage in the United States. From the middle of the nineteenth century, wealthy individuals like Louise Curtis Bok, Elizabeth Sprague Coolidge, Isabella Stewart Gardner, Henry Higginson, and Jeanette Meyer Thurber, among many others, opened their checkbooks and their homes for musicians and composers, orchestra associations, and opera societies.[11] Many of these patrons, women especially, committed vast sums of money and time to an art form to which they were firmly devoted. Not until the mid-twentieth century, however, did large private philanthropic foundations enter the picture. Compared to wealthy individual giving, the foundations institutionalized and bureaucratized arts programming into professional, organizational missions.

While some scholars and former foundation officers have begun documenting the mainstream work of the Rockefeller and Ford Foundations, there has yet to be a thorough study of these two institutions' arts and culture programs. Similarly, there has been very little analysis of the NEA's music program, despite it being the largest division by budget. Each organization took its own path to music funding, but they all had ambitions toward some public good or societal benefit.

The Rockefeller Foundation, the oldest of the three, was established in 1913 by John D. Rockefeller, explicitly "to promote the well-being of mankind throughout the world."[12] Rockefeller had made a significant amount of money in the oil industry, and he was possibly the wealthiest American of all time.[13] Under the guidance of his advisor, Baptist minister Frederick Taylor Gates, Rockefeller revolutionized philanthropy in the United States. Within the foundation's first year, he donated $100 million—followed by another $82.8 million in 1919—turning the foundation into the largest philanthropic enterprise in the world at the time. Those contributions combined amounted to roughly $3 billion in current value. The Rockefeller Foundation surpassed the net worth of both the Russell Sage Foundation (est. 1907) and the Carnegie Corporation (est. 1911).

The Ford Foundation was established two decades later in 1936. It was, and continues to be, a private, nonprofit institution "incorporated for charitable, educational, and scientific purposes" for the "advancement of human welfare."[14] While formed by an initial gift of $25,000 from Edsel Ford—son of Henry Ford, founder of the motor company—the company did not control the foundation, nor did the foundation have control of the company. When Edsel and Henry Ford died in the 1940s, their stock bequests turned the Ford Foundation into the largest philanthropic organization in the world, with assets estimated around $480 million ($8.4 billion in 2017).[15] As of 2018, it is the second largest foundation, after the Bill and Melinda Gates Foundation (est. 2000), although with recent trends in private philanthropy, its status may change.

Both the Ford and Rockefeller Foundations, however, originally disregarded the arts from their philanthropic missions. Instead, they devoted their resources to efforts such as the alleviation of global hunger, the expansion of American higher education, and the eradication of hookworm. Not until after World War II did they start giving substantial funds to the arts and humanities. The Rockefeller Foundation began projects in new music, like the Louisville Orchestra commissions, operas and ballets at New York's City Center, and the work of the "creative associates" at the State University of New York at Buffalo. It also gave a massive $15 million grant to the Lincoln Center (the equivalent of roughly $130 million in 2017) and $1 million to the Kennedy Center. The Ford Foundation in 1966 granted a colossal sum of $80.2 million ($620 million) to sixty-one American orchestras. According to its annual report, this was "the largest single amount ever given to the arts by any foundation."[16] It also held several concert artist and vocal artist competitions between 1959 and 1969, which resulted in new music commissions. In total, between 1953 and 1976, the Ford Foundation gave more than $140 million ($1 billion) to the field of music, while the Rockefeller Foundation granted more than $30 million ($210 million).[17]

The origins of large-scale government arts funding also began around the same time as the Ford Foundation's establishment, but without initial permanency. During the Great Depression, the Works Progress Administration and its Theater and Music Projects employed thousands of artists to paint murals on the sides of buildings, perform stage plays in parks, and hold symphony concerts in railway stations.[18] It operated twenty-eight symphony orchestras and offered 225,000 performances for 150 million people. The Works Progress Administration was a powerful and memorable symbol of government work in the arts, sparking public interest and demonstrating that the arts could be a national concern. Unfortunately, momentum staggered.

Similar to Ford and Rockefeller, not until after the war and into the 1960s did the federal government firmly enter the arts and establish an independent agency. The confluence of arts activity among the three institutions in the midcentury was no accident. Scholar Gary Larson suggests three major trends in the field that led to the NEA: first, greater organization of the "arts lobby"; second, solidification of a federal arts plan into a highly rationalized framework; and third, evolution from an extreme hands-off government arts policy to an activist stance that favored ambitious federal involvement.[19]

Presidential and congressional support dramatically increased. Senators Claiborne Pell (D-RI), Jacob Javits (R-NY), and Hubert Humphrey (D-MN), as well as Representative Frank Thompson Jr. (D-NJ) were stalwart and indefatigable arts advocates in Congress. With President John F. Kennedy's election, First Lady Jacqueline Kennedy began inviting internationally renowned musicians like Pablo Casals to the White House, cultivating an arts-friendly environment. Through

Executive Order 11112, President Kennedy formed the Advisory Council on the Arts. President Lyndon B. Johnson developed this body into the National Council on the Arts after Kennedy's assassination. Two years later in 1965, the NEA was established by the Arts and Humanities Act, written and passed by Congress. Its annual budget began at $5 million ($40 million in 2017), but by 1976, it was well over $90 million ($390 million), an upward trend it continued until 1982 when it received its first cut under President Ronald Reagan.[20] Between 1965 and 1976, the NEA granted over $110 million ($800 million) in the field of music, its largest program in the arts.[21]

Setting the Stage: The Early Cold War

As many scholars have recounted, growing tensions with the Soviet Union and the emergence of the Cold War had a large—albeit often unclear and indirect—impact on music and the arts.[22] Historian Donna Binkiewicz has characterized the cultural environment of the 1950s as a time when the United States was accused of having become "conformist, materialist, complacent, and aesthetically deplorable."[23] According to Representative Frank Thompson Jr. (D-NJ), the country needed to make "Washington the cultural center of the world," which "would be one of the very best and most effective ways to answer the Russian lies and defeat their heavily financed effort to have Communism take over the world."[24] In other words, the United States needed to launch its own cultural *Sputnik* and show it wasn't a country of "gum-chewing barbarians."[25] As musicologists Emily Abrams Ansari and Danielle Fosler-Lussier have both demonstrated in their work on the State Department's cultural sponsorship, the federal government took proactive, multifaceted approaches to music patronage and the cultivation of an American image abroad.[26]

But the issue was not just about the United States investing more in music and the arts. Less studied has been the political and economic impacts the Cold War environment had on other funding institutions and the ways they approached the making of, and listening to, music. Beginning in the 1950s, both political parties raised suspicions against private foundations. Republicans believed that some foundations used their resources to support communist causes; Democrats worried that the wealthy employed the larger ones as tax shelters. Foundations were stuck in a tough place and critics were ubiquitous. Under the revisions implemented by the Revenue Act of 1950, foundations could lose their tax-exempt status if their records showed that they mainly served for capital accumulation or if they diverted income to donors through tax evasion schemes.

In 1953, the same year as the Rockefeller Foundation's first large-scale music and arts grants, the Cox and Reece congressional investigations challenged foundations' favored tax positions, as well as a number of charities and schools. Representative Brazilla Carroll Reece (R-TN) accused Ford, Rockefeller, and Carnegie of being involved in a "diabolical conspiracy" with educational institutions such as Columbia University, Harvard University, the University of Chicago, and the University of California to impose socialism on the American people.[27] Political scientist Joan Roelofs attributes these investigations to a "populist reaction against the corporate-liberal-internationalist thrust of the 'Eastern Establishment.'"[28] The specter of McCarthyism loomed large, and despite the fact that Congress enacted no directly negative sanctions on the foundations, the investigations generated anxiety and uncertainty in the field of grantmaking.

The case against them continued in the House in 1961, again focusing on issues of tax evasion and the concentration of wealth in the hands of a few. Representative Wright Patman (D-TX) investigated, in particular, foundations' competition with small businesses, their use to commit fraud, and their international activities. Patman questioned Ford's grants to members of Robert Kennedy's staff after his assassination, as well as a grant for voter registration efforts by the Cleveland Congress of Racial Equality.[29] After the House investigations, the Senate continued to pursue the topic. One proposal, referred to by Senator Walter Mondale (D-MN) as the "death sentence amendment," capped a foundation's life span to forty years. Submitted by Senator Albert Gore Sr. (D-TN), father of the later U.S. vice president, it was ultimately defeated.

Admittedly, isolating the precise impacts of these congressional investigations on Ford and Rockefeller's arts grantmaking is a difficult task: whether laws concerning foundation operations had direct effects on arts expenditures, or whether the Cold War environment of paranoia pushed foundations toward more conservative projects is hard to say. Nevertheless, there were at least some archival traces and insider histories that revealed how the investigations and legislation impacted the field.

For instance, officers sometimes cross-checked grantees for potential communist affiliations. The Bennington College Composers' Conference—a grant that supported chamber music workshops—was one of several examples where Rockefeller Foundation officers referenced participants' names with indices such as the McCarran Committee hearings on Communist tactics in controlling youth organizations (1952), the Velde Committee hearings (1953), the McCarthy Committee composite index (1953), and the McCarran Committee hearings on subversive infiltration of the radio, television, and entertainment industry (1952), *inter alia*.[30] In later years, the list of indices grew longer to account for newer potentially "subversive" organizations. The fact that Rockefeller officers wrote comments next to certain individuals suggested that these references were not pro forma.[31]

At the Ford Foundation, long-time director of the Office of Reports Richard Magat noted that the trustees, "believing it desirable to make a highly visible public impression with safe and popular grants," produced the $550 million ($5 billion in 2017) "Christmas package" to support college faculty, hospitals, and medical schools in the mid-1950s.[32] A year after the conclusion of the Cox and Reece investigations, these large, "popular," and "safe" grants were a form of "image repair" reinforcing Ford's contributions to the public good. In 1965, the $80 million grant to symphony orchestras also served the dual role of providing a nonthreatening and publicity-generating grant while allowing the foundation to spend a large amount of money in a short time period to avoid significant capital gains taxes. In program director Paul Ylvisaker's oral history, he recounted how Ford Foundation vice president W. McNeil Lowry wanted a "blockbuster" and that "nobody was going to stand in the way of this thing" because "how could you say anything against symphonies?"[33] Ylvisaker noted the strong connection between trustees and membership on the boards of symphony orchestras, as well as the grant having an impact in "the social pages."

These examples demonstrated that congressional investigations and the resulting legislation had, at a minimum, two impacts on Ford and Rockefeller's arts grantmaking: first, the background screening and more careful selection of grant recipients, and second, the support of "popular" and "safe" projects as a way to quickly spend money from the selling of stocks. These changes to the field were meaningful not only because of the contested political environment—the gamut from McCarthyism to anti-Establishment and populist sentiment—which Congress codified in rules and regulations, but also the shifts that occurred within individual actors' worldviews, from risk loving to risk aversion, from the pursuit of innovation to a more level-headed conservatism. The relationships between the Cold War and their attitudes were inseparable and mutually constitutive.

The Growing Cultural Movement

At the same time, the United States experienced—what the mainstream press called—a "cultural explosion" during the 1960s and 1970s.[34] An influx of artists, writers, and musicians who had emigrated from Europe before and during World War II contributed to this growth. Famous composers such as Arnold Schoenberg, Kurt Weill, and Erich Korngold had fled Nazi Germany as a result of the monstrosities committed against Jews. Although the United States did not welcome all emigrants with open arms, these artists nevertheless contributed greatly to music written at universities and in Hollywood.

Additionally, a number of significant reports on the performing arts added fodder to the cultural boom; they galvanized the arts community by providing economic data to justify greater support. The reports included studies by August Heckscher, the Rockefeller Brothers Fund (RBF), and Princeton professors William Baumol and William Bowen.[35] The RBF publication "The Performing Arts: Problems and Prospects," for instance, proclaimed that the arts were necessary to attain "the emotional, intellectual, and aesthetic satisfactions that constitute [human beings'] higher needs."[36] As former NEA music director Fannie Taylor noted, the fact that the RBF report was made by a "prestigious organization caused it to become front-page news," and as a result, the arts experienced a "tremendous expansion of interest."[37] A large amount of money and political energy moved into the nation's cultural development.

Princeton economists Baumol and Bowen moreover supplied an economic theory justifying the necessity of arts funding.[38] In their first article, "On the Performing Arts: The Anatomy of Their Economic Problems," they contended that there were "fundamental reasons to expect the financial strains which beset the performing arts organizations to increase, chronically, with the passage of time."[39] The sector lacked "productivity improvements," which meant that there was "no offsetting improvement in output per man-hour, and so every increase in money wages is translated automatically into an equivalent increase in unit labor costs."[40] Baumol and Bowen illustrated precisely this theory with their example that a Beethoven string quartet needed the same number of musicians to perform it in the present day as it did in the nineteenth century.[41] Yet while the musicians could not play the work in half the time (i.e., a productivity improvement), their wages—and thus the costs—had increased.[42] The theory became known as Baumol's cost disease, or the Baumol effect, and it helped explain the increasing expensiveness of the performing arts, offering a reason they could not survive on ticket sales alone.

The cultural boom of the 1960s, however, was followed by a retrenchment toward the end of the 1970s. One of the causes was the aforementioned unfriendly political climate. Another was the economic downturn, which limited resources and what foundations did with those resources. The recession that began in 1973 sharply reduced the market value of foundation assets from between 30% and 60%.[43] The Tax Reform Act of 1969 had imposed an excise tax on foundation investment income and established a minimum payout rate, in addition to other regulations.[44] Finally, the incremental easing of tensions with the Soviet Union under détente decreased pressures of supercharging both the military industrial complex and the cultural explosion.

There are several reasons that 1976—the U.S. Bicentennial—thus serves as an appropriate conclusion to this book. First, the Rockefeller Foundation and NEA celebrated the occasion with some of its largest grants in the field of music—the NEA gave commissions and awards to composers, jazz musicians, and folk musicians, and the Rockefeller Foundation produced a hundred-LP collection to celebrate two hundred years of music in the United States. Second, the Ford Foundation and NEA experienced significant leadership changes: Ford's vice president W. McNeil Lowry had retired in 1974 (Lowry was contemporaneously compared to the Medici of arts philanthropy), and the NEA's second chairman Nancy Hanks stepped down in 1977 after supervising an exponential growth of the federal agency during her tenure. Third, after the Bicentennial, the arts and music budgets of the Ford and Rockefeller Foundations shrank in size, from tens of millions of dollars to just a few million dollars a year. A reduction in the number of arts and humanities staff accompanied the budget decreases. Therefore, between the 1950s and 1970s, the arts field underwent a catalytic expansion, with the establishment of some roots, followed by a period of decline and uncertainty about the future.

The Critical Role of Institutions and Individuals Supporting Western Art Music

Ask the Experts investigates three heretofore underexamined organizations by analyzing thousands of archival documents, memoranda, and correspondence, and interviewing officers and consultants past and present. Its interdisciplinary approach engages with debates surrounding the sociology of art and music and the sociology of expertise, awards, and recognition most recently elucidated in the work of Michèle Lamont, Gloria Origgi, Harry Collins, and Robert Evans. This sociocultural approach examines what sociologist Pierre Bourdieu refers to as the "field of cultural production" to understand how this system of grantmaking produced its outcomes.[45]

Over the past two decades, there has been a large surge in the critical examination of Western cultural institutions.[46] "Cultural production" is not a straightforward process, nor is it easily achieved through official policies, especially with higher-order organizations like private foundations and government agencies. Institutions are composed of individuals, and while individuals often come to agree on codified rules and policies, institutions are never monolithic. Due to organizational structures and hierarchies, some individuals are more powerful and influential than others. A government agency, for example, actively seeking to "produce" a specific culture would need a high degree of autonomy and capacity, with an explicit agenda that all members abide by.

Yet this institutional cohesion was rarely achieved in toto, and one did not find complete consistency in policy at the NEA, Ford, or Rockefeller Foundations. As sociologist Paul DiMaggio observed, the NEA at the time was usually reacting "to the pressures upon it rather than boldly articulating visions concrete enough to serve as bases for action."[47] Any analysis of the field of cultural production cannot reduce its unit to the level of institution, but must push further to the individuals that made up these institutions. As musicologist Eduardo Herrera reminds us, institutions are "peopled."[48] Thus, it was never just the "Rockefeller Foundation" that shaped the course of music history, but the officers and directors. Individuals were the levers and motors that operated these institutions. They too were connected to a broader network of people at other funding bodies, nonprofit organizations, and government agencies.[49]

Ask the Experts focuses on not only individuals working within institutions but also how they came to concentrate on elite and professional support of "Western art music." This style of, and approach toward, musical composition, performance, and listening goes by many different names—twentieth-century American society often refers to it simply as "classical music."[50] The music has historical roots in Western Europe (i.e., primarily Austro-Germany, France, and the Italian states), with the typical account rehearsing the changes between monophony and polyphony in the "Middle Ages" to the present.[51] It is not my intention to articulate all the differences that actually make up "classical music," "Western art music," or "serious music"— terms I use interchangeably—because music has always been a product of many social, cultural, economic, and political processes. Instead, I focus on Western art music's position in the American midcentury, as a predominantly noncommercial musical practice, distinguished by what musicologist H. Wiley Hitchcock famously referred to as its "cultivated" nature.[52] In *Ask the Experts*, Western art music took generally two main forms: first, orchestral, symphonic, and operatic performances and commissions, and second, newly written and performed modernist, avant-garde works. "Modernism" refers not just to the contemporary and present, but also to an artistic stance of pursuing the "modern."

Western art music provided a crucial link in the grantmaking system: composers and performers determined the music's high aesthetic value and cultural capital, and the nation's largest and wealthiest foundations and the federal government employed these composers and performers. In particular, composers of both serial and electronic music, working in elite university environments, capitalized on the scientific, mathematical, and technological allure of their compositional styles, which foundation officers found attractive. A strong collaborative bond united Western high art music with grantmaking after World War II, perpetuating ideologies of privilege and elitism in the system.

Western art music stood in contrast to other musical and cultural practices in the United States. The focus on classical music was to the almost complete exclusion of non-Western musics, jazz, and folk music, with the notable exception of several NEA programs. There was a clear lack of diversity—racial, geographic, gender-based, and social—in the funding system. U.S. society experienced not just the radical shifts in political and cultural attitudes as a result of the Cold War, but also the civil rights movement, the black arts movement, second-wave feminism, the Vietnam War, and the LGBT movement throughout the 1950s, 1960s, and 1970s. The NEA, in contrast to the Ford and Rockefeller Foundations, paid special attention to geographic and racial minorities—which it defined as persons from "four major ethnic or racial groups: blacks, Spanish-Americans, American Indians, and Asian-Americans."[53] In a grantmaking field that white men predominantly governed, the NEA exhibited several exceptions among its officers, including chairman Nancy Hanks and music director Walter Anderson.

Chapter Overview

The arts and music programs of Ford, Rockefeller, and the NEA could each be subjects of books in their own right, but much would be lost without comparing their work side by side. By examining all three, one can see the large overlap in the employment of the same consultants and experts, the officials who moved in and out of these institutions, the relationships between public and private sources of arts funding, and the different prioritizations of genre, style, and innovation. These arguments could not be made by looking at each organization in isolation.

How did they ask the experts? Part I of this book discusses two kinds of experts: first, performing artists, composers, and leaders who served as consultants and peer reviewers, and second, foundation and NEA officers who institutionalized this system of grantmaking based on models of scientific objectivity. Part II illustrates how Ford, Rockefeller, and the NEA carried out their visions of shaping music making in the United States in their own distinctive ways, whether through matching grants, university music centers, or jazz and folk music.

The overarching theme of Part I (Chapters 1, 2, and 3) is "Who Were the Experts?" The first of these chapters begins with several definitions and understandings of expertise, as well as its relational and social aspects. The first chapter then investigates the role of artists and arts managers as "contributory experts." Grantmaking institutions invited consultants and panelists to help them make cultural policy. One Rockefeller Foundation vice president referred to his music advisory committee as his "wise men."[54] They provided the "knowledge and stature" to guide the foundation in "the most creative and promising direction." These experts, in turn, determined and defined artistic excellence and quality. These "wise men" decided the fate of hundreds of millions of dollars in music, choosing which kinds of music and which composers and performers received foundation and government money. Experts evaluated criteria they believed to be objective, such as budget data, project feasibility, and measured outcomes, in conjunction with their own subjective criteria, such as individual taste and preference. Peer and expert review provided a system of legitimization and authority while concentrating power in a remarkably small and overlapping network of artists.

The second chapter elucidates the previously opaque and little-understood roles of foundation and NEA staff and officers, or "philanthropoids" as famous American writer Dwight Macdonald referred to them in a *New Yorker* article from the period. These officers included program directors Walter Anderson (NEA) and Norman Lloyd (Rockefeller); vice president W. McNeil Lowry (Ford); and chairmen Roger Stevens (NEA) and Nancy Hanks (NEA). Foundation and NEA officers, as well as board of trustee members, can be considered "interactional experts"—even if they did not regularly self-identify as "experts"—with tremendous influence in the operation of the system. They decided the kinds of outside voices that were heard in the process. They were gatekeepers, interlocutors, and translators between the outside consultants they recruited and grant applicants. They wielded the almighty red and black pens and their Rolodexes were a who's who of asked experts.

The third chapter discusses a number of issues regarding coordination, cooperation, and competition between the federal government and private philanthropic organizations. As a federal agency, the NEA was mandated to serve broadly the interests of all citizens, groups, and communities. Private foundations, on the other hand, could decide to uniquely tailor their chosen missions. Regardless of differences in institutional practices and operation, however, the NEA, Ford, and Rockefeller collectively served as weathervanes in the field. Their "seals of approval" guided the decision making of individual patrons, smaller foundations, state art agencies, and multinational corporations. Furthermore, their matching requirements concentrated winners and excluded losers because most often, matching grant recipients already possessed other sources of social and economic capital. After the Tax Reform Act of 1969, foundations and the federal government found even more reasons to communicate and cooperate with one another, including at high-powered meetings in New York like the Rockefeller Foundation's "How Can Foundations Help the Arts?" meeting in 1974.

The second half of the book explores "experts in action." While all three institutions utilized a core group of experts in similar ways, they also accomplished their own separate goals. Chapters 4, 5, and 6 demonstrate how experts in action supported different kinds of music in the United States.

The fourth chapter focuses on the Rockefeller Foundation and its support of university new music centers and contemporary chamber ensembles. Most notably, composers at Columbia University, Princeton University, the University of Chicago, and Mills College served dually as outside experts *and* commissioned artists and performers. For example, Milton Babbitt, Otto Luening, and Vladimir Ussachevsky benefited greatly from their involvement in the Rockefeller Foundation and the Columbia-Princeton Electronic Music Center. This chapter offers new insights into a commonly understood historiography of twentieth-century music in the United States: the dominance and prestige of avant-garde music and serialism at American universities. Rockefeller's commitment to new music centers demonstrated their desire to develop and expand regional centers across the country and to support key artists. The composers and performers, in turn, justified their work initially through the Soviet threat and rivalries with European electronic studios, and later with experimentalism, innovation, and creativity. The new music ensembles solidified a musical circuit that crisscrossed the country, making stops at many Rockefeller-funded centers. The foundation revealed ways it was both an advertent and inadvertent patron of what writer and *New Yorker* critic Winthrop Sargeant pejoratively referred to as "foundation music."

The fifth chapter examines the Ford Foundation's predominantly economics- and finance-based expertise, and the way it sustained the country's largest and most expensive performing arts institutions: orchestras, opera companies, and conservatories. Ford accomplished its goals primarily through the funding tools of matching grants and endowments. It designed its matching requirements with the hope of diversifying organizations' sources of funding and expanding everyday citizens' involvement and commitment to local arts. Based on the expert advice of economists and arts administrators, Ford intended endowments to be a permanent source of income for orchestras and conservatories, if they managed the invested principal properly. In practice, however, wealthy individuals on boards of trustees for institutions such as the Boston Symphony Orchestra and the Juilliard School solidified their personal, social connections to elicit five-, six-, and sometimes seven-figure gifts. In general, ordinary citizens and the local community did not participate, and as a result, broad-based support never materialized. Orchestras and conservatories came back knocking on the foundation's door again and again.

The last chapter returns to the NEA and its jazz program, Expansion Arts division, Bicentennial fellowships for "jazz/folk/ethnic" artists, and Folk Arts division. While the NEA mirrored a policy of matching requirements in its Treasury grants— which by and large supported mostly symphony orchestras—it also provided several millions of dollars to otherwise underrepresented and undersupported artists and communities. Not only were the NEA's officers keenly committed to helping jazz and folk music, but also they brought in experts from urban, suburban, and rural communities to work as program directors. Vantile Whitfield and A.B. Spellman—key figures in the black arts movement of the 1970s—became directors of its Expansion Arts division. These experts recruited panelists of a broader geographical, racial, and gender representation, and similarly funded more diverse musicians and artists. The NEA was not a perfect archetype of egalitarian grantmaking—more than nine-tenths of its music funds during the 1960s and 1970s went to Western art music genres. But compared to the Ford and Rockefeller Foundations, which rarely provided funding to jazz or the music of minority communities, the government agency was a lifeline to otherwise unseen and unheard cultural practices.

Finally, the epilogue discusses recent developments in arts funding and philanthropy. The field has undergone notable changes since the 1970s, with new trends of giving, political readjustments, and the questioning of the role of experts in decision making. The divergent paths of Rockefeller and Ford—where the former discontinued its arts program and the latter rebranded its cultural work in terms of addressing "inequality"—is a revealing outcome of the increasing social and economic legitimation of arts funding. The NEA experienced its first budget cut under President Reagan, and in the 1990s, amid the culture wars, Congress slashed its budget nearly in half. The culture wars generated a hostile environment for governmental arts funding, which continued into the new millennium. Private contributions increasingly took up the slack, but not without their own challenges. There are now three times as many foundations as there were in the 1970s.[55] New philanthropists are exploring options such as limited liability corporations, donor-advised funds, and metrics and outcomes-based funding. With increasing economic and political inequality and decreasing civic engagement, it might be time to re-evaluate the government funds foregone because of tax-deductible charitable contributions, and the ways the federal government is better suited to provide and distribute resources more equitably. Finally, in a world of growing social media influence and influencers, and claims and counterclaims of "fake news," an ethics of expertise is more critical, as is a discussion on the future role of the expert.

Conclusion

A number of moral and ethical questions arise given the structure of arts grantmaking based on expertise after World War II. The first was the role of government money in a U.S. capitalistic system that had historically viewed arts support as a matter of private initiative. When the federal government entered the field in 1965, it worked closely with private philanthropies and individuals—in fact, many of its initial leaders came from the foundation world, including Nancy Hanks. The NEA made the vast majority of its grants on a matching basis, for fear that the government crowded out private funding. But the matching system was biased toward organizations that already had the capacity to elicit other sources of funding. How and whether the government should redistribute money to a wider variety of recipients were questions of equity. Furthermore, how and whether private foundations, as nonprofit organizations that received tax benefits, should distribute their money to a diversity of grantees were also issues of cultural pluralism and democracy.

A final set of questions revolves around the worthiness of grant recipients, powerfully intertwined with arguments involving quality and merit. Over the past decade, greater attention has been paid to challenging the assumptions or taken-for-grantedness of meritocracy. Do we believe that we live in a meritocratic world where those who work the hardest and who are the most talented are the ones who are most successful? In the United States, society venerates rugged individualism, coupled with the American dream of supposed bootstrap lifting. Yet scholars, and sociologists in particular, have pointed out ways when merit is not enough, when hard work only gets you so far in systems of inequality and disproportional access to resources.[56] Other factors based on social background, race, physical appearance, connections, gender, disability, or being lucky enough to have that "x-factor" play a strong role.[57] The U.S. art world of the 1950s, 1960s, and 1970s was similarly nonmeritocratic. Social networks were especially important when it came to knowing who's who. Considering how difficult it was to "assess" or "evaluate" a work of art—further complicated by the evolving aesthetics of modernism and avant-gardism in "serious music"—evaluators could hide behind the veil of expertise or objectivity to justify their decisions. As I repeat again and again in *Ask the Experts*, I am not questioning anyone's motives or expertise in this book. Artists and arts lovers sacrificed their money, time, and lives, with the best of intentions and with a passion and dedication toward artistic mastery that was undeniable. But so did many other artists who did not benefit from this arts grantmaking system. They equally too could have been seen as experts but were not.

Ultimately, this book contributes to our understanding of U.S. history and the role of music in American society in several important ways. It offers an in-depth investigation of the environmental circumstances that supported Western high art musicians and organizations; it suggests a method to analyze a network of relationships between artists, arts managers, arts advocates, and audiences; and it provides a critical examination of the relationships between large performing arts venues, new music centers, universities, and the musical avant-garde in twentieth-century

America. I generate a detailed analysis of the definitions and understandings of various terms such as cultural pluralism, democracy, taste, and, most significantly, expertise.

The questions I pose are those central to many humanists and historians concerned with aesthetic evaluation and the power that networks of artists and grantmakers can exercise in producing and judging art. They are also relevant to the wider public, especially in current protestations that "the arts are underfunded in this country," as well as allegations that "we waste too much money on the arts." Finally, I hope that issues of funding excellent and diverse cultural practices are deeply relevant to current policymakers and arts philanthropists. Legitimized forms of culture can be problematically chosen to represent images of both national and local identity. Yet Western music is only one example of the many kinds of art produced in the United States. When art is called upon to serve the multiple functions of creative inspiration, economic stimulus, and community expression, an examination of the field of cultural production and the rules of the game is critical—the resulting insights and conclusions allow us to better understand the consequences of our policies. Art, after all, is at the intersection of aesthetics and social change.

Who Were the Experts?

1

DEFINING EXCELLENCE, QUALITY, AND STYLE

Consultants as Contributory Experts

AS MOST SCHOOLCHILDREN come to understand, social interactions operate according to certain established rules of engagement. They learn that pushing, biting, and hair pulling are not acceptable; that adults with clipboards have the power to scold and punish; and that performing well in one's studies generally results in some form of reward, whether verbal affirmation, signs of affection, or trips to Disneyland. Rules are pervasive and are deeply (if not always fully) understood. Sometimes rules are codified ("raise your hand before speaking; ask permission before going to the bathroom"), while at other times, they are not ("you never said I couldn't climb on top of the jungle gym!"). Importantly, rules function under social hierarchies based on power, legitimacy, and authority, whether among the children themselves or among the children, their school teachers, and their parents. Without a doubt, rules also apply well beyond the school classroom, governing social interactions on all levels and in a range of spheres. The National Endowment for the Arts (NEA), the Ford Foundation, and the Rockefeller Foundation were no exception during their large arts grantmaking period of the 1950s, 1960s, and 1970s. Apply for a grant and you may be chosen, based on formal and informal rules and guidelines.

At the heart of the system was the power of *expertise*. Arts experts of many different kinds determined which artists were worthy of funding, which art forms were

Ask the Experts. Michael Sy Uy, Oxford University Press (2020). © Oxford University Press.
DOI: 10.1093/oso/9780197510445.001.0001.

important to support, and which projects were of so-called quality and excellence. Their expertise was legitimized through extensive practice, in addition to formal education and other credentials bestowed by entrusted institutions. Experts provided a useful service based on their knowledge and experience, but they also indirectly provided a legitimizing function, attaching their prestige and influence to arts grantmaking decisions. The foundations and the government fragmented expertise across various people: chairmen, trustees, program directors, panelists, and contracted consultants all shared a piece of the pie. Yet the grantmaking structure also rarely spelled out the kinds of experiences and training needed to be an expert in music. The rules were not always clear.

One way to better understand the field and the relationships among actors is to peel away layers of decision making like the skins of an onion. Different layers corresponded to separate forms of expertise. At the first layer, outside consultants and panelists recommended for or against individual grants; they served and advised as judges for competitions; and they attended conferences and decided future policies. In the terminology of sociologists Harry Collins and Robert Evans, they were "contributory experts" because they were artists who directly provided specialized knowledge, judgments, and opinions based on their experiences in the arts.[1]

At a layer deeper were foundation and NEA staff who ran the organizational bureaucracy. Their tasks were multiple: they screened thousands of grant applications, explored new fields for spending, selected institutions and people to carry out the work, and followed up on grants once they were made. In the words of Collins and Evans, they were "interactional experts" because they were not practicing artists, but, more often, "generalists" with knowledge about the arts. Their backgrounds were in government work, academia, or the nonprofit world. One of their most important responsibilities was to decide which consultants and outside experts to trust. With the power to control their divisions and assemble such expert panels, foundation and government officers were like the schoolteachers on the playground. Clipboards in hand and Rolodexes within reach, they were at the heart of arts grantmaking during this period.

The impact of arts experts on American twentieth-century music was profound. As the record demonstrated, foundation and government officers largely drew from a limited group of composers, music professors, and managers of performing arts organizations. The formation of power in this small and concentrated field preshaped and predetermined decision making. One reason for this outcome was that officers normally engaged consultants through the personal recommendation of other consultants. First-degree connections were critical. Social networks based especially on prestigious affiliation facilitated the establishment of restricted expert groups to the exclusion of others active in the arts, including artists of non-Western music, amateur music makers, folk musicians, and jazz artists. Moreover, because the high art field and academia in general were dominated by white, male managers and composers, the system of first-degree referral perpetuated the exclusion of women and minorities, who lacked both the cultural capital and social capital to participate. The inclusion and exclusion of voices mattered in decision making.

At the same time, the employment of consultants as experts provided the *appearance* of disinterested knowledge and objectivity, based on discourses of management and meritocracy prevalent at the time. Experts at the NEA, Ford Foundation, and Rockefeller Foundation codified particular sets of subjectivities, casting them as examples of universal excellence in music and the performing arts. While subjectivity played a role in all exercises of judgment, using experts for external objectivity was different in evaluating aesthetic choices compared to perhaps scientific ones. When experts determined a project's quality based on its "fiscal soundness," its "multiple sources of funding," or its "audience capacity," then the assessment was more a quantitative analysis than one based on artistic merits. When the evaluator derived quality from the project's innovation, boldness, or creativity, then his or her social upbringing and personal values played a large role in the success or failure of the grant.

The extensive reliance on expertise in the system shaped the way grantmaking institutions decided the future of music in the United States. Expert opinion influenced patterns of production and consumption, as well as the relative social and cultural importance of differing aesthetics. The interaction among experts, rules, and discussions of artistic quality provides a critical framework with which to examine the institutions' impacts on the arts world.

Definitions of Expertise and Experts

Today, the topic of "expertise" is a hot-button issue. Historian Tom Nichols observes that people dismiss expertise "with such frequency, on so many issues, and with such *anger*."[2] His arguments are particularly resonant in a country debating the impacts of "fake news," climate change denialism, and suspicions against elite universities. To Nichols, the death of expertise is about "the aggressive replacement of expert views or established knowledge with the insistence that every opinion on any matter is as good as every other."[3]

Part of the problem is that satisfying definitions for the terms "experts" and "expertise" are difficult to establish. Differences between experts and nonexperts may be found in their training, knowledge, social network, or talent, and these can be measured in terms of intelligence, registered brain activity, skills, personal management, and creativity.[4] Psychological research has played a particularly important role in the field of expertise, focusing on differences in mental capacities and the use of psychometric tests (e.g., aptitude or personality tests) to evaluate innate conditions before an individual's training or practice.[5] These tests, however, remain contested due to the question of whether they can be designed to assess inherent capacities free of cultural biases. Furthermore, although there are studies that show that genetic inheritance is a relative component for skills or talent in music and sports—and even these conclusions remain controversial—they say nothing about what it means to have expertise in music or art.[6]

Alternatively, a sociological approach to expertise evaluates relationships between experts and nonexperts (or laypersons) and *among* experts. Sociologists such as Robert Merton, Pierre Bourdieu, and Max Weber have sought to explain the ways and reasons that certain individuals and certain ways of thinking or acting are rewarded more than others.[7] Among one of Merton's most influential ideas is the "Matthew effect," citing a tendency whereby grants are given to those who've been awarded other recognitions in the past.[8] "Halo effects," a phrase coined by Edward Thorndike, are also a type of confirmation bias that help explain prestige or quality that is derived by association, for example, with graduating from, or teaching at, an Ivy League school, or working with a well-respected authority.[9] It's important to note that the Mathew and Halo effects demonstrate sociological and psychological biases that go beyond simply assessing someone's level of expertise. As Harald Mieg points out, relationships among experts and laypersons not only imply gradients or degrees of expertise but also differences in other social dimensions, such as privileges and power.[10] Bourdieu's concept of habitus, or the ways an individual's socialization and access to resources and different forms of capital are shaped, and continue to shape his or her actions, provides an overarching understanding of the powers at work in grantmaking institutions.[11]

The majority of sociological research, however, has tended to focus either on fields such as the history of science or on the professionalization of certain occupations such as medicine and law. When research has examined aspects of musical expertise, it has looked into the development of savant composers, like Mozart, or the role of hereditary family structures, like those of Bach and Strauss.[12] Missing are in-depth historical analyses of arts institutions and the grants that support them, interrogating how composers and performers come to be seen and awarded as creative artists by individuals working within systems of patronage.

Collins and Evans have attempted to move current social understanding of expertise beyond just the *relational*, so that "the process of coming to be called an expert [has] more to do with the possession of real and substantive expertise."[13] This move has significant value for anyone interested in art's role in society. Their analysis is reliant on Michael Polanyi's idea of tacit knowledge, "the deep understanding one can only gain through social immersion in groups who possess it."[14] The significance of tacit knowledge is that humans know more than they can tell, and that the transfer of tacit knowledge requires extensive personal and social contact.[15] What results from an explanation of tacit knowledge is Collins and Evans's Periodic Table of Expertises, which provides a typology of different kinds of expertise (specialist expertises), how they are acquired, and how they are judged (meta-expertises and meta-criteria).[16]

Collins and Evans distinguish between two kinds of specialist tacit knowledge: "contributory expertise" and "interactional expertise." As its name suggests, contributory expertise is possessed by those who are able to "contribute to the domain to which the expertise pertains." For example, a contributory expert is a thermonuclear physicist actively working and experimenting in the field of thermonuclear fusion.[17] By contrast, Collins and Evans propose an underrecognized form of "deeply tacit-knowledge-laden expertise," which they name interactional expertise. Often possessed by sociologists, journalists, or critics working in a field, interactional expertise is one in the "*language* of a specialism in the absence of expertise in its *practice*."[18] Although Collins and Evans do not refer to it as such, interactional expertise can be considered discursive, with interactional experts able to function and "pass" as knowledgeable, without directly adding new knowledge.[19] This interpretation by no means suggests that interactional experts are frauds or interlopers: far from the case, interactional experts can provide deeply informed perspectives on problems within a field. They serve as interpreters or translators between a specialized field and a wider audience, and they act as historians, journalists, or anthropologists, offering greater knowledge on the operations and culture of a particular community.

Using Collins and Evans's typology, one fruitful way of applying this understanding is to the differences in the kinds of experts employed in grantmaking. Outside consultants and panelists can be seen to give predominantly contributory expertise to the system, and institutional staff and officers as providing predominantly interactional expertise. Officers and staff (as interactional experts), in the words of philosopher Gloria Origgi, deliver a "second-order epistemology": they are an authority to check indirectly—or on a second level—the reliability of information or an evaluation.[20] Oppositely, contributory experts provide a first-order epistemology, contributing to the domain to which their expertise pertains. This categorization does not discount the fact that outside consultants can also provide interactional expertise, and that some staff, for example, Norman Lloyd at the Rockefeller Foundation and Walter Anderson at the NEA, were artists and provided contributory expertise. But for the most part, officers, while capable of eloquently discussing issues regarding musical performances, commissions, or recordings, were not artists themselves. They were not directly contributing or producing new art.

The Role of Consultants and Panelists at the Rockefeller and Ford Foundations

As the first institution to begin granting large-scale amounts of money to music projects in the United States, the Rockefeller Foundation started its earliest consultation with experts after World War II. Program directors overseeing the performing arts took from other Rockefeller divisions, such as agriculture and medicine, the practice of using consultants. Between 1948 and 1963, the foundation employed two music advisory committees. Virgil Thomson led the first, and the second included Leonard Bernstein and Aaron Copland, among others. Recommendations made by foundation consultants had a direct and substantial impact on the projects that Rockefeller funded.

Associate director John Marshall recorded in his officer's diary that he hosted composer and music critic Virgil Thomson for dinner at his New York apartment in December 1948.[21] Thomson had just premiered his second opera with Gertrude Stein, *The Mother of Us All* (1947), and was chief critic of the *New York Herald Tribune*. Among the topics of discussion at the dinner were the state of contemporary music in the United States and the problems of issuing recordings and publishing scores. Thomson recommended five other leading composers for a small conference to be held by the foundation in New York, including professor and dean at the University of Oklahoma Harrison Kerr, Columbia professors Otto Luening and Douglas Moore, Yale professor Quincy Porter, and Harvard professor Randall Thompson. Thomson knew all of these composers through professional channels and had recently worked with Luening and Moore through their position on the committee of the Alice B. Ditson Fund, which had commissioned *The Mother of Us All* (Luening also conducted its premiere).[22]

Luening, Porter, and Thomson attended the music conference with Rockefeller officers Marshall, Edward F. D'Arms, and David Stevens (director of humanities, which covered the arts, also see Box 1.1). D'Arms's diary recorded in detail the conversations and debates, noting that Virgil Thomson "did most of the talking and did it extremely well."[23] Much of the discussion centered on the realities and constraints of recording and publishing new music. Practical suggestions included a grant to the American Music Center in New York City for a study regarding the publication of modern American music and its relationship with recording. Marshall's notes focused on Luening's specific recommendation to finance "larger local symphony

---

BOX 1.1

KEY OFFICERS AT THE ROCKEFELLER FOUNDATION

- **John Marshall**: associate director of the humanities division (which also covered the arts) (1933–62)
- **Edward F. D'Arms**: associate director of the humanities division (1955–57)
- **Kenneth W. Thompson**: vice president (1961–74)

---

orchestras," citing specifically the case of Louisville.[24] The Louisville Orchestra indeed received a large Rockefeller grant of $400,000 ($3.7 million in 2017) for composer commissions in 1953, after the music conference. The grant to the Louisville Orchestra marked a huge increase in the Rockefeller Foundation's humanities budget and it was, at the time, the largest amount ever given to a music program by any foundation. It is hard to imagine, though, that Louisville was on the officers' radar as a "large local symphony orchestra," no matter the rising national coverage, had Luening not made a direct recommendation. Marshall's correspondence with Thomson, Luening, and Porter less than two months after the conference confirmed that the foundation's new consideration of proposals in contemporary music emerged directly out of the conference, "which very usefully served to illustrate the kind of action which it might be advantageous for the foundation to consider."[25]

With the election of Rockefeller president Jacob George Harrar, a re-evaluation of the foundation's goals occurred, resulting in a program for the performing and creative arts.[26] Harrar acknowledged that since it was impossible to cover the field with regular staff, the foundation planned to "use the technique of the appointment of consultants or small committees of leaders in the several branches of the creative and performing arts in order to have the benefit of expert judgment."[27] The practice of using consultants, as he well knew from the agriculture division, was one that had "served the foundation well in other fields" and brought in the "weight of opinions from outstanding authorities."

The use of experts for each domain of knowledge (e.g., performing arts vs. agriculture vs. medicine), as sociologist Anthony Giddens argues, is tightly connected to dilemmas posed by an increasingly complex world.[28] Specialization allowed experts to become authorities in their field. Furthermore, as sociologist Harald Mieg contends, experts certified the "legitimizing use" of certain products or services.[29] In the case of the Rockefeller Foundation, consultants legitimized certain musicians and artist organizations.

Two years later, the Rockefeller Foundation formed its new Music Advisory Committee by inviting a core group of well-known, influential composers, a music critic, and a musicologist/dean: Leonard Bernstein, Aaron Copland, Lukas Foss, Paul Hume (*Washington Post*), and Raymond Kendall (dean of the School of Performing Arts, University of Southern California). The committee provided initial direction for program policy and projects. As Rockefeller's vice president Kenneth W. Thompson noted in his invitation, the purpose of the committee was to bring "a small community of four or five 'wise men' who might meet" with the foundation at least once or twice a year.[30] It is difficult not to pause and note the racial background and gender of these "wise men" who essentially served as gatekeepers for the earliest rounds of music funding given by a large philanthropic institution in the United States. Their strong influence manifested in their ability to set the agenda and to determine where the Rockefeller Foundation put its money.

As vice president Thompson cited, the first meeting was a "tour d'horizon" of possible programming and grants. He concluded that "only through working with men of knowledge and stature was it likely that the foundation's program could evolve in the most creative and promising direction." The Music Advisory Committee met with Thompson and two foundation officers, Gerald Freund and Boyd Compton.[31] One example of the committee's recommendations was a program to selected U.S. symphony orchestras to lengthen their seasons and give premieres of works by young composers. Aaron Copland provided the initial idea, and in fact, Thompson referred to it as the "Copland Plan." The foundation provided three appropriations totaling $850,000 ($6.6 million in 2017). Lukas Foss made another suggestion to support university music departments. Foss himself was at the University of Buffalo and that year had submitted a grant proposal for what became the Creative Associates program, supported by the foundation.[32]

The Music Advisory Committee proposed another set of grants in a "composer-in-residence" program for artists to work closely with orchestras.[33] The first experiment placed composer John Huggler with the Boston Symphony Orchestra and it led to an initial $96,000 ($760,000 in 2017) grant the year later. In the trustees' docket, the recommendations of Copland, Bernstein, and Foss, described as "distinguished musical artists," justified the support of this grant, as well as of the earlier programs that extended orchestral seasons. The docket included reference to the very large Ford Foundation grant to symphony orchestras the same year, 1965, and how the Rockefeller program differed: Rockefeller supported composers, while Ford gave aid to the orchestral musicians' salaries and benefits.

By contrast, the Ford Foundation relied slightly less on outside consultants and experts in setting its grant policy and direction. Programming at Ford was more firmly within the control of the officers, and especially, in the hands of vice president W. McNeil Lowry (see Box 1.2). Lowry's own goal was to open the lines of communication and promote the sharing of information between officers and artists,

BOX 1.2

KEY OFFICERS AT THE FORD FOUNDATION

- **W. McNeil Lowry**: vice president of the humanities and the arts division (1964–74)
- **Edward F. D'Arms**: program officer of the humanities and the arts division (1957–69) (previously associate director at the Rockefeller Foundation)

hoping then to build a strong network with the Ford Foundation at the center. One of the ways he accomplished this aim was by employing artists as judges for young musicians competitions, including vocal and instrumental soloists (1959), opera singers (1962), and concert artists (1971).[34]

The awards to performing artists were not open to direct application, but through nomination by foundation-invited musicians, conductors, critics, and music teachers. Ford permitted nominators to recommend no more than two candidates, and the foundation asked for a "brief critical evaluation" of each one. Nominees then sent in a biographical form, which included a statement of artistic aspirations, tapes or recordings, and two letters of reference. A panel of professional musicians, acting as consultants to the foundation and judges for the program, thereafter reviewed the nominations and, following preliminary screening, invited a smaller number of nominees for taped or live audition.

In the letter sent to prospective judges, Lowry wrote, "the job of the panelists will be time consuming and perhaps even arduous but, we hope, ultimately gratifying to those who help us with this task."[35] Ford reimbursed panelists for expenses and paid them an honorarium of $125 ($1,000 in 2017) for each day spent reviewing applications and attending panel meetings in New York City. Unlike the panelists and reviewers of the NEA, the foundation kept its judges anonymous and confidential. Additionally, Ford asked judges to withhold any mention of possible or eventual participation in the program; their own nominees were furthermore ineligible for consideration. Among the judges for the first competition in 1959 were well-known composers, performers, and managers, including Leonard Bernstein, Rudolf Serkin, Isaac Stern, Blanche Thebom, and Robert Whitney.

According to a document titled "Background of the Concert Artists Program," Ford saw an advantage in operating these individual grant programs itself:

> The use of an elaborate nominating system, the opportunities to analyze the artists' own statements of purpose, and the chance to observe the professional judges at work in their selection—all these things deepen the staff's insight

into particular fields and into the career patterns of artists. They also engage the foundation at the center of a network.[36]

In line with the foundation being at the center, Lowry specified his views on the relationship between the foundation and its consultants, "baptizing" them as the "reporters from the field of the arts."[37] Ford staff, according to Lowry, were "intellectual bankers," and as "a banker necessarily [had] somewhat more detachment from the sufferings and problems of his clients," consultants needed to be "reporters and spokesmen" for these "pains and travails." According to a later internal report, Ford designed all staff work and grantmaking "to create continuing networks and communications points for artists and artistic directors both to free them from isolation and to give focus and shape to efforts aimed at artistic development."[38]

Lowry characterized the Ford Foundation not only as a "communications center," but also as a "clearing house," evident in the officers' frequent site visits, "unstructured conferences" at the offices in New York, and correspondence with artists and organizations. Staff reached out to arts groups and smaller foundations, serving as "consultants" in their own right, often offering fundraising strategies and "technical assistance" such as management training. Lowry argued that "collateral and somewhat intangible" components of the program were actually more supportive of the arts and artists than the grants themselves.[39] While the NEA also provided technical assistance to its grantees, its large and comprehensive system of panelists marked a different approach to employing experts than the Ford Foundation or the Rockefeller Foundation. Nevertheless, NEA chairman Nancy Hanks acknowledged that she derived the use of panelists, consultants, and "professional advisers" from the experiences of private foundations themselves.[40] After all, Hanks's background was at a foundation, as trustee and vice chairman of the Rockefeller Brothers Fund.

Panelists at the National Endowment for the Arts

The National Foundation on the Arts and the Humanities Act of 1965 authorized the NEA to establish panels of experts to assist the agency. Unlike Ford and Rockefeller, however, which operated as nonprofit, private entities, the NEA faced a high degree of scrutiny from a number of governmental overseers, including the Office of Management and Budget, and elected officials, including the president of the United States (who appointed the chairman and members of the National Council on the Arts [NCA]) and members of Congress (who drafted and voted on the agency's authorization and appropriations bills).

In its initial meetings, members of the NCA extensively discussed the importance of outside consultants to aid council members and Arts Endowment (NEA) staff. The NCA—made up of twenty-six presidentially appointed members—advised the NEA chairman on agency policies and programs and reviewed and recommended grant applications and funding guidelines. The proposed NCA panel resolution established two categories of experts: those who assisted the NCA and the Arts Endowment on a regular basis concerning general matters, and those who assisted on a temporary basis with implementing specific projects.[41] The chairman—with recommendations from the NCA—appointed the first group of experts, representing "distinguished and experienced knowledge in the arts." The second group served on a limited basis, with no definite term of service, but was still appointed by the chairman with the approval of at least one council member.

Similar to the Ford Foundation, the NEA was conscious of the public role that panelists played in networking and strategy. According to the resolution, expert advisers served a function beyond specialized knowledge: they acted as outreach for the NEA to help build its legitimacy and geographic reach.

> We need as complete a list of prospective expert advisers as possible—in all the major art forms, and with a good geographic representation so that we can be assisted on specific projects in specific areas throughout the country. These experts can also help us in stimulating community support for the work we undertake; they can act in a liaison fashion with the communities we wish to assist; they can broaden public interest in the endowment.[42]

Over the next year and a half, though, the NEA began to feel internal and external pressures to establish a permanent music panel as had been done in the other arts categories. Early correspondence between chairman Roger Stevens and Aaron Copland revealed that music was the one field within the council that had failed to set up a panel of experts. The council had previously felt that with Leonard Bernstein and Isaac Stern as NCA members, it had covered its bases. Stevens wrote, however, that "since several of our most important programs have been under attack [the National Chamber Orchestra, the Jeunesses Musicales program], I feel that a completely independent committee made up of outstanding people in the field of music should be assembled to review our programs." At the conclusion of the letter, Stevens offered Copland chairmanship of the panel, "as a great public service to this country and to the field of music," and so, the NEA established its first Music Advisory Panel in 1967.[43] At the NCA's tenth meeting, Stevens announced the further inclusion of "twenty distinguished leaders" to the music panel, including Lukas Foss and Paul Hume.[44] With Bernstein on the NCA, Copland the chair, and Foss and Hume on the panel itself, the leading voices of the NEA strongly resembled those of the Rockefeller Foundation's Music Advisory Committee (established four years earlier).

Almost immediately, the precise role of panelists was contentious. Chairman Stevens argued that it was important for the panelists to feel that their contributions were substantive and that the council heard their opinions. The panelists declared that if they spent the time serving on the music panel, they deserved the right to examine the grant proposals first. Stevens acknowledged that if the NCA approved a project without the panel knowing, then the panel might justifiably feel excluded and embarrassed. The NCA demanded, however, the power to make the final decision.

At first, Stevens did not feel compelled to release the identities of panelists publicly, although he recognized that as a government agency, the Arts Endowment could not withhold any names. He feared that if identified, panelists might receive undue influence or pressure before the completion of a project.[45] Yet Stevens's standards were not always consistent. He had no problem, for example, with using panelists' identities to legitimize the rejection of certain applications, deflect any expectation that a project would be automatically supported, or defend against prior NCA actions, especially if the inquiries came from members of Congress. For example, Stevens's correspondence with Representative Charles Joelson (D-NJ) showed deference to the panel. He assured Joelson of the "very distinguished" nature of this group of experts, and that anyone, after seeing the panel's membership, would be completely satisfied with the music field's representation.[46]

The reconsideration of panel structure and procedure occurred under chairman Nancy Hanks (1969–77), the most powerful woman in arts grantmaking during this period, and her music director Walter Anderson, the most powerful African American in government arts grantmaking (see Box 1.3). The greatest challenge in systematizing the panel system was tied to the rapid growth of the NEA and the increasing number of applications it received. Under Hanks, panels consisted of no

---

BOX 1.3
KEY OFFICERS AT THE NATIONAL ENDOWMENT FOR THE ARTS

- **Roger Stevens**: inaugural chairman (1965–69)
- **Nancy Hanks**: chairman (1969–77)
- **Michael Straight**: deputy chairman (1969–77)
- **Walter Anderson**: director of music (1968–83)

fewer than eight and no more than sixteen members and included a chairman (or cochairmen) and a possible vice chairman.

Panelists served a one-year term for up to four years with staggered rotation. They could also serve on more than one panel at a time. The use of panels throughout the NEA, however, varied from program to program. Directors decided the size of panels, the length of service of each panelist, and the time of appointment. For example, deputy chairman Michael Straight at one point criticized the music panel for being "far too large" and needing more frequent rotation.[47] Greater turnover perhaps counteracted the entrenchment of vested interests, but it also prevented the continuation of institutional knowledge.

The NEA implemented stricter criteria for the selection of panelists throughout the 1970s, a product of external pressure from Congress and arts organizations, and internal pressure from staff and council members.[48] It formalized the criteria as:

1. Professional competence
2. Ability to assess applications through personal knowledge and experience
3. Geographical diversity
4. Diversity of backgrounds and viewpoint
5. Available time for panel meetings and for assistance between meetings

The NEA expected panelists to meet four times a year, and it paid for transportation costs, a per diem of $25 ($150 in 2017), and an honorarium of $50 a day to each panel member.[49] Panelists signed an appointment affidavit and confidential financial statement, and sent a short personal biography.

The director's network and range of contacts played a significant role in the kinds of people that the NEA approached for consultation. The deputy chairman solicited panelists from recommendations by members of the NCA, state arts agencies, and national organizations, but the major responsibility fell on the individual program directors. Directors further asked for referrals from panel members themselves, and according to deputy chairman Straight, "their views [were] given primary consideration."[50] Thus, the system was self-reinforcing because grantmakers based their network for new and prospective panelists on personal and first-degree connections.

While music director Anderson valued as much as possible "highly artistic input," he asserted to give greater preference to members who knew "how to cut through red tape, avoid extraneous conversation, attend all meetings without dropping in and out, and work in an extremely efficient manner"—therefore, he prioritized what he called the panelists' "management skills."[51] Anderson's preference for formality, efficiency, and reliability over aesthetic or artistic concerns was important. The emphasis on management skills also had consequences because of the large year-by-year increases in applications. As Anderson wrote, above all, "this group would 'move' on all our objectives with the utmost speed." Under these criteria, Aaron Copland was the perfect fit to have led the music panel in its early days. As Howard Pollack argues in his biography of Copland, the composer's "tact" helped him "chair innumerable organizations, committees, juries, and panel discussions" during the course of his life.[52]

A survey of panel operations for the music division revealed that voting was done by a voice vote, proceeding one at a time after evaluation of each application (rather than at the end, after a discussion of all the projects).[53] Therefore, the order in which panelists reviewed the projects had a potential impact on the amount of money they allocated, and the panel evaluated later projects in comparison to earlier ones. Additionally, the time of day that voting occurred mattered due to "a possible general fatigue factor, i.e., after a long day(s) of dealing with nothing but applications." Programs tried to minimize this problem through careful structuring of agendas that permitted adequate time for discussion and frequent breaks.[54] Additionally, the music program prescreened applications in subcommittees "to identify obvious rejections prior to the panel meeting." The division listed alphabetically all applications, however, including those rejected, before the full NCA for discussion and vote.

Some council members and NEA staff critiqued the panel structure and how it, at times, operated. For example, NCA member Gunther Schuller wrote to Hanks after attending a meeting, "having stayed 'til the bitter end" that he was left with

the uncomfortable recognition that the constitution of the panels is terribly crucial ... and that this particular music panel is not really on or up to the level commensurate with the decisions it is asked to make.[55]

Schuller had previous experience as a panelist himself (in addition to his consultancy for the Ford and Rockefeller Foundations). In this letter, Schuller criticized what he saw as the weaknesses in the system that prevented panelists from making the most informed, conscientious decisions.

In specific detail, Schuller wrote that at the panel meeting he was present at, the morning went well with good attendance and "healthy pro and con discussion, input from all directions." But as the day proceeded, "the decisions became increasingly arbitrary, thoughtless, down to the point of irresponsibility." He attributed part of the problems due to voting when the majority of the panel was absent, or when the committee was swayed "by one or two vocal members who, let's say, represented a negative vote, when one or two equally vocal members representing a positive vote happened to be absent." Schuller also criticized a "casualness" or "lack of seriousness that pervaded the atmosphere," but which might also have been "circumstantial" or "bad luck" due to the fact that some of the "more seasoned, wisest and articulate members of the panel were the ones who had to leave early." He concluded that there should have been "a cut-off point beyond which important decisions or votes ought to be postponed." But he also came to realize how important the selection of panelists was.

While many musicians and academics who have sat on selection committees or panels can sympathize with Schuller's criticisms, one other consideration that shouldn't be ignored was that among the topics discussed that afternoon was a grant to the Association of Independent Conservatories of Music. Schuller addressed his letter to Hanks privately as a "concerned" member of the NCA, but he served also, at the time, as president of the New England Conservatory, and during the panel meeting, he voiced opinions in support of the association. Hence, Schuller had a stake in the "seriousness" of discussion and of the panelists involved. Even given this context, however, Schuller's concern was one shared by other panelists and officers. Walter Anderson's response to him reiterated the worry of panelists who departed early, the lack of a quorum when carrying out business, and the negative consequences of making decisions at the end of long, successive days of intense discussion.[56]

As Schuller well knew from his participation as an expert for the Rockefeller Foundation, the deliberation process and the selection of consultants also had a strong impact in the decision making of the private foundations. A particularly illuminating example of the strong impact of outside consultants on the development of a project was Rockefeller's Recorded Anthology of American Music (RAAM). The ways the foundation and its experts structured debates and discussions greatly shaped the final product.

The Rockefeller Foundation and RAAM

RAAM was a 100-LP collection released between 1976 and 1978 in celebration of the U.S. Bicentennial.[57] It included an astounding 1,200 musical titles by 500 composers, performed by 1,600 musicians. With a total playing time of over eighty hours, the anthology covered a wide range of music, from Virgil Thomson and Gertrude Stein's *The Mother of Us All*, to Eubie Blake and Noble Sissle's *Shuffle Along*, to Ricky Ford's jazz album *Loxodonta Africana*. The Rockefeller Foundation contributed $4.9 million ($21 million in 2017) to RAAM, originally conceiving the project as "a gift from the foundation to the American people."[58] According to a foundation program officer, the public could find in the anthology "all the strands of music which make up the fabric of American musical experience."[59] Musicologists, leading critics, composers, and performers wrote extensive liner notes, which amounted to six 300-page volumes.

The choice of repertory and the selection committee deciding the repertory, however, were early sources of contention. Two general divisions arose: contemporary composers viewed the project as a way to record new music that was not commercially viable, while musicologists and historians wanted the project to serve as a wide-ranging compilation of American music of all styles, encompassing the country's two-hundred-year history. For example, composer and foundation consultant Mario di Bonaventura saw the project as a Marshall Plan for new music.[60] By contrast, musicologist Charles Hamm, a dedicated supporter of a broad-based vision, perceived RAAM as an opportunity to include unrecorded popular songs, folk music, and the music of African Americans, women, and other racial minorities.[61]

Similar to the power that panelists at the NEA wielded in approving or rejecting grants, the employment of outside consultants in RAAM had major implications for the inclusion and exclusion of repertory. American musicologists in particular were strongly influential in the anthology's outcome. The three musicologists who played a significant role were H. Wiley Hitchcock, Charles Hamm, and Richard Crawford. Their participation counterbalanced the power of composers who wanted to focus predominantly on contemporary music. Initially, composers advocated for up to 75% of the anthology to be devoted to "serious" composers of concert music. Due to the musicologists' influence, however, there was a significant increase in the number of records devoted to popular music, jazz, religious music, and music of earlier time periods. In the end, "Concert and Art Music" represented only 35% of the records, while almost one-fifth of the music was written before 1900, demonstrating an appreciation of more historical examples. The lesson learned was that the musicologists' impact was direct and consistent with their presence on the committee.

The final product was still an incomplete realization, though, of the foundation's own search for broad representation, especially with respect to the music of minorities and women. Absence mattered just as inclusion mattered for the musicologists. The lack of women and experts of color, as seen in Table 1.1, correlated with the underrepresentation of music composed by women and artists of color in the anthology. Despite a striking diversity of genres, RAAM still reflected a very Anglo- and Euro-centric understanding of the United States.[62]

Of the sixteen original editorial committee members, only two were women: Cynthia Hoover, curator of the Division of Musical Instruments at the Smithsonian Institution, and Eileen Southern, a professor of Music and Afro-American Studies at Harvard (the first tenured black woman in Harvard's Faculty of Arts and Sciences), who resigned from the committee before the initial release of ten records due to "differences in opinion with her colleagues."[63] Composer and

TABLE I.I

RAAM Editorial Committee

- Don Roberts, chairman (music librarian, Northwestern University; former president, Association of Recorded Sound Collections)
- Milton Babbitt (composer; professor of music, Princeton University)
- David Baker (composer; professor of music and director, Institute of Jazz Studies, Indiana University)
- Neely Bruce (composer, choral director, and associate professor of music, Wesleyan University)
- Richard Crawford (musicologist; professor of music, University of Michigan)
- Ross Lee Finney (composer; professor emeritus, University of Michigan)
- Richard Franko Goldman (conductor and composer; president emeritus, Peabody Conservatory of Music)
- David Hamilton (music critic, *The Nation*; former editor, W. W. Norton and Company)
- H. Wiley Hitchcock (professor of music, Brooklyn College, CUNY; director, Institute for Studies in American Music)
- Cynthia Hoover (musicologist and curator, Division of Musical Instruments, Smithsonian Institution)
- Herman E. Krawitz (producer; adjunct professor, School of Drama, Yale University)
- Gunther Schuller (composer and conductor; president emeritus, New England Conservatory of Music)
- Mike Seeger (performer, teacher, and collector of traditional mountain music)
- Michael Steinberg (director of publications, Boston Symphony Orchestra; former music critic, *Boston Globe*)
- Warren Susman (cultural historian; chairman, Department of History, Rutgers University)

director of the Institute of Jazz Studies at Indiana University David Baker was the only person of color after Southern left, and he and Gunther Schuller were responsible for producing most of the jazz music in the anthology. Given the significant number of these recordings—twelve compared to initial proposals for three or four—Schuller and Baker's involvement underscored, yet again, the importance of committee membership.

In RAAM, the music of nonblack, ethnic minorities included only six recordings: one each of Puerto Rican and Cuban music in New York, two compilations of the music from eleven Native American tribes, one of songs by Slavic Americans, and one of archival music from Spanish New Mexico. Just two composers of Asian descent were represented: Chou Wen-Chung and Earl Kim. Additionally, women were gravely underrepresented. While there were many female performers, the only two female composers included were Amy Beach and Ruth Crawford Seeger.

The Rockefeller Foundation's concern for cultural pluralism and gender representation, though, was evident in the arts division's own appropriation requests to the board of trustees, and in officers' correspondence with consultants. As a Bicentennial project, officers proposed that RAAM should encompass "the genius and vitality of *Americans of many periods and ethnic backgrounds*, much of which ha[d] been ignored in the past and deserve[d] to be brought to light."[64] In another internal document, the foundation recognized that "Americans . . . have been historically neglectful in sufficiently recognizing *the contribution of blacks, other ethnic groups, and women*."[65]

A multiracial editorial committee with equal numbers of men and women would not have guaranteed a proportional representation of race and gender in the anthology. Nor would a committee predominantly composed of white men preclude the selection of music by women or racial minorities. But as the representation of musicologists showed, the inclusion of other voices mattered. It resulted in an anthology that was more diverse in terms of time period and genre than the original proposals. The membership list of the editorial committee showed instead a prioritization of successful and established artists and influential and well-connected musicians over gender or racial diversity. The fact that most were male and white was, in part, the product of a network based on personal referral, just as it was also due to the fact that the vast majority of composers working within extensions of the Western classical tradition were white and male, that the academy was largely white and male, and that officers and trustees at the foundation were largely white and male. The employment of these eminent composers, conductors, and administrators had such merits as providing a source of legitimacy and authority to bolster the editorial committee's decisions. But the selection of these members was not an inevitable outcome. Many other experts could have been included as well.

A Concentrated Field of Outside Consultants and Experts

The most important fact to note about the foundation and government arts structure of expert consultants and panelists during this period was the high degree of overlap. To take just one constellation as an example, Figure 1.1 details membership

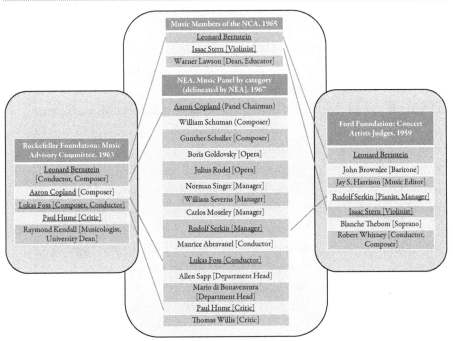

Music Members of the NCA, 1965
Leonard Bernstein
Isaac Stern [Violinist]
Warner Lawson [Dean, Educator]

NEA, Music Panel by category (delineated by NEA), 1967
Aaron Copland (Panel Chairman)
William Schuman (Composer)
Gunther Schuller [Composer]
Boris Goldovsky [Opera]
Julius Rudel [Opera]
Norman Singer [Manager]
William Severns [Manager]
Carlos Moseley [Manager]
Rudolf Serkin [Manager]
Maurice Abravanel [Conductor]
Lukas Foss [Conductor]
Allen Sapp [Department Head]
Mario di Bonaventura [Department Head]
Paul Hume [Critic]
Thomas Willis [Critic]

Rockefeller Foundation: Music Advisory Committee, 1963
Leonard Bernstein [Conductor, Composer]
Aaron Copland [Composer]
Lukas Foss [Composer, Conductor]
Paul Hume [Critic]
Raymond Kendall [Musicologist, University Dean]

Ford Foundation: Concert Artists Judges, 1959
Leonard Bernstein
John Brownlee [Baritone]
Jay S. Harrison [Music Editor]
Rudolf Serkin [Pianist, Manager]
Isaac Stern [Violinist]
Blanche Thebom [Soprano]
Robert Whitney [Conductor, Composer]

FIGURE 1.1 A network of consultants and panelists.

for the Rockefeller's Music Advisory Committee (1963), Ford's Concert Artist Judges (1959), and the NEA's Music Panel (1967). Leonard Bernstein, Aaron Copland, and Lukas Foss (underlined in Figure 1.1) served as consultants for more than one institution in this subset. This figure hardly captures, however, the amount of intertwinement that extended beyond this subset. Zeroing in on the NEA's music panel shows that William Schuman, Gunther Schuller, Julius Rudel, Allen Sapp, Mario di Bonaventura, and Maurice Abravanel also extensively consulted with the Rockefeller Foundation and they all played a large role in the execution of specific projects (e.g., Sapp with the Buffalo Creative Associates and di Bonaventura, Schuller, and Schuman with RAAM). Schuller, in fact, consulted for all three institutions, likely because of his activity across multiple musical genres—as the pioneer in "Third Stream"—and his presidency at the New England Conservatory. The constellation also leaves out many other consultants who were influential in this system, including Peter Mennin (Peabody Conservatory and Juilliard), Milton Babbitt (Princeton), and David Rockefeller Jr. (philanthropist and performer).

The network further reveals the large representation of artists and managers working in a Western high art tradition, the concentration of men at socially and culturally elite institutions on the East Coast (mostly near, or in, New York City and Boston), as seen in Table 1.2, and the underrepresentation of women and racial minorities.

TABLE 1.2

Key Consultants' Institutional Affiliations

Maurice Abravanel	Metropolitan Opera, Utah Symphony, Tanglewood Music Festival
Leonard Bernstein	Harvard University, Curtis Institute of Music, New York Philharmonic, Tanglewood
Mario di Bonaventura	Dartmouth College
Aaron Copland	Tanglewood
Lukas Foss	Curtis, Tanglewood, UCLA, University of Buffalo
Paul Hume	University of Chicago, *Washington Post*, Georgetown University
Julius Rudel	Mannes School of Music, New York City Opera
Allen Sapp	Harvard, Wellesley College, Buffalo
Gunther Schuller	New England Conservatory, Tanglewood
William Schuman	Juilliard, Lincoln Center
Rudolf Serkin	Curtis, Marlboro Music Festival

The interconnectedness of this network of U.S. composers has further been documented in other scholarship. For example, musicologist Carol Oja identifies a "deep stylistic conservatism" in the American Prix de Rome, underscored by the "makeup of selection juries, which privileged certain composer networks" in New York (Juilliard and Eastman), Boston (Harvard), and Chicago, and included the "earliest waves of American composer-academics."[66] She argues that the "homogeneity of the fellows was narrowly defined" and that there were no Jews, African Americans, or women. In another study, Jann Pasler examines the "political economy" of American composers at universities after World War II and NEA awards.[67] Pasler shows the strong influence of composers at specific northeastern universities, especially Columbia, Eastman, Juilliard, Princeton, and Yale. Her history demonstrates how male modernist composers "integrated themselves into the fabric of American universities in the 1950s and 60s and then maintained their aesthetics through their monopoly on grants, fellowships, and other awards," to the exclusion and near absence of women on these panels.[68] And Emily Abrams Ansari's work shows the ways composers like Copland and Schuman, among others, used government agencies to advance their own personal and aesthetic agendas.[69]

Greater gender and racial representation eventually became important, but mostly at the NEA. For instance, in a letter from Hanks to Senator Lee Metcalf (D-MT),

Hanks emphasized the racial diversity of the NEA's panels, including "Americans of Philippine, Japanese and Chinese extraction, full-blooded Indians, and 12 Spanish-speaking citizens, including the Deputy Director of the Institute of Puerto Rican Culture."[70] She also noted that women and African Americans were represented on *every* panel and that the music planning panel in particular had six women. Among past chairmen and cochairmen were Judith Raskin for music planning and music opera, Margaret Hillis for music choral, and David Baker and Jean Ritchie, both for jazz/folk/ethnic. The NEA, however, was an exception, and was influenced by the tremendous work of Hanks (a woman) and Walter Anderson (an African American), as well as external pressures from Congress, state arts agencies, and other social and cultural groups.

The goal is not to homogenize the types of music that composers wrote at elite universities or to accuse any individual of malicious intention—or even conscious decision among staff or panelists. Instead, focus should be placed on the legitimacy and authority accrued from elite institutional affiliations.

Two issues persist: first, in what sense these experts were exercising expertise in their fields and what criteria of excellence they applied, and second, an understanding of the social networks that facilitated the establishment of these groups of experts—that is, why these lists look the way they do.

One illustration of the first issue was the criteria used by NEA panelists as they reviewed grant applications. While many panelists indeed had intimate knowledge of the field—that is, "contributory expertise"—and understood well its problems, their domains of expertise did not always align with the types of grants. More often, they applied a "referred expertise," or an expertise taken from one field and indirectly applied to another.[71] Furthermore, the criteria they often used did not always correspond to aspects of artistic quality or excellence, in whatever way these terms could be defined.[72]

For example, the earliest minutes of the NCA meetings revealed that rarely was "artistic quality," per se, actually evaluated by panelists. More often, "quality" in an interdisciplinary setting was interpreted as financial security, program organization, or how well the project fit into existing program criteria and guidelines. If someone brought up artistic quality, they relied on their personal experience with (or even second-hand knowledge of) the organization. In a lingo familiar to many grant-makers, they wrote that "X" organization did "good work"; they hired the "best talent"; their artistry was of the "highest quality." On the other hand, the most often cited criterion for rejection of a proposal was that it did not fit within the current guidelines of the funding institution.[73] There were certainly also rejections based on quality—poor performance, lack of innovation, faulty management—but these represented far fewer cases. Thus, given the fact that most rejections were because they

did not fit within existing programs and that panelists and staff worked in cooperation to set program policy and direction, those most directly involved in the process determined the rules of the game. Considering the number of panelists in the
orchestral field, it was perhaps no surprise that among the first recommendations of
the newly created NEA music panel was an appropriation of $250,000 ($1.8 million
in 2017) to professional symphony orchestras, when previously they had received
nothing.[74]

The second issue regarding social networks concerned affinity, access, and rein-
forcement. Membership within these groups of experts was primarily based on
first-degree connections: preexisting members recommended and endorsed prospective consultants, usually by personal invitation. Taking the example of RAAM,
Richard Crawford noted that his adviser Wiley Hitchcock brought him onto the
project. Joshua Rifkin, another consultant, attributed his consultancy to Rockefeller
director Norman Lloyd, who mentored him when Lloyd was education director at Juilliard and Rifkin was an undergraduate.[75] Herman Krawitz, president of
New World Records (which produced and released RAAM), also noted that consultant and composer William Schuman was president of Juilliard when Lloyd
taught there. As Krawitz recounted, he was directly connected to Rockefeller president John Knowles, who knew Krawitz from a fundraising event at the Vincent
Memorial Hospital in Boston.[76] Krawitz also worked with committee member and
composer Gunther Schuller during the Metropolitan Opera's union negotiations,
and he regarded committee member and composer Milton Babbitt as his private
music mentor. Krawitz relied especially on Babbitt and David Hamilton (another
colleague from the Metropolitan Opera) for guidance on the editorial committee.

The tight-knit circle with Leonard Bernstein, Aaron Copland, and Lukas Foss was
another example. Bernstein and Copland were, for some time, lovers, and Howard
Pollack suggests that "without Bernstein, Copland probably would not have found
so large a public for his music; without Copland, Bernstein certainly would not have
written the kind of music he did."[77] They began corresponding when Bernstein was
nineteen and a student at Harvard, after meeting at an Anna Sokolow dance recital
in New York for Copland's birthday.[78] Foss and Bernstein's friendship was also
close and long-lasting. The two composer-conductors met as students at the Curtis
Institute of Music, and they were both prodigies at Tanglewood—where Copland
also taught for many decades since its inception.[79] Three years before Bernstein,
Foss, and Copland were brought together as the Rockefeller Foundation's Music
Advisory Committee, the latter two spent six weeks in 1960 in the Soviet Union, as
part of a U.S. State Department program.[80]

At the NEA, correspondence revealed that it was Copland who suggested
to chairman Stevens that Norman Singer would be a good member of the opera

subcommittee, along with Boris Goldovsky and Julius Rudel, and that Gunther Schuller should be chairman for an "unofficial advisory committee" on jazz.[81] As mentioned, at the Rockefeller Foundation Virgil Thomson made the early recommendations for the humanities division to contact Otto Luening and Quincy Porter. A similar system of referral also happened at the Ford Foundation. For example, in musicologist Paul Michael Covey's examination of Ford's Composers in Public Schools program, he reveals that to join the committee, current members suggested further individuals to recruit. Covey's work shows that the network of artists was rather limited, and that first-degree connections were significant, even if the program espoused a "nonpartisan stylistic attitude" and "ecumenical approach" in supporting tonal and atonal music.[82]

Several outcomes resulted from this form of social networking: a degree of insularity and self-reinforcement, and benefits that accrued from the powers and privileges of decision making. Sociologist Raymond Murphy attests that one of the desired outcomes of the monopolization of expertise is social closure: the exclusion and separation of experts from nonexperts.[83] As Schuller pointed out when he served as a consultant, "I cannot refrain from noting that I am so often in the position of recommending people or institutions for projects which I myself am vitally interested in."[84] Thus, tight social networks, often based on university or elite affiliation, facilitated the establishment of a group of outside consultants exercising their expertise to the exclusion of other voices, including those of laypersons, people without strong organizational attachments, and, significantly, women and minorities. Deliberation and debate could perhaps expand or push certain disciplinary and aesthetic boundaries, but for the most part, the system resisted change. Women and racial minorities lacked not only the cultural and social capital to contribute to this legitimacy but also the capital to even participate.

Finally, expertise was a renewable resource that magnified one's cultural, social, and symbolic (fame and celebrity) capital. Experts did not expend or deplete their expertise with each use. To the contrary, expertise grew every time an expert utilized it. The more the foundations and government entrusted and called upon someone to be an expert, the more he (rarely she) became famous and well known (as long as he comported to certain accepted standards of behavior and protocol). Philosopher Gloria Origgi refers to this phenomenon as exhibiting "aristocracy," where the rich get richer.[85] Due to the innumerable quantity of artists and arts groups, seeing and hearing everything was impossible. So a few artists became household names and garnered the most honors and awards. This was not to deny their tremendous talent, craft, hard work, or experiences; it was to comment on one of the operating principles of the structure from which they benefited. In a similar way, NEA and foundation officers, as "interactional experts," had a list of go-to consultants or panelists, as "contributory experts," for whatever issue was at hand. And when the interactional experts did not know someone, they asked for recommendations from contributory experts they already trusted or those who they had heard of before. Therefore, what characterized the system of expertise in arts grantmaking and evaluation during this time period was not simply objective knowledge and experience, but also fame, exclusion, and social networks.

2

GATEKEEPING FROM WITHIN

Grantmaking Officers as Interactional Experts

IN A SERIES of articles published in the *New Yorker* in 1955, Dwight Macdonald penned a satirical—nonetheless sharp-witted—account of the Ford Foundation's "philanthropoids." Macdonald used the neologism—taken from Frederick Keppel, former president of the Carnegie Corporation—to categorize the roughly fifty individuals at Ford who made the "crucial decisions in the foundation's work" and decided how to award more than $60 million ($550 million in 2017) each year.[1] The "philanthropoid" was "the middleman between the philanthropist and the philanthropee," and his profession was "the giving away of other people's money." Macdonald lampooned officers who "dictate the systolic flow of memoranda that is the blood stream of a modern foundation" and, perhaps meanly, chastised officers who "would deal with the problem of a man trapped in a burning house by subsidizing a study of combustion."[2] He interviewed one former officer who recalled that working at the foundation was like a "never-never land," because there "weren't any of the ordinary benchmarks that people can use in real life to see how they're doing." The officer said there was no way of telling whether the money the foundation spent was being used wisely or not. There was no competition and no criticism.

Even while Macdonald focused on the Ford Foundation, his description of the occupational duties and existential anxieties of serving as a philanthropoid were

Ask the Experts. Michael Sy Uy, Oxford University Press (2020). © Oxford University Press.
DOI: 10.1093/oso/9780197510445.001.0001.

applicable to the Rockefeller Foundation and, to an extent, the National Endowment for the Arts (NEA). More often, these grantmaking officers were *not* practicing artists, but instead former government officials or academics who served as "generalists." In other words, they were interactional experts. Contrasting with consultants who moved in and out of the process, staff members tended to hold their positions over longer periods of time, providing a level of stability and consistency to programs and missions. Their ability to determine fields of funding and select who to include and exclude in the decision making meant that they were powerful and influential figures.

Peeling back further the layers of arts grantmaking reveals how foundation and NEA staff provided a second-order epistemology to the system. They possessed the discursive knowledge and experience to maintain the operations of the arts field, and they served as an additional (i.e., second-order) checkpoint to evaluate the quality and legitimacy of information provided by contributory experts. As "philanthropoids," they acted as interpreters between the specialized world of artists and producers and a wider American audience and public. Given their power to spin their Rolodex of consultants and their control over the everyday functioning of the foundations and the NEA, officers played a significant and critical role as gatekeepers.

Officers' educational and personal backgrounds impacted their outlooks, preferences, and ideologies. The vast majority of them came from careers and backgrounds that prioritized objectivity and corporatization, and their goals in the arts also reflected an attempt at rationalizing the subjective. Especially at the two foundations, staff employed the entire arsenal of management discourse to codify a particular set of subjectivities—ones that they and their consultants held. Thus, they interpreted art, access, and diversity according to certain worldviews, deeply influenced by their networks and upbringing, as well as the political and social climate of the postwar years. In this regard, the ideas of Pierre Bourdieu and Michèle Lamont provide useful insights when connected with recent social psychological research on implicit associations and bias by Mahzarin Banaji and Anthony Greenwald.

In an effort to bring to life the personal histories of these individuals, in this chapter are interspersed short "character pieces" as biographical vignettes of key figures. Nancy Hanks (NEA, Box 2.1), Walter Anderson (NEA, Box 2.3), W. McNeil Lowry (Ford, Box 2.2), Edward F. D'Arms (Ford and Rockefeller, Box 2.5), and Norman Lloyd (Rockefeller, Box 2.4) each had a tremendous impact on the music and performing arts programs of their organizations. Hanks and Anderson were truly exceptional because they differed so greatly from the usual template of their peers: Hanks was one of the most prominent women in a male-dominated administrative field, and Anderson was one of the most influential African Americans. D'Arms was a unique example because he began his career at the Rockefeller Foundation, helping to build its humanities program, before moving to the Ford Foundation under a similar role. Lloyd was the first *artist* (as opposed to social scientist or generalist) to lead a division of a major foundation. All of these individuals were important checkpoints in a concentrated network that linked officers with consultants with grant recipients (also see Box 2.6).

A Typology of Staff, Officers, and Their Functions

The NEA and Ford and Rockefeller Foundations operated as hierarchical organizations divided by program areas. At the top were the chairman of the NEA, the president of Ford, and the president of Rockefeller. They oversaw directors (also known as vice presidents at Ford), who, in turn, oversaw their own associate and assistant directors, not to mention secretaries and other clerical workers. Figure 2.1 is a visual representation of the structures of each institution: the top boxes contain officer positions with responsibilities over the entire organization, and the bottom boxes contain positions that were division specific (e.g., arts and humanities, international affairs, agricultural sciences, etc., at Ford and Rockefeller; music, dance, theater, etc., at the NEA). Because position titles sometimes changed and varied, the term "officer" was used to refer to any staffed positions (from the chairman to assistant program directors).[3] Officers of the organization contrasted with the board of trustees or National Council on the Arts (NCA) members, who did not serve as

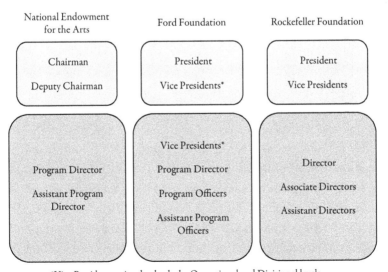

*Vice Presidents existed at both the Operational and Divisional levels

FIGURE 2.1 Organizational structure of the NEA and Ford and Rockefeller Foundations.

full-time paid professionals but as advisers and overseers; officers differed as well from clerical workers, who did not have decision-making capacities; and they were distinct from outside consultants and panelists, who were not employees, even if they were sometimes paid.[4] "Staff" refer broadly to the divisional officers (i.e., those in the bottom boxes).

The chairman of the NEA was appointed by the president of the United States and confirmed by the Senate for four-year terms. He or she also served as the chairman of the NCA, a body consisting of presidentially appointed individuals to advise the chairman on policies and programs. Early discussions in the House of Representatives centered on the authority of the chairman—they initially considered constraints for fear that he or she might become a "cultural czar."[5] Ultimately, however, Congress decided to vest "full authority for making awards in the chairperson, who was to be held accountable to the president and to the authorizing and appropriating committees of Congress for the actions of the agency."[6]

As an institution that focused solely on the arts, the NEA was different from the Ford and Rockefeller Foundations, both of which supported other program areas like biomedical research and education. Yet while the disciplines overseen by the NEA chairman differed in scope to those of the foundation presidents, functionally and symbolically, their leadership positions were similar: they were management roles that required a broad, generalist perspective. At all three institutions, the chairman/president oversaw, and even sometimes directly appointed, the directors of each division. For example, according to Ana Steele, who began working at the NEA in its first days, chairman Roger Stevens signed off on all program directors and panels.[7] Program directors, and in some cases council (NCA) members, suggested prospective panelists, but the chairman approved them all. While presidents of the two private foundations did not have such a controlling hand in these types of decisions—likely due to the much larger size of their institutions—they still represented the interests of each program director, especially at meetings of the board, when officers requested larger grant appropriations.

Below the top leadership, directors and associate directors of the Ford and Rockefeller Foundations and NEA played significant roles in the management and operation of each program at the divisional level, from deciding goals and policies, to advising grant applicants, to supervising panelists and outside consultants. At the NEA, deputy chairman Straight recalled that he attended panel meetings, proposed nominations for panelists and members of the NCA, and served as the primary coordinator for communication with members of Congress.[8] At Rockefeller, Howard Klein included among his roles as assistant director the screening and evaluating of proposals and new grants, as well as the evaluation

BOX 2.1
NANCY HANKS (1927–83)

Our orchestras will not become fossils like the dinosaur. On the contrary, they will be dynamos.[a]

Nancy Hanks was the second chairman of the NEA and the National Council on the Arts (1969–77), after Roger Stevens. Under her leadership, the budget of the NEA expanded from roughly $7 million in 1969 ($47 million in 2017) to $94 million in 1977 ($380 million in 2017). The staff also increased from roughly three dozen people employed by Stevens to over 215 by the time of Hanks's retirement. She supported the growth of existing programs like Music, Theater, and Dance, and established new programs for Museums and Expansion Arts. She also fostered the development of state arts agencies and regional arts programs, with an "arts for all Americans" vision for the NEA.

After graduating magna cum laude from Duke University with a degree in political science, Hanks served in a number of government agencies including the Office of Defense Mobilization before working as assistant and associate to two Rockefeller brothers, Nelson and Laurance. She was executive secretary for the Special Studies Project of the Rockefeller Brothers Fund, project coordinator for the report "The Performing Arts: Problems and Prospects," and eventually vice chairman for the organization before being appointed to the NEA. According to government scholar Margaret Wyszomirski:

[Hanks] had been thoroughly schooled in the consultative, networking style of foundation work . . . [involving] the forming of expert panels, coordinating advisory committee decisions, integrating diverse viewpoints, and distilling bountiful information and opinion into an acceptable and practical product.[b]

The same year Hanks became chairman, she also became president of the Associated Councils of the Arts, an organization dedicated to supporting and developing the arts in the United States and Canada.

Deputy chairman Michael Straight described Hanks as protective of her staff as if they were her family, which he thought was an inherited disposition attributed to her time working with the Rockefellers. "Within its walls, she was the head of a family rather than the chairman of a government agency. . . . Nancy was ruthless in disregarding established procedures and the needs of others when she wanted something for her family."[c] She also worked tirelessly and relentlessly and expected similar from her staff. According to the Arts Endowment's history, Hanks was the fourth-highest female appointee in the Nixon administration.[d]

[a]Folder: Speech: Amer. Sym. Orch. League June 19, 1974—Memphis, Tenn., Box 3, A1 Entry 5, Record Group 288 (RG288), The National Archives at College Park, Maryland (Archives II).
[b]Margaret Wyszomirski, "The Politics of Art: Nancy Hanks and the National Endowment for the Arts," in *Leadership and Innovation: A Biographical Perspective on Entrepreneurs in Government*, ed. Jameson W. Doig and Erwin C. Hargrove (Baltimore: Johns Hopkins University Press, 1987), 179.
[c]Michael Straight, *Nancy Hanks, An Intimate Portrait: The Creation of a National Commitment to the Arts* (Durham, NC: Duke University Press, 1988), 174.
[d]Mark Bauerlein and Ellen Grantham, eds., *National Endowment for the Arts: A History 1965–2008* (Washington, DC: National Endowment for the Arts, 2009), 39.

of existing programs.[9] The "Guidelines for Foundation Staff" issued by Ford noted that in developing grants, program officers were "expected to be professionally and intellectually knowledgeable in the field involved, and sensitive to the social implications of a proposed program action."[10] Officers needed to be aware of broader foundational and divisional perspectives and policies. "Requests for Grant Action" at Ford "set forth the rationale for approval of the grant requested by the prospective grantee and designated the responsible program officer." The standard format included a cover sheet with basic data and the recommended action, a brief précis, a description of the grant's objectives, and a description of how the grant fit in with existing activities.

Chairman Hanks noted in her request for additional funds to the Bureau of the Budget that responsibilities of the program staff included a large amount of technical assistance (management training, fundraising strategies, public outreach, etc.) to potential grantees. "Our program people spend virtually three-fourths of their time advising and counseling. One of our most important functions is to assist the arts groups in becoming better organized. . . . This is just as important a part of our program as actual dollars in grants."[11] Ford provided technical assistance as well, seeing a significant part of its work as providing "effective administration and fiscal management systems" for performing arts organizations.[12]

The Rockefeller Foundation stood somewhat apart from Ford and the NEA, due to its frequent changes in staff and divisions (see Table 2.1). Compared to the relative stability at the other two institutions, which allowed for greater long-term planning and execution, the Rockefeller Foundation had a more fragmentary and ad hoc approach to its arts grantmaking. Prior to the establishment of its arts division in 1964, eventual director Howard Klein described the foundation's work in the arts as "helter-skelter, responding to a crisis here or there, making an impact occasionally," but without any continuity or long-term planning.[13] Unlike Ford's program, which was under the leadership of Lowry from its establishment in 1957 until his retirement in 1974, the Rockefeller Foundation's arts division only existed as a distinct program

BOX 2.2

WILSON MCNEIL (MAC) LOWRY (1913–93)

> In the last twenty years, the Ford Foundation with the leadership of Mac Lowry, has
> served as a direct patron on a Medicean [i.e., the Medici family] scale. . . . McNeil
> Lowry has been the single most influential patron of the performing arts that the
> American democratic system has produced.[a]

W. McNeil Lowry joined the Ford Foundation in 1953 initially to head its education
program. In 1957, he became director of the humanities and the arts division, the first
program at a major philanthropy devoted to supporting the arts. In 1964, he was promoted to vice president of the division, as well as vice president of policy and planning for the foundation. Under his leadership, the Ford Foundation distributed over
$60 million ($460 million in 2017) to humanities scholarship and $320 million ($2.5
billion in 2017) to individual artists, artistic institutions, and performing arts organizations, including over $80 million ($620 million in 2017) in a single year to symphony
orchestras. Among other programs of special interest to Lowry were dance and the
development of regional theaters.

    Lowry received his bachelor's degree in 1934 from the University of Illinois and his
PhD in English in 1941 from the same institution. He also taught there from 1936 to
1942 before serving as a lieutenant in the U.S. Naval Reserve and writer for the Office
of War Information during World War II. Before beginning his tenure at the Ford
Foundation, he was associate director of the International Press Institute in Zurich,
Switzerland. He retired from the Ford Foundation in 1974.

---

[a]"An Album of Autograph Tributes Honoring W. McNeil Lowry," Folder L, Box 8, A1 Entry 3, RG288,
Archives II.

for the periods between 1964 and 1970, and from 1973 until the early 1980s. During
other periods, the humanities or social sciences divisions evaluated arts grants, lend-
ing an even greater interdisciplinary character.

    Turnover in staff at Rockefeller also resulted, at times, in a changed outlook on
previous grantees. For example, with the joining of the division of humanities and
social sciences under Kenneth W. Thompson, officers took a different perspective
on the relationship between the foundation and the American Symphony Orchestra
League (ASOL). After nine years of support, beginning in 1954 for conductor and
music critic workshops, the new division declined four further proposals. Deputy
director Chadbourne Gilpatric wrote to the ASOL president that the result was
largely due to changes that had taken place in program objectives and foundation
priorities, including "what may be favored for support in the creative and performing

BOX 2.3
WALTER ANDERSON (1915–2003)

Walter Anderson, composer, pianist, and music professor, was the second director of music at the NEA, after Fannie Taylor, who claimed to have recommended him to chairman Roger Stevens. Anderson graduated from Oberlin Conservatory, the Cleveland Institute of Music, and the Tanglewood Music Center. In 1946, he was appointed head of the music department at Antioch College, and was the first African American to chair a department outside of the historically black colleges. At the NEA, Anderson directed the music staff, had the largest budget, and oversaw the greatest number of panels.

Long-serving NEA officer Ana Steele recounted that Anderson was "extraordinarily creative, an endless stream of ideas, with energy to burn. He was charming in the best sense of the word, fun to be around, very smart, very verbal (he wrote the world's longest letters, trust me)."[a] And she recalled how he also was "insistent [and] good at pressing his points . . . always with a smile on his face with a little steel behind the smile." One of Steele's most vivid memories was when Anderson set up a hot griddle at a meeting of the music panel and cooked up a large stack of pancakes, fixed with butter and maple syrup. "Platefuls were handed up and down the panel table, their contents (there was juice and coffee, too) packed away by a surprised, delighted, and well-fed panel by the time the meeting ended. To my eye, it didn't seem to interrupt or dilute, in any way, the panel's work. Unforgettable."[b]

---

[a]After examining the NEA's archives, I can certainly corroborate this statement. Interview with Ana Steele, 14 12 2014.

[b]Ibid.

TABLE 2.1

Timeline of the Rockefeller Foundation in the Arts, 1932–73

1932	Division of humanities
1962	Division of humanities and social sciences
1965	Division of arts
1970	Division of arts and humanities
1973	Division of arts

arts."[14] Gilpatric stated that the declination was in no way a negative evaluation on the organization's performance based on previous grants, nor on the merits of the current submitted proposal. Nevertheless, the changes in the division corresponded with an end to grants for the league's workshops.

BOX 2.4
NORMAN LLOYD (1909–80)

Norman Lloyd became director of the newly established division of arts in 1965, and continued in the position as it remerged with the humanities division in 1970, until his retirement in 1972, shortly following a heart attack.[a] Lloyd was a self-described "artistic gadfly," with degrees in music education from New York University (NYU). He was a pianist, composer, conductor, teacher, and author. He had taught at the NYU School of Education and Sarah Lawrence College, and was director of education at the Juilliard School of Music, as well as dean of the Conservatory of Music at Oberlin College, before joining the Rockefeller Foundation. Lloyd was the first director of an arts-specific Rockefeller department. While the foundation had given arts and music grants in the preceding years, they were administered by directors and associates with backgrounds in the humanities or social sciences—none had any professional artistic experience. In addition to authoring and editing works including *The Fireside Book of Favorite American Songs* and *Fundamentals of Sight Singing and Ear Training*, Lloyd also composed and conducted dance scores and music for over thirty documentary and experimental films, and he published on the topic of music education in the *Juilliard Review, Dance Observer*, and *Film Music*.

    Conductor, performer, and musicologist Joshua Rifkin recalled Lloyd as one of his teachers at Juilliard when he was an undergraduate composition student. Rifkin remembered Lloyd as one of his defenders and protectors, especially because Rifkin was often in trouble with the administration because of his devotion to European serialism and other avant-garde music. Rifkin remembered Lloyd as "one of the nicest human beings," and it was Lloyd who reached out to him several years later to serve as a consultant for the Rockefeller Foundation as it developed its recording project of American music.[b]

[a] "Norman Lloyd," http://rockefeller100.org/biographical (Accessed 19 11 2015).
[b] Interview with Joshua Rifkin, 10 09 2015.

Educational and Cultural Backgrounds, Preferences, and Habitus

The most prevalent foundation officer was the generalist, who decided on grants and worked in the large divisions. Rather than focusing on one field or specialty alone, they regularly exercised judgment in domains outside their expertise. For example, an officer with a PhD in the cultural practices of Southeast Asia could still preside over a division that oversaw the economic development of the Caribbean. Furthermore, due to the overlap between the arts and humanities and the social sciences at Ford and Rockefeller, as opposed to the NEA, humanists and social scientists often decided on the earliest grants to musicians and arts organizations. Officers in these divisions may have had a proclivity toward certain art forms more than others, but overall, they did not possess specialized arts training, nor were they active arts practitioners. (For a timeline of key officers at each of these institutions, see Figures 2.2–2.4 at the end of this section.)

Officers' educations reflected how foundations prioritized the credentials provided by elite universities and institutions. The vast majority of officers came from middle- or upper-middle-class backgrounds, were from the northeastern United States, were white and male, and were part of social networks with high barriers to entry. As a result, how their socialization and experiences impacted their prejudices and decision making necessitates closer examination. Officers rationalized and contained the arts within management discourses of objectivity, and this impetus was a product of their own social and educational pedigrees. Furthermore, officers' generally advantaged socioeconomic, urban, and white upbringings, along with the privileged position of Western art music, coincided with their patronage of this aestheticized and legitimized art form more than any other.

According to sociologist Pierre Bourdieu, individuals' "habitus" is a product of their socialization, from their family, to their education, to the political, economic, and cultural environment in which they grew up.[15] An Ivy League education is different from a public school education, as an East Coast education is different from a midwestern education (n.b., "different" implies neither "worse" nor "better"); similarly, one's experience and access to resources, like wealth and a parent who encouraged attendance of performances at the Metropolitan Opera, impact one's familiarity with, perspectives on, and attitudes toward opera.[16] Sometimes people understand their habitus as part of their identity, or social group membership. In the words of philosopher Kwame Anthony Appiah, "among the most significant things people do with their identities is use them as the basis of hierarchies of status and respect and of structures of power."[17]

Furthermore, the way individuals see the world and how it works is persistent despite changes in social and economic circumstances, no matter where individuals live, what they do, or how much money they make. People bring their experiences with them—whether they are fond memories or traumas they prefer to lock away. Individuals are not at liberty to do whatever they want or think however they want; how one is socialized impacts—although does not necessarily determines—one's beliefs and preferences. Therefore, the social and educational backgrounds of foundation officers were consequential, having a core bearing on what they viewed as legitimate projects for funding.

More recently, social psychologists Mahzarin Banaji and Anthony Greenwald demonstrate how socialization directly influences people's prejudices, which in turn affect—often unconsciously—how they evaluate others and others' work. Through an implicit association test, they show humans' "hidden biases," demonstrating empirically the fact that an individual's habitus affects his or her preferences or actions, and that these attitudes are durable and resistant to change.[18] While widely used in showing the automatic (versus reflective) preferences and mental associations individuals have with respect to race or gender, the test also reveals "group-based preferences, stereotype, and identities that may not be accessible to conscious awareness."[19]

Due to the natural tendency of human beings to make associations and form categories, it is difficult to listen to music or identify a composer without placing a genre or label on it. Listeners categorize composers as classical, jazz, Romantic, or modern. Critics add qualifiers like avant-garde and Second Viennese School, but these descriptors don't significantly change the "camp" or "category" to which composers belong.[20] Importantly, different categories carry different aesthetic weight in cultural practice, which can change the way people hear things or associate certain genres with negative or positive stereotypes. Think, for example, of the moral panic that arose with rap in the 1990s or the belief that listening to Mozart makes babies smarter. Banaji and Greenwald refer to "ingrained habits of thought that lead to errors in how we perceive, remember, reason, and make decisions" as "mindbugs."[21] These blind spots prevent people from seeing (or hearing) in what ways their decisions are not truly objective, despite appearing to be so, and in what ways education and socialization determine what individuals endorse and support as legitimate.

An analysis of the habitus of Ford Foundation officers offers critical insight. Internal reports completed by Mary Brucker and Merrimon Cuninggim, advisers and consultants for Ford, show data of "The Foundation's People and Their Work."[22] (Cuninggim also came from the foundation world, having served as president of the Danforth Foundation.) Their statistical analysis looked at demographic criteria such as age, previous work experience, and length at the institution. According to their analysis, the foundation was a relatively young organization, with a vast majority in the thirty-one- to fifty-year-old brackets; moreover, most had worked for the foundation for less than ten years, with the greatest number working less than five. Nearly half had previous experience in business and industry, almost a third had teaching experience, a fifth had been in academic administration, and another fifth in some branch of government.[23]

Brucker and Cuninggim characterized professional staff as "intelligent, articulate, knowledgeable, often erudite, and at ease in 'intellectual circles' (whatever they are)." In the *New Yorker* articles, Macdonald also described the Ford "philanthropoids" as "youngish, earnest, sincere (as social workers, rather than advertising men, use the term), unpretentious, and, above all, friendly."[24] Brucker and Cuninggim attributed their ease as a product of the high levels of education that many had received, with one-third having a master's as their terminal degree, and one-quarter having a PhD or equivalent. Less than 10% had not attained a bachelor's degree. Among the most represented undergraduate colleges were (in descending order) Harvard, Yale, New York University, Oberlin, Columbia, Princeton, and Fordham. Among the most represented institutions for graduate study (in descending order) were Harvard, Columbia, Yale, Princeton, Cornell, Chicago, the University of California, Berkeley, the University of Michigan, and the University of Pennsylvania. As Brucker and Cuninggim observed, it was "indeed heavily weighted toward the Ivy League, but diluted with some virile, largely Eastern, strains." The authors additionally categorized the staff based on their political characteristics:

> Their social and political outlook, too, seems pretty much of a piece—middle-of-the-road, armchair suburban liberal; usually voting Democratic but casting an occasional gander at the Republicans; non-joiner but staunchly upright; scornful of Rotary but having many Rotarian values.[25]

BOX 2.5

EDWARD FRANCIS (CHET) D'ARMS (1904–91)

Edward F. D'Arms was a key individual with careers in both the Rockefeller Foundation and the Ford Foundation arts and humanities programs. D'Arms graduated Phi Beta Kappa from Princeton in classics, studied at Oxford (Oriel College) on a Rhodes scholarship, and returned to his alma mater for a doctorate. He also taught classics there and at the University of Minnesota and the University of Colorado before serving as an army major in France and Germany during World War II. Beginning in 1947, he was assistant director of humanities (later becoming associate) for the Rockefeller Foundation. In 1957, he moved to the Ford Foundation, serving twelve years as a program officer until 1969.

Once moving to Ford, D'Arms was directly involved in the early establishment of its Humanities and Arts program, as well as a music panel. In fact, among D'Arms's early recommendations for the panel were Quincy Porter (Yale) and Virgil Thomson (Harvard), undoubtedly consultants he drew on from his experiences at Rockefeller.[a] He justified their employment in objective terms, however, as "established composers who had also concerned themselves with problems of publication." A second project involving the extension of opportunities for professional solo and ensemble instrumentalists included panel recommendations for Isaac Stern, Yehudi Menuhin, Rudolf Serkin, and Peggy Glanville-Hicks. These artists were all musicians that D'Arms knew from Rockefeller and who eventually assisted Ford and the NEA in their grants as well.

[a] From Edward F. D'Arms to W. McNeil Lowry, 07 04 1958, Subject: Purposes and Personnel of a Music Panel, Folder: Music Conference: May 23–24, 1958, Box 36, Series XI, FA640, FF, RAC.

By the last, they likely meant that while the staff espoused values of service, they did not want to see themselves as overly idealistic. They had a stronger faith that their work was based on objective data and supportable facts—something they had learned to value during their education.

At the Rockefeller Foundation, the high educational attainment of its officers was also evident in the makeup of its humanities division. Director Charles B. Fahs received his BS, MA, and PhD in political science from Northwestern University and had extensive experience in Japan and the State Department before joining the foundation in 1946.[26] His program began with three officers, John Marshall (MA in English from Harvard), Chadbourne Gilpatric (BS from Harvard, Rhodes Scholar at Oxford, with a focus on India), and Edward F. D'Arms (see Box 2.5), before doubling with the addition of three more specialists: Robert Crawford (BA from Yale, MA and PhD from Princeton) was a specialist in Middle Eastern and African affairs, Boyd Compton (BA and MA from Princeton) was a Far Eastern specialist with experience in South and Southeast Asia, and Robert July (PhD) had experience in African studies at the University College of Ibadan, Nigeria.[27]

The generalist and nonarts backgrounds of these staff members were critical. Using the terminology of social psychology, they relied on a "referred expertise," or the use of an expertise learned in one domain (social science and humanities) and applied within another (art). The strong intellectual and academic interests of the Rockefeller Foundation's officers were furthermore evident in a five-year review undertaken, focusing on the models of expertise and knowledge attainment provided by university settings.[28] The confidential report evaluated each of the foundation's divisions. Concern within the humanities and social sciences touched upon the difficulty of finding obvious measurements for evaluating progress, which, for example, officers more easily accomplished in the agriculture program by quantifying crop yields.

Officers used the same grant evaluation forms regardless of division, meaning that in practice, they rated arts grants according to the same utilitarian or scientific purposes as grants in medicine or international development. They rated applications on a five-point scale according to a rubric that looked at relevance to program objectives, innovative value of proposal, degree of risk, financial feasibility, probability of success, and potential for other benefits.[29] Additionally, they judged the grant's goals based on its capacity to generate new knowledge; provide a new application of, or disseminate further, existing knowledge; test existing hypotheses; innovate services; establish new training, service, or research programs; and support creative work. Officers rated the value of proposals as high, above average, average, below average, or low. Given these criteria and the officers who passed judgment, it was clear that the foundation attempted to rationalize the arts with the same objectivity as its other departments.

BOX 2.6
ADDITIONAL ROCKEFELLER FOUNDATION OFFICERS

Charles Burton Fahs (1908–80)
Fahs received his BS (1929), MA (1931), and PhD (1933) from Northwestern University. He was a specialist in Far Eastern studies, beginning as an instructor in Oriental affairs at Pomona College, before becoming an assistant professor. He also served as an analyst for the Far Eastern Division of the Office of Strategic Services during the war, and he received the U.S. Medal of Freedom. He began as an assistant director of the humanities at the Rockefeller Foundation in 1946, was promoted to associate director in 1949, and was director from 1950 to 1962. He left to join the U.S. Information Agency at the U.S. embassy in Tokyo.[a]

Chadbourne Gilpatric (1914–89)
Gilpatric graduated from Harvard in 1937 and then went to study as a Rhodes Scholar at Balliol College, Oxford. He pursued further graduate studies at Princeton and Harvard but did not complete formal degrees. During the war, he served in the U.S. Army as a captain. He joined the Rockefeller Foundation in 1949 as an assistant director of humanities, becoming an associate director in 1956. In 1964, he left the New York office to serve as a visiting professor of philosophy at the University of Delhi. He filled a number of roles including member of the Task Force in Higher Education of the Indian National Education Committee and member of the Indian Agricultural Research Institute. He retired in 1972 while on the field staff of the foundation in India.[b]

John Marshall (1903–80)
Marshall received his AB from Harvard in 1925 and began teaching there as an assistant English instructor and executive secretary at the Medieval Academy of America. He received his MA in 1928. He joined the Rockefeller Foundation in 1933 as assistant director of humanities and in 1940 became the associate director. His signature arts program at the foundation was the $400,000 Louisville Orchestra commissions. He left the humanities to serve as the influential director of the Villa Serbelloni (also known as the Bellagio Center) from 1959 to 1970. During their time, he and his wife, Charlotte Trowbridge Marshall, hosted hundreds of distinguished scientists, scholars, and artists from all over the world.[c]

Kenneth W. Thompson (1921–2013)
Thompson obtained his AB from Augustana College in 1943 and his MA (1948) and PhD (1950) from the University of Chicago. He alternated between the University of Chicago and Northwestern University as assistant and associate professor of political science and international relations. He joined the Rockefeller Foundation first as a consultant for social sciences in 1953, then steadily rose from assistant director in 1955 to

associate director in 1957, director in 1960, and finally vice president in 1961, where he continued for more than a decade through 1974. He left the foundation to become the director of the Miller Center at the University of Virginia, Arlington.[d]

Boyd Compton (1925–2011)

Compton graduated with an AB from Princeton (1948) and then received an MA in Far Eastern studies from the University of Washington (1951). He joined the Rockefeller Foundation as a consultant in 1958 and after a year was appointed to assistant director of the humanities. He read, wrote, and spoke Indonesian, Russian, and Dutch, and published a volume of translations from Chinese. In 1967, he left the foundation to become director of the Environmental Arts Group, a major program at the new School of Arts at New York University. The group was an experimental workshop for artists exploring new forms of media, which was also designated to develop freshman courses on sensory perception and "environmental awareness."[e] He joined the group along with Rockefeller grantee Morton Subotnick, both of them having worked together on the Mills College Performing Group and Tape Music Center.

Gerald Freund (1930–97)

Freund was born in Berlin in 1930 but moved with his family to the United States by way of Holland and England. He graduated from Haverford College in 1952 and returned to the United Kingdom on a Fulbright scholarship to attend St. John's College, Oxford, where he earned his DPhil in 1955. A Rockefeller Foundation grant allowed him to remain there for an additional two years as a senior scholar and research fellow at St. Anthony's. Prior to joining the foundation as a consultant, Freund went back to his alma mater to become an assistant professor of political science, and he published two books, *Unholy Alliance* (1957) and *Germany Between Two Worlds* (1961). He was assistant director for humanities and social sciences at the Rockefeller Foundation beginning in 1961 and became associate director in 1964, moving to full-time status in the newly established arts division in 1965. After leaving the foundation in 1969, Freund later served as dean of Humanities and the Arts at Hunter College, as well as director of its new Arts Center.[f] In the 1980s, he was the first director of the MacArthur Foundation's "genius grants."

Howard Klein (1931–)

Klein was born in New Jersey and grew up in Maryland and Washington, DC, where he began private piano studies with Daisy Fickénscher.[g] He completed undergraduate work at Murray State College, Kentucky, before moving to Southeastern Louisiana College (now University), graduating in 1952 with a Bachelor of Music. One of his classmates was jazz pianist Bill Evans. He served in the U.S. Air Force from 1953 to 1957 and, upon discharge, began studying and teaching piano at Juilliard. He earned a BS in music in 1960 and a master's in 1962, and he joined the faculty teaching music theory in the dance division. From 1962 to 1967, he was a reporter and music critic for the *New York Times*. While at the *New York Times*, the Rockefeller Foundation hired him as a consultant for its composer-in-residence program. He joined the foundation as assistant director in 1967, under Norman Lloyd. He became director in 1972 and was known especially for his support of creative artists in music, theater, dance, film, and video art. He retired from the foundation in 1986 due to health reasons. After his departure, he consulted for the Wallace Foundation, the Pew Charitable Trust, the MacArthur Foundation, and the NEA.

Additional Ford Foundation Officer
Marcia Thompson (1923–2018)
Thompson was born in China, where her father worked for the Standard Oil Company.[h] She attended the Katherine Gibbs Secretarial School and began working as an assistant to the editor of the *New York Times Magazine*. While on assignment with the International Press Institute in Zurich, she met W. McNeil Lowry. They both joined the Ford Foundation in 1953. As noted in her obituary in the *New York Times*, she worked with Lowry to create "the framework for unprecedented, nation-wide expansion of professionally and fiscally sound initiatives, notably in the performing arts."[i] The programs she oversaw at Ford concerned the financial health and long-term stability of the largest performing groups, from the Symphony Orchestra grants in 1965 to the endowments for conservatories during the 1960s and 1970s, and lastly the creation of the National Arts Stabilization Funds. She retired from the Ford Foundation after three decades in 1983.

[a]Folder 87: Fahs, Charles B., Box 2, FA485 Rockefeller Foundation Biographical File, RF, RAC.
[b]Folder 109: Gilpatric, Chadbourne, Box 3, FA485, RF, RAC.
[c]Folder 207: Marshall, John, Box 5, FA485, RF, RAC.
[d]Folder 317: Thompson, Kenneth W., Box 7, FA485, RF, RAC.
[e]Folder 54: Compton, Boyd H., Box 1, FA485, RF, RAC.
[f]Folder 100: Freund, Gerald, Box 3, FA485, RF, RAC.
[g]Interview with Howard Klein, 29 03 2019.
[h]"Unsung Advocate for the Arts," http://laffsociety.org/News.asp?PostID=1000 (Accessed 28 08 2019).
[i]"Marcia Thompson," *New York Times*, April 10, 2018.

Finally, the approach of focusing on areas where officers or contracted consultants were expert, to an extent, limited the types of programs that they funded. D'Arms wrote a memorandum on staff procedures and duties while at Rockefeller.[30] (He very likely brought these ideas with him to Ford when he became an officer there, three years later.) D'Arms suggested remarkably that the humanities division at the

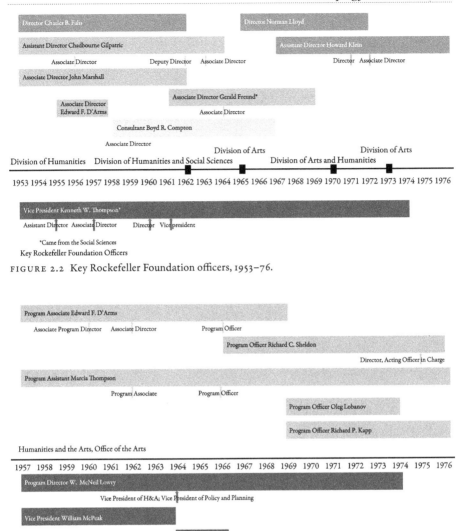

FIGURE 2.2 Key Rockefeller Foundation officers, 1953–76.

FIGURE 2.3 Key Ford Foundation officers, 1957–76.

Rockefeller Foundation limit its programs "to subjects in which officers [were] or [could] soon become reasonably expert and in which they [could], in their travels, concentrate essentially on the operational functions of their responsibility." Using this focused approach, he predicted that a small number of projects within a few fields could be carefully analyzed and proposed to the trustees. "This would make our projects more definitely selective and would be likely to assure consistently high quality with a minimum risk of disappointment or failure." Therefore, the limitation of program areas to the domains of expertise the staff possessed indicated a risk-averse and limiting approach to grantmaking.

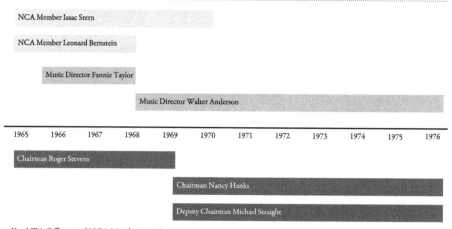

Key NEA Officers and NCA Members in Music

FIGURE 2.4 Key NEA officers and NCA members in music, 1965–76.

At the foundations especially, the emphasis on "objective" criteria to evaluate grants in the arts (as they were in other divisions) and the "generalist" backgrounds of most staff trained in social sciences or economics degrees at Ivy League schools substantially impacted the programs that officers developed and maintained. Not only did they exhibit a largely conservative approach to the arts, but also, due to the perceived high artistic value of Western classical music, foundations predominantly focused on symphony orchestras, opera companies, and university-based new music centers. Relationships among staff and consultants, as well as staff and boards of trustees, demonstrated how officers' habitus and unconscious biases shaped the decision-making process. Additionally, it was not that habitus only mattered for officers and not for consultants, but that one could hide one's preferences through the discourses of impartiality and meritocracy. By contrast, the fact that an artist might be an advocate of his or her own practice was clear from the beginning.

Relationships Between Staff and Consultants

Officers wielded significant power in their relationships with consultants. While in most cases at the Rockefeller Foundation and NEA (Ford officers used panelists to a lesser extent) staff did not decide themselves on the outcome of grants or of grant amounts, they nevertheless played a decisive role in the way that panelists understood what was acceptable and unacceptable.

In sociologist Michèle Lamont's examination of competitive, interdisciplinary academic fellowships, she finds an important role in program officers' selection of screeners and panelists, their assembly of individual panels, and their supervision over panel deliberations. Lamont makes a convincing case that these discretionary powers were some of the strongest determinants of competition outcomes because they could change the balance of ideological and disciplinary priorities within a panel. Since definitions of quality, originality, and excellence varied by institutional affiliation, discipline, and intragroup membership, the types of grants that officers chose were greatly impacted by the people they involved. For example, the bias of homophily ("love of the same") was significant because it meant that one appreciated work that most resembled one's own. According to Lamont, senior and established academics often defined excellence as work that "spoke most to them," which was often akin to "what was most like them."[31]

Furthermore, Lamont suggests that the determination of institutional rules as well as the enforcement of these rules in panel deliberations affected the frame and hardware in which selection and interaction occurred. Program officers (or their elected panel chairs), for instance, supervised deliberations by ensuring the flow of discussions, allowing panelists to express their opinions in an equitable and orderly manner, and guaranteeing that applicants received a fair hearing.[32] As panelists quickly learned the rules of engagement, they came to understand what constituted acceptable behavior, in what ways they could voice agreement and dissent, and roughly the amount of time to spend on each application. Lamont notes that the program officers she interviewed uniformly stressed the importance of "collegiality," and that panelists who were personable were more desirable.[33] The underlying possibility that if they did not abide by these rules they would not be invited back was one way of policing or regulating conduct.

Lamont's narrative is also reflective of the way program officers ran the NEA and Ford and Rockefeller Foundations. At the NEA, for example, chairman Hanks noted to her directors that "the most productive meetings [were] based on well-structured agendas and background material supplied well in advance [by the staff]."[34] By contrast, "informal 'policy discussions' were not possible when people were not advised in advance of what they were to think about nor when everyone came into the meeting without at least a simple common point of reference." When the NEA staff felt that the panelists had made a mistake in deciding on a project, the director suggested that the panel re-evaluate its selection, in effect, implying that the panel had got it wrong. And while staff for the most part upheld panel decisions, there was also the possibility that panelists would not be invited back to participate, since directors (in consultation with the chairman and the deputy chairman) chose panel membership and rotation.

At the Rockefeller Foundation, a particularly illuminating example of staff-panelist relations occurred when Arthur Mendel, head of the Department of Music at Princeton, applied for a grant to use computers to analyze ten masses by composer Josquin Desprez. Mendel wanted to convert the Renaissance musical notation into "computer-accessible notation," or punched cards, to solve "some elementary problems in the theory of contemporary twelve-tone and non-twelve-tone composition."[35]

To evaluate the proposal, long-term Rockefeller consultant Martin Bookspan recommended to associate director Gerald Freund that new experts should be sought for their advice: Arthur Berger (Brandeis, Music Department), Richard Franko Goldman (conductor), Goddard Lieberson (Columbia Records), and Michael Steinberg (music critic, *Boston Globe*). As Bookspan wrote, "I hate go to back to the same people time after time for opinions about various proposals, and so let's try a few new ones on this one."[36] (Bookspan acted more like a part-time staff member who specialized in music, rather than a consultant that was hired for one-off projects.) Freund accepted all of Bookspan's recommendations apart from one. For whatever reason, Freund crossed out the name of Lieberson. Freund additionally recommended Stefan Bauer-Mengelberg (IBM), Alan Rich (*New York Herald Tribune*), and composer Iannis Xenakis.

Several aspects of this process were important to note: first, the conscious effort to use different experts and not to rely on the same ones to evaluate every project—an anxiety due to the fact that this practice had hitherto not been routine; second, foundation staff members decided by consensus, and on an individual grant basis, which experts were evaluators—the process was ad hoc, rather than systematized; and third, foundation staff maintained significant discretionary power, serving as final gatekeepers.[37]

Most revealing was how Bookspan and Freund decided to overrule the recommended rejection of at least one of the experts.[38] Richard Franko Goldman's response had been the most damning: "The project seems to me not only completely without value, but to represent an extreme case of one of the gnawing diseases of our society: the travesty of scholarship and service to the arts."[39] Goldman did not see what could be accomplished by computers that individual study or performance did not similarly achieve, and he viewed the project as overly academic and interesting only to those personally engaged. To Goldman, it represented "a perfect example of the sort of thing on which money is often spent today, and for which no money should be made available."

In addition to Freund's marginalia that Goldman was "too strong" or had "a misunderstanding at best," brief intraoffice correspondence between Freund and Bookspan demonstrated their questioning of Goldman's judgment. Rather than addressing the critiques that Goldman posed regarding the validity of the proposal, Freund wrote to Bookspan that Goldman's "ardent letter" led him to question the "man's judgment" and that even if there were "many factions among music professionals," the foundation's advisers still needed to "exercise more balanced judgment in evaluating proposals."[40] Bookspan cautiously agreed, writing that Goldman may have "gone off the deep end in a few of the things he said," but that they should not "dismiss his reaction as hysterical."[41] Bookspan acknowledged that Goldman's was "a point of view that I'm sure we'll find articulated by others, too," and that whatever the decision, their investigations and research "ought to be pretty exhaustive." Bookspan concluded at length:

> Just a word about Goldman himself. I don't know him at all well, but the few occasions on which I've had any contact with him he has struck me as a thoughtful, sincere and intelligent man. I think he arrived at his appraisal of the Princeton proposal only after very serious consideration of it. And I'm sure his reaction is genuine.

By contrast, the letters of recommendation that Freund and Bookspan received from Berger and Bauer-Mengelberg, while positive, were vague in their evaluations and reasons for support. Bauer-Mengelberg wrote, "I am not familiar with the particular work being done in stylistic analysis, but the goals seem appropriately modest."[42] Ultimately, Princeton received the research funding. Kenneth W. Thompson, at the time acting director for humanities and social sciences, signed the grant-in-aid for $15,000 ($120,000 in 2017) one month later. And despite the negative critiques against Goldman's judgment, he continued to serve as a consultant for the foundation, playing an especially large role in its Recorded Anthology of American Music.

The critical role of Rockefeller program directors in this example, though, was just one instance of *every* grant decision that officers made within the divisions. Foundation and NEA staff decided who to involve in the decision-making process, whose opinions and evaluations were reasonable or unreasonable, and how individuals interacted with each other. While not always as heavy-handed as this case, their influence as second-order gatekeepers was tremendous. From the opposite perspective of the decision-making hierarchy, staff also negotiated their roles with those higher up in command, and thus their relationships with trustees is also worth further inquiry.

Relationships Between Staff and Boards of Trustees

At the top of the chain were the boards of trustees of the Ford Foundation and the Rockefeller Foundation, as well as the NCA, which oversaw the NEA. They determined foundation and Arts Endowment governance, program areas, and professional standards. Trustees and council members had ultimate say in grants, and their approval was needed for the largest and most expensive ones. Yet, even though the proverbial buck stopped with them, trustees were also a step removed from the grantmaking. While they sometimes made their own recommendations, for the most part, they were not directly involved in the administrative, day-to-day, operational functioning of the institutions. They did not pick up the phone; they did not schedule or attend routine meetings; they did not talk shop in the corporate cafeteria. Therefore, the working relationships trustees developed with foundation and NEA staff were vital.

Trustees occupied an even rarer and more solidified social position than officers. According to William Whyte Jr.'s analysis of "What Are the Foundations Up To?" in *Fortune* magazine, of the forty-seven trustees at Ford, Carnegie, and Rockefeller, in 1955, twenty-nine were businesspeople, bankers, or lawyers; nine were educators; three were scientists; four were foundation executives; and one was an architect.[43] There was only one woman, Mrs. Margaret Carnegie Miller. Fifty-five percent of the trustees went to an Ivy League college, and of that group, 82% went to Harvard, Yale, or Princeton. Thirteen of the forty-seven, or over a quarter, were trustees of other foundations. Sociologist Inderjeet Parmar's own recent analysis of Ford, Carnegie, and Rockefeller Foundation trustees shows that they were "a core part of the power elite of the United States—unrepresentative, unaccountable, yet highly influential in the nation's foreign relations, undermining pluralistic notions of competing elites."[44]

Much like the role of outside consultants, trustees served as another source of experience and expertise (usually from a wide variety of fields, including the sciences, business, and government). They broadened the range of generalist knowledge while still representing their respective personal, professional, and social interests. They were interactional experts par excellence. By contrast, members of the NCA, while also bringing with them connections, experience, and influence, were quintessential contributory experts, including some of the nation's most well-known artists.

During the earliest years of the NEA, when the staff was limited and there were not yet any panelists, the NCA functioned in a much different manner, taking on the role of both staff and consultants, and recommending and debating their own grants and special interests. Ana Steele, at the time a secretary, recalled in an interview that "the Council was very active in helping carve out the shape and scope of what became the Arts Endowment's programs, and, in some cases in those very early years, in determining (urging) some grant recipients as well."[45]

The two most vocal NCA members representing the field of music were violinist Isaac Stern and conductor-composer Leonard Bernstein. Until the establishment of the first music advisory panel under Aaron Copland, the charismatic Stern, in particular, significantly influenced the several large grants proposed in music. Chief among his suggestions were the Carnegie Hall-Jeunesses Musicales program to send gifted young soloists to tour the United States; a National Chamber Orchestra at Carnegie Hall to help find and train orchestra section leaders and concert masters; and a Kodaly Fellowship Program and Institute based on the work of the Hungarian music educator.

Stern's presidency of Carnegie Hall and his experiences as a world-renowned violin virtuoso undoubtedly influenced the first two of these proposals. But despite Stern's prominent positions, the grants encountered strong resistance from established concert managers and orchestras who feared that the NEA was taking over their jobs, or that it was poaching their best musicians. Ultimately, the Jeunesses Musicales program and National Chamber Orchestra proposals failed. Nevertheless, Stern's strength of personality showed how in the NEA's earliest days, it awarded grants not through a peer-review panel process, but by the judgment of a limited number of individuals. The emergence of panels was a response to, and a turn away from, the controversial nature of decision making as undertaken by members of the NCA. In other words, the NEA exchanged their functions as contributory experts for their advice as interactional experts.

At the foundations, for the most part, trustees endorsed the decisions and recommendations of the arts and music staff, but there were also times when relations were not so smooth. One of the most controversial trustee appropriations at the Rockefeller Foundation was for $200,000 ($1.5 million in 2017) to the Business Committee for the Arts (BCA), founded by David Rockefeller to encourage corporate donations to the visual and performing arts.[46] One officer in particular, associate director Gerald Freund (the same officer who oversaw the grant to analyze Josquin masses at Princeton), was upset about such a large grant going to a new and untested organization. In interoffice correspondence with director Norman Lloyd, Freund wrote:

> No item of any program I have been associated with here disturbs me as deeply as this one. The wisdom of an RF [Rockefeller Foundation] item for a new organization, officially headed by one of our trustees [Douglas Dillon, trustee of the Rockefeller Foundation and chairman of the BCA], and inspired by a member of the Rockefeller family [David] is for officers above my level to judge. That goes too for the fact that the RBF [Rockefeller Brothers Fund] is the other principal funding source—a combination I have repeatedly been told here was undesirable. . . . To me it is simply ironic that an organization made up of some of the wealthiest businessmen in the country leading some of the most lucrative corporations in the country whose declared purpose it is to raise funds for American cultural activities should turn to the RF and succeed in obtaining basic operating costs.[47]

Freund's letter pointed to several tensions in the relationships between staff and trustees. First, he was upset by the fact that the foundation gave such a large grant to a single, new organization when "over the past months one institution after another in the arts . . . had to be deprived of funds." Second, the selection of the BCA in particular pointed to a distrust concerning the impartiality or objectivity of the grantmaking process since its chairman Douglas Dillon was also a Rockefeller Foundation trustee, and its founder, David, was a member of the Rockefeller family. These connections represented a clear conflict of interest. And third, the process became fractured because the division of labor between staff and trustees was disrupted. The staff members sidestepped the due diligence normally undertaken in their evaluation of applications to accommodate the objectives of certain trustees.

As scholar Mary Anna Culleton Colwell points out during this time period, foundations across the field practiced "wide variation" when it came to trustee relationships and whether trustees could serve on the boards of both a grantmaking institution (e.g., the Rockefeller Foundation) and a grant-receiving organization (e.g., the BCA).[48] Some foundations didn't consider overlapping membership to be a conflict of interest and even relied on trustees' personal experiences with groups to inform decisions, while others had fairly strict guidelines, including voting eligibility and exclusion from discussions pertaining to such grants. Colwell also suggests that recipient organizations sought foundation trustees to join their own boards "precisely because they improved their access to that foundation, and to the foundation sector as a whole. . . . Having foundation trustees on the board of directors provided 'credibility.' "[49]

While these examples of Stern's NCA proposals and the Rockefeller Foundation's BCA grant were ones when staff members perceived of trustees overstepping the line or acting in a conflict of interest, the historical record generally did not show frequent disagreement. At one end of the spectrum they may have found certain pet projects to advocate, while on the other end, they simply rubberstamped the results of panel and staff deliberations. Nevertheless, their power should not be underestimated. Trustees and council members were significant sources of interactional and contributory expertise in the concentrated network of actors involved in the U.S. arts field.

A Further Thought on Expertise

As documented in these two chapters, foundations and the NEA brought panelists and outside consultants into the decision making because of their extensive experiences as arts practitioners—that is, as those actively contributing to the making of art. As NEA general counsel Robert Wade stated, "The interests of the arts required a maximum contribution from the leaders in each field"; consequently, NCA members and consultants should not have disqualified themselves as participants in arts organizations and projects supported by the NEA just because they served on the council or on panels. Instead, they were simply to have been "alert to avoid any action" that could be interpreted as furthering their own interests or those of an organization with which they were affiliated.[50] The point was not to question hidden motives or the actual expertise that experts possessed, but to be more cognizant of how expertise could be used in unfair or exclusionary ways.

Returning to the ideas of sociologists Collins and Evans, they propose one more fruitful way of thinking about expertise, focusing on the differences between expertise in the sciences and expertise in the arts, and specifically, on a special kind of "meta-expertise" known as connoisseurship. Citing the Chamber's Dictionary definition of the term, Collins and Evans write that a "connoisseur" is "a person with a well-informed knowledge and appreciation." Connoisseurship is judgment honed by exercise and experience within a domain. In music, for example, a connoisseur could be someone with the ability to distinguish a Haydn symphony from a Mozart symphony or a thirteenth-century motet from a fifteenth-century motet, or in the case of arts grantmaking, someone who knows a fiscally responsible arts group from a wasteful one. In the words of Bourdieu, connoisseurship is an "unconscious mastery of the instruments of appropriation which derives from slow familiarization and is the basis of familiarity with works."[51] Yet what is significant about connoisseurship is that this meta-expertise is much more concerned (and confined) to art (and food and wine) than it is to science. Rarely are there connoisseurs of thermonuclear fusion or sciurine reproduction.

Elaborating further on this distinction between the presence of arts connoisseurs and their absence in the sciences, Collins and Evans refer back to the role of interactional expertise. In science, which is directed toward a truth more than a reaction or conceptual idea, "competition is between those with contributory expertise and everyone else," while in art, "competition [is] between those with interactional expertise, on the one hand, and ordinary folk on the other."[52] Put another way, journalists who report on sciences rarely define the meaning of the work, usually instead summarizing and describing; arts critics, however, regularly attempt to interpret meaning. As Collins and Evans write, one of the defining features of the "provocative arts," that is, certain avant-garde art, is the artist's intention not to deliver information, but to engender reaction. If this is indeed the case, then those who are best positioned to judge the art work are not other artists, but art critics (or grantmaking officers), who possess a greater breadth of interactional expertise. At the same time, the art critic also stands in contradistinction to the general public, who possesses neither the contributory nor the interactional expertise to judge the work of art. (Of course, this understanding is a particular [modernist] ideology itself of the nature, purpose, and social role of avant-garde art.)

Therefore, the premise of grant applications in the arts conflicts with the peer-review process in science and academia more generally, whereby projects submitted by contributory experts—like thermonuclear physicists and mammologists, or composers and performers—are best judged by other contributory experts. Extending this logic, it is the connoisseur with interactional expertise and years of experience that should judge the proposed art project.

What still remains largely unresolved, though, are the impacts of taste, preference, and aesthetic ideology. The challenges loom large in light of the considerable impacts of habitus, mindbugs, and tight social networks that limit access to decision making while valuing elite educational pedigrees. Nonetheless, arts grantmakers, artists, and citizens concerned with cultural policy should continue to question these normative, theoretical, and practical issues.

Conclusion

> Democracy cannot dominate every domain—that would destroy expertise—and expertise
> cannot dominate every domain—that would destroy democracy.[53]
> —COLLINS AND EVANS, *Rethinking Expertise*

Critical to an understanding of the way that expertise operates is an examination of the systems under which it functions. In this chapter and the previous one, experts—made up of foundation and NEA chairmen, presidents, officers, outside consultants, and panelists—were shown to have supported certain kinds of music, artists, and groups. They limited changes to the status quo and the system was self-reinforcing, especially in terms of how foundations and the government derived and legitimized networks of expertise.

Inderjeet Parmar's analysis of the significant impact the Ford, Rockefeller, and Carnegie Foundations had on U.S. foreign policy in the twentieth century reveals the ways institutions functioned, with specific goals, and supported specialized knowledge. According to Parmar, the networks of grant recipients, government agencies, established academic institutions, and philanthropic foundations produced " 'legitimate' scholars linked with 'legitimate' ideas and policies endorsed by or at least engaged with 'legitimate' organizations" like the International Monetary Fund, the World Bank, and the U.S. Department of State.[54] The networks became "system-maintenance systems" whose vested interest was self-perpetuation—through the renewal of grants, through the continuation of existing policies, and through the buttressing of certain ideologies. Networks maintained the status quo, and if there was reform, it was "intrasystemic."[55]

A comparison can be made between Parmar's analysis of foreign policy and this examination of experts in the field of arts grantmaking. If the arts field of the 1950s, 1960s, and 1970s indeed was a system of self-maintenance and self-perpetuation, then re-evaluation of how this system has changed and whether it needs to be reassessed in view of evolving social issues and priorities is necessary. Exclusion and social closure occurred as a result of an arts field based on first-degree connections, and qualifications derived from training and experience at elite cultural and educational institutions. In these examples, foundations and the government left out nonmale and nonwhite people. But the story did not end there. During the 1970s, members of Congress, arts organization leaders, and directors of state arts agencies demanded greater representation of race, gender, geography, and overall diversity. The fact that the NEA was a federal government agency meant that its operation as a public institution required transparency and was subject to criticism. The Rockefeller and Ford Foundations, by contrast, despite congressional investigations in the 1950s and 1960s, maintained a level of operational opacity.

This analysis is not simply about questioning the good intentions of experts in the system, even if there were substantial monetary, cultural, and social awards to be gained. The arts encompassed a largely nonlucrative field that survived on the countless hours donated by artists, managers, and practitioners. Good intentions can hardly be challenged. The tremendous amount of experience and knowledge that experts in the arts possessed can, and should, be commended. Likewise, by no means does this study critique high educational attainment from prestigious institutions. Expertise and elite credentials regularly overlapped because of the necessary investment of large amounts of time and energy to acquire both. Expertise, however, goes beyond good intentions and university degrees.

A deeper awareness of artistic expertise can contribute to a richer lens on history, as well as a wider path to critical questions regarding the role of experts. Through this lens, society can re-examine persistent themes in American cultural history. For example, questions of democracy, meritocracy, and egalitarian distribution raise issues linked with a broader sense of equality. What would justice look like in an arts funding structure? Whose voices are represented and who reaps the benefits? It is not a simplistic answer of equally and evenly distributed resources. The critique concerns the functioning and setup of the system and the results that it supports, rather than the actions or ideologies of any given individual.

The epigraph of this conclusion provokes several moral issues on the role of experts in American society. The dollar amounts and disproportionate allocation of funds in budgets to Western high art genres compared to folk arts, the music of ethnic minorities, and jazz painted a picture of inequality, making it difficult to ignore the way that other cultural groups were excluded from the system. Part of the problem was the institutionalized role of expertise in evaluating noninstitutionalized artistic genres: jazz ensembles and folk musicians, for example, were not initially connected to the same kinds of service organizations and lobby groups that orchestras and opera companies had. Nor is this analysis a critique against orchestras and opera companies, which understandably and legitimately pushed for the greatest amount of public and private sources they could obtain. Grant recipients within the system should be praised for their tenacity in promoting their artistic endeavors, their dedication to high standards, and the progress they made in securing monetary resources.

Concerning the broader issue of justice in arts funding, however, the problems of the system provoke greater action toward inclusivity and pluralism. The problems require the acknowledgment that the status quo was insufficient in guaranteeing the inclusion of the many different cultural groups that worked in this country and that membership in panels and in groups of experts and specialists had an impact.

Fortunately, the role of experts in democratic societies has been the subject of some political theory, pointing toward their role in public governance and deliberation. Frank Fischer's *Democracy and Expertise* argues that an expert's role is to help citizens understand issues and to improve their abilities to debate public issues, rather than to make decisions on citizens' behalf. Citing American philosopher John Dewey, Fischer suggests that experts on a "technical front . . . would identify and analyze basic social and economic problems," while on the "political front, citizens and their political representatives would democratically set out an agenda for dealing with them."[56] Fischer cites that in recent years, the public's trust in professionals and experts has declined. Citizens sometimes accuse them of "lacking solutions relevant to the diverse range of interests in society as a whole," while experts use their power and authority to "buffer economic and political elites against challenges from below."[57] Thus, a re-evaluation of experts' role in contemporary society is needed.

Fischer focuses on the possibilities of "deliberative experiments" in citizen juries and consensus conferences in the sciences, but actually, these strategies are even better placed in the fields of arts and culture. Citizen juries or panels are multiday events that provide people with the opportunity to debate a certain social issue with the help of expert discussions and interviews. Consensus conferences are usually longer, where citizens can decide themselves the questions and issues they tackle. They are also more open to the public and involve greater cross-examination of experts.[58] Owing to the evaluative and normative nature of "facts" in the arts, the possibilities of expert-facilitated citizen deliberation are noteworthy. A form of democratic representation that appears as mere tokenism might become truly meaningful and permanent in the long run. Issues of high art and low art, commercial art and non-commercial art, serious art and popular art, and whether these binaries actually mean anything should be discussed.

As scholar Robert Arnove writes, "intellectuals" (but just as easily, experts and academics) represent both important instrumentalities of "cultural domination" and "potential agents of revolutionary change."[59] Intellectuals can place their expertise at the service of dominant groups, working toward preserving the status quo, or they can work with the marginalized, to tell stories that have been ignored in the past and to participate in the collective struggles of transforming an unjust society. These are the questions that we must ask of ourselves and of our work.

> Art often has not earned its way in the marketplace. For
> centuries it relied on patronage, the benevolence of a church
> or ruler; in the modern era it has turned to generous wealthy
> patrons for support: individuals, foundations, and corporations
> continue to build the cultural resources of our nation today.
> In this past decade the federal and state governments have
> recognized and shouldered their responsibility to serve as
> nonauthoritarian catalysts—to help close the gap between
> earnings and expenses without ever dictating artistic policies.[1]
> —ANNUAL REPORT, National Endowment for the Arts, 1975

3

PLURALISM AND PUBLIC-PRIVATE RELATIONSHIPS IN THE

FIELD OF CULTURAL PRODUCTION

THIS CHAPTER'S EPIGRAPH from the National Endowment for the Arts's (NEA's) annual report encapsulates many of the issues at stake within the public and private relationships of arts and music funding after World War II: in the modern era of American free market capitalism, wealthy philanthropists, private institutions, and the government emerged as new patrons for the arts, in contrast to previous benefactors such as the church and the crown; the United States was a system that relied on a mixture of public and private funds to support the arts; and state intervention in a society founded upon the ideals of democracy were purposely different from countries under authoritarian and communist regimes.

Private initiative has been a guiding principle of civil society and social endeavors in the United States from its earliest days, and the federal government has protected these rights under the First Amendment. Political scientist Joan Roelofs notes that the civic sector operates in numerous areas of social, cultural, and economic life. For instance, it has historically picked up the slack caused by industrial decline through support of hospitals and arts centers; it has provided goods that the market would not otherwise support, like opera productions or British television dramas; and it has been a source of jobs and benefits.[2] In other words, the civic sector appears to eschew the dangers of the profit motive, while simultaneously avoiding government overreach and guaranteeing individual citizens' right to free speech and association.

Ask the Experts. Michael Sy Uy, Oxford University Press (2020). © Oxford University Press.
DOI: 10.1093/oso/9780197510445.001.0001.

Philanthropic foundations are an example of citizens freely assembling, and they occupy a unique legal position to pursue their own goals while serving the "public" good, as required by their tax-exempt status. "Foundations, along with the organizations that they support," according to scholar on the subject Joel Fleishman, "are the great secret of the dynamism of America's civic sector . . . providing the capital that powers innovation and diverse experimentation."[3]

As wealthy institutions that are not beholden to a public constituency (boards of trustees and officers are not elected by popular vote, nor are policies approved by citizen referenda), private foundations have possessed the privilege and power to direct large sums of money toward special causes. The "Big Three" (Carnegie, Rockefeller, and Ford) have since the beginning of the twentieth century led public and social missions as diverse as establishing schools of health and hygiene, developing the vaccine to prevent yellow fever, and offering microloans to citizens of developing countries. Foundations have exercised great latitude and speed, with the power to take action sometimes more quickly than the federal government. They act without federal appropriations or authorizations bills, and without the supervision of either the Office of Management and Budget or the House and Senate Committees on the Budget. While the government has passed laws regarding congressional and public oversight over the past century, foundations have largely operated behind closed doors. A degree of mystery and secrecy have obscured their activity.

In analyzing the landscape of music grantmaking in the United States between the 1950s and 1970s and how private foundations fit into the funding ecosystem, sociologist Pierre Bourdieu provides another useful theoretical lens. His idea of the "field of cultural production" takes into account all relationships among different actors working during a particular time, encapsulating the social spaces where interactions, transactions, and events occur among individuals, institutions, states, and other groups.[4] He argues that the relationships between actors and institutions are strongly impacted by society's structures. Laws, unspoken social agreements, and traditions shape society.

One of the most dominant ideas that governed U.S. arts funding during this time period—not to mention, since the founding of this nation—was that of *pluralism*. Then and now, "pluralism" was and is an ambiguous term, with its own plurality of meanings. Generally speaking, pluralism was used analogously to "diversity." This diversity, however, had two different facets, depending on whether one looked at the grantmakers or the grant receivers. On the one hand, there could be a pluralism of funding sources—for example, an organization was sponsored by the NEA, PepsiCo, local foundations, and bequests. On the other hand, there could be a pluralism of funding recipients—for example, the Mellon Foundation funded Harvard, the American Council of Learned Societies, and doctoral student fellowships.

Furthermore, during this time period, what both U.S. grantmakers and grant receivers sought to achieve was "cultural pluralism." As sociologists Antonia Pantoja, Wilhemina Perry, and Barbara Blourock defined in the 1970s, "cultural pluralism" was the aspiration to build a society where "culturally different groups . . . can fully experience both the positive and distinctive attributes of their given and ascribed differences without the penalties of loss of status, educational, social, or political disenfranchisement."[5] Cultural pluralism also sometimes went by the term "multiculturalism." In all cases, the goals of "arts funding *pluralism*" and "cultural *pluralism*" were marked by diversity and difference, rather than assimilation or monopoly.

After World War II, interactional experts at Rockefeller, Ford, and the NEA strongly shaped cultural and funding pluralism through their establishment of certain structural homogeneities that then dominated the decision making of all three institutions. They employed two specific tools: first, foundation and government officers required their grants to be matched by other financial sources, and second, they met and coordinated their work through interorganizational meetings and correspondence. Matching requirements were the skeletal framework of American public–private funding, mandating grant recipients to diversify their donors. Such heterogeneity was supposed to be economically prudent, as one would diversify an investment portfolio, for example. But these requirements actually had the unintended effect of reducing and concentrating the number of grantees, as not all organizations had the financial and organizational means to undertake broad fundraising efforts. Expert use of matching grants, in reality, counteracted foundation and government goals of cultural pluralism.

Amidst the Cold War and the precarious climate established by congressional investigations into private foundations, the three institutions also found themselves coordinating to an even greater degree. From the end of the 1950s, foundations increasingly got stuck between a rock and a hard place: from the perspective of liberal critiques, they served as tax shelters for the wealthy; from a conservative viewpoint, they supported disruptive political ideologies. "Expenditure requirements" (minimum annual giving) and "expenditure responsibility" (legal liability for a grantee's actions) pushed foundations to be more cautious, and to work more closely with other philanthropic institutions. Through negotiations and interpersonal relationships, expert-arts administrators segmented and differentiated foundation and Arts Endowment activities and areas of focus. NEA staff invited Rockefeller and Ford officers to the earliest National Council on the Arts (NCA) meetings. The first NEA chairman Roger Stevens wrote regularly and informally to his institutional counterparts. And the Rockefeller Foundation organized meetings, as it did with the key gathering "How Can Foundations Help the Arts?" in 1974, including many of the largest and wealthiest stakeholders.

While arts grantmakers after World War II generally did *not* provide grants to the same projects, they did tend to fund the same individuals and organizations, especially those focused on Western art music. The increase in government funding *initially* had little impact—specifically concerning the arts budgets of the Ford and Rockefeller Foundations—but eventually correlated with a decline. The NEA stood as one example of the possible "crowding out" effect, whereby rising public sector spending drove down private sector spending in the arts, at least for Ford and Rockefeller.[6] The worsening economic conditions of the 1970s exacerbated the decreasing aid from the two largest foundations, and a loss in their leadership and perceived impact. On the other hand, government funding also sparked an *increase* in contributions made by state arts agencies, corporations, and smaller foundations. So, while some areas experienced crowding out, others underwent stimulation.

The arts grantmaking world in general was difficult to penetrate. As government studies scholar Margaret Wyszomirski suggests, an arts policy "iron triangle" solidified in the 1970s under chairman Nancy Hanks, who contacted orchestras and museums, soliciting them to lobby the national government for increased appropriations.[7] In return, Hanks promised larger grants. While the NEA made efforts in jazz, folk, and ethnic music, the notion that they, Ford, and Rockefeller served a broad "public" cognizant of issues of gender, race, and geography was an inaccurate characterization.

By coordinating their efforts informally, the interactional experts avoided direct project overlap, at the same time largely sustaining the powerful performing arts ensembles of the Western European tradition. Admittedly, their programs reflected the worldviews of individuals, each with their own vision of how to better humankind. But they represented yet another small and concentrated network of expert-decision makers coalescing and maintaining their power through formal and informal means. The result of these two structural homogeneities—matching grants and coordinated expert gatherings—produced a distinct lack of cultural pluralism, as well as failed efforts at funding pluralism in the field of music.

The Field of Cultural Production

> The tastes actually realized depend on the state of the system of goods offered; every change in the system of goods induces a change in tastes. But conversely, every change in tastes resulting from a transformation of the conditions of existence and of the corresponding dispositions will tend to induce, directly or indirectly, a transformation of the field of production.[8]
> —PIERRE BOURDIEU, *Distinction*

At its most basic, a field is an arena in which interactions, transactions, and events occur. Examining a field means uncovering relationships between actors and institutions, as well as the way society is structured in general: formal and informal laws, the educational system, the availability of social services, and the branches of government. Additionally, to look carefully into a field of power is to analyze cultural tastes and preferences and how those differ among individuals and among social groups.[9] Different fields interact with each other, from politics to economics to education. The arts operate within the "field of cultural production," which is similar too to sociologist Howard Becker's idea of an "art world," or "the network of people whose cooperative activity . . . produces the kind of art works that art world is noted for."[10]

A first step in analyzing the field of cultural production is to look at the distribution of capital, or different resources available to individuals and organizations. In the arts, several of the most important resources are symbolic capital, cultural capital, and social capital. Examples of symbolic capital include prestige, celebrity, and honor. Society recognizes one artist over another artist, and there develops a hierarchy—or inequality—among artists. Society builds hierarchies even if tastes and distinctions are arbitrary.[11] A specific kind of symbolic capital is cultural capital, and it is often found in two forms: first, as objects, like works of art (a painting, a musical score dedicated to a specific patron, or a sculpture), and second, as titles, such as educational degrees. As a kind of symbolic capital, think of the ways owning Da Vinci's *Mona Lisa* gives the Louvre an aura of prestige and status, or how a master's in creative writing from the University of Iowa adds allure to a writer's reputation.[12] Cultural capital in the form of educational attainment takes large investments in time and practice, and unlike economic capital (e.g., cash money), it is not directly transferable between people. A doctorate could take six years to complete, and PhD holders cannot simply donate their degree to a sibling like they could Venmo $20 for last night's dinner.[13] Last, but certainly not least, social capital is derived from human relationships and networks with other people. Artists who are friends with powerful politicians, wealthy donors, or other possessors of capital are more powerful in the field than those without such connections.

Fields shape and are shaped by the way people see the world. They work together. When the Pulitzer Prize Committee chooses *DAMN.* by Kendrick Lamar as the 2018 winner, the field experienced a change in the way individuals see and hear rap music. There is not just economic capital to be made through record sales, but also a change in cultural capital as some people may want to own special edition rap records or study rap music in school. Lamar may also become more famous and influential to future generations of rappers, within the African American community, or in American society in toto. Changes in the field, though, are not usually instantaneous or immediately detectable in the way people see the world. Just because Lamar wins the Pulitzer Prize doesn't mean that he suddenly becomes the next Aaron Copland (Pulitzer, 1945) or Charles Ives (Pulitzer, 1947). Similarly, a new government policy to support jazz programs does not instantly change performers' or listeners' attitudes toward, or consumption of, jazz.[14]

In the postwar period, an analysis of the field and the distribution of capital illuminates how government and foundation officers' focus on partnerships and pluralism in the United States had the effect of increasing *density*—or concentrating and reducing the number of grantees—within the field of arts funding. The enforcement of matching policies impacted the way grantees designed and implemented their projects. They also restricted and narrowed the range of organizations and cultural products that had the capacity to apply for such institutional grants. Thus, one consequence was that high art institutions that were already well connected with symbolic and social capital within the larger field of power benefited, while those without such resources stood on the sidelines. Experts and consultants produced a field that rewarded already influential and capital-rich members of society—experts were catalysts and positive influences on the dissemination and promotion of particular composers, schools of music, and performing arts organizations.

Foundation Work in the Arts Field Before the NEA

While both the Rockefeller Foundation and the Ford Foundation were established to provide an outlet for some of the accumulated riches of America's industrial boom in the early twentieth century, they did not originally believe that the arts, or music in particular, could be part of their social missions. Instead, they focused primarily on areas like medical health, agricultural and natural sciences, overseas development, and international relations. Foundations centered early concerns on providing funds for research with quantifiable data and outcomes. Other goals focused on how private and capitalist initiatives were best suited to help the government solve social problems. As historian Kathleen McCarthy has argued, "Philanthropy needed to strike at the root causes of social problems, test solutions, turn the best over to government, and then move on to fresh fields—ideas poorly suited to either the arts or the humanities."[15]

In the 1950s, the Rockefeller Foundation articulated its distinct role in promoting the "public interest" as a private, independent organization. In its 1953 annual report it claimed that it was "nonpolitical and nongovernmental in character" and that its policies and decisions were in the hands of a board of trustees composed of "responsible citizens, who contribute time and a lively interest to its activities and who select officers and professional staff to carry out their policies."[16] Yet the foundation also claimed a dual role. It was "private in that it was not governmental" and it was "public in that its funds were held in trust for public rather than private purposes." As a social institution, it reflected "the application to philanthropy of the principles of private initiative and free enterprise," and in a free society, "the widest diversity of individual and group effort" was encouraged "in order that citizens may share directly in the privileges and responsibilities of free institutions."[17]

A few years later, the foundation indicated its resistance to serving as a funding top-up for governmental activities. Discussing the "marginal utility" of foundation grants, Rockefeller officers considered the "critical disadvantages" of absorbing private funds into a national plan. "A reduction of support [by the government] to an institution receiving a foundation grant would mean, in effect, that foundation funds were paying for the marginal expenditure of the national budget."[18] Instead, the foundation was better at making grants to organizations that treated the financial assistance as a "windfall," allowing the organization to undertake efforts beyond what was originally planned.

Similar to the Rockefeller Foundation, the Ford Foundation was accustomed to working independently from the national government, and in its report, "An Enlarged Program in the Arts," it demonstrated a similarly cautious view of Washington.[19] One of Ford's primary concerns was the potential threat of public servants with no artistic background or experience controlling and bureaucratizing the arts. According to its evaluation of the field, "the U.S. government would never be likely to let artists participate in its decision as full partners." Instead, Ford saw itself as providing a useful precedent and example of a "private institution that could establish standards" and possibly even "mechanisms for the subsequent expenditure of federal monies."

In fact, Ford officers even considered establishing their own "full-scale endowment of a private National Council on the Arts" that would seek a congressional charter.[20] (Ford's plan was completely independent of the NCA that the government later founded.) Ford vice president W. McNeil Lowry proposed the initial idea to Ford's board of trustees and outlined plans to contribute as much as $500 million ($4 billion in 2017) toward its endowment. The surprisingly high amount would allow it to grant $12 to $15 million ($100 million) each year. Ultimately, after much internal exploration and discussion, the trustees chose not to pursue the proposal. The board decided instead to "keep the operation [of arts funding] inside the foundation."

Nevertheless, Ford officers remained wary of the impact the federal government could have in arts funding. It concluded from its own analysis of state support in France, Great Britain, Denmark, and Italy that

Government programs in the arts concentrate largely, though not exclusively, on the deficit financing of institutions; favor institutions in some fields much more than those in others; are often dominated by an overly traditional view of art; lack flexibility in adding or removing grantees; and suffer from bureaucratic weaknesses and timidities both through the high cost of administration and through official dogmatism.[21]

The problem was not just with money, but "the ability of a bureaucracy to grasp the artistic facts of life." Instead, Ford believed it had "both adequate financial resources and a staff intimately involved in the various fields of the creative arts."

When the federal government established the NEA, however, both foundations had to deal with the realities of a third actor on the stage. The year 1965 marked an important moment because it was the end of Rockefeller and Ford's decade-long independence absent of Washington's intervention. The emergence of the NEA heralded a significant structural change in the field, with the new agency backed by the power and authority of the federal government and the NCA.[22] Changes in levels of funding, the distribution of resources, the possession of cultural and symbolic capital in the form of leadership, expertise, and influence—all of these factors were at stake as the ground shifted.

Early Interactions Among the NEA and Ford and Rockefeller Foundations

The federal government had not played an active part in arts funding since the Works Progress Administration and the Great Depression, leaving a gap of roughly thirty years to be negotiated. Initially, foundations responded by re-emphasizing the critical importance of their own arts programs. Rather than curtailing private funds or crowding out the field, the federal government's entry actually encouraged further private giving by Ford and Rockefeller, in addition to other contributions from individuals and organizations.

For example, the Rockefeller Foundation responded to the passing of the National Arts and Humanities Act by emphasizing that the "significance of foundation funds [became] greater as more public funds [were] invested."[23] Officers saw funding in the arts as no different from funding in other areas that the government had entered, including agriculture, education, international development, and science. As the foundation's president noted in his annual message, "the highly selective assistance characteristic of foundations can be of decisive influence in demonstrating its inherent value. . . . [T]he foundation dollar can furnish new leverage, proportionately far greater than the fraction of overall support it represents," and "now that more public funds are becoming available, this is also likely to happen in the arts."

At the Ford Foundation, president Henry T. Heald addressed his officers and directors by writing that "the foundation should not eliminate its activities . . . merely because government agencies move into these fields and support the same or related objectives."[24] Instead, Ford reacted positively by establishing a communications liaison between it and the "relevant government agency" (i.e., the NEA) through its Office of Policy and Planning. The vice president of this office was, in fact, W. McNeil Lowry, the same vice president for the arts and humanities.

Lowry and Heald had indeed met for two hours with government representatives from education, public affairs, and the arts and humanities in April 1965.[25] Lowry was initially concerned that federal entry into the arts field would take away publicity from his own $80 million Symphony Orchestra Program, accepted by the board that year. (The NEA, however, stayed away from funding orchestras for at least its first two years.) Among Lowry and Heald's main conclusions were that the Ford Foundation would maintain "its own independence and autonomy as a private philanthropy organization" and that there would be no "slackening" in its efforts despite government expansion. Moreover, none of the foundation's work "should be carried out in such a way that would invite Washington officials to make proposals for Ford Foundation grants or to use the Ford Foundation as a means of developing particular government interests." The only exception to this rule was "the mixture of private and public activities aimed at related objectives," which Ford and the NEA eventually carried out in arts education and the American Film Institute.

In addition to its cooperative work with the NEA, Ford had its own ambitions as to how it might work with the Rockefeller Foundation.[26] Within vice president Lowry's Policy and Planning division, officers discussed how the three institutions could provide differently sized grants. One proposed that the Rockefeller Foundation stand at the "middle ground of philanthropic investment" because it was best "equipped to handle the $1/4 million, the $1/2 million and even the $1 million grant without much difficulty." On the other hand, Ford officers "should concentrate much more in the area of the large grant and in small grantmaking. . . . [They] should make fewer, larger, longer and better grants." The working assumption— shared by Rockefeller as well—was that Ford's budget was significantly larger than Rockefeller's and thus had more room to underwrite big grants. By contrast, the Rockefeller Foundation could fill in the gap for medium-sized grants, and so the two foundations could occupy different philanthropic spaces. As a point of comparison, Rockefeller officers viewed their role in terms of program focus, rather than money. For example, Rockefeller saw itself "particularly well suited to direct support of individual creative artists," as it did with its university new music centers.[27] In this area, it was in a far better position than the NEA or the Ford Foundation, which had, according to an internal memo, "repeatedly demonstrated its ineptness in this field."

The federal government's officers and experts encouraged further meetings with their foundation counterparts. The NCA invited representatives from the large private institutions to its earliest meetings. Lowry was present at its second meeting, as well as Lukas Foss, long-time consultant for the Rockefeller Foundation and music director of the Buffalo Philharmonic Orchestra. Norman Lloyd, director of the arts division at Rockefeller, also came to an early meeting as chairman Roger Stevens's "special guest." In a letter from Frederick Gash (Business Committee for the Arts and consultant on development and resources for the NCA) to Lloyd, Gash wrote that he thought Lloyd was "lucky to get the invitation because, sitting in on some of the debate, watching the council cut up the $4,000,000 pie, ought to be fascinating to one who spends as much dough, and consults only his shadow."[28]

Stevens confided to the NCA that he planned to send foundations "confidential letters" periodically, "which would tell them of projects that we were working on, so that they wouldn't have duplication of effort."[29] He continued, "there is no point in our spending money on something that they want to do, and in general we tried to work out a cooperative working arrangement." Rather than collusion, Stevens's efforts at a "cooperative working arrangement" sounded more like coordination. Specifically regarding the Ford symphony grants, Stevens asked for approval from the council to telegram Lowry and state that "the NCA did not contemplate aid of that kind in the immediate future." Stevens acknowledged that after the Ford grant, "anything we do for symphony orchestras would be an anti-climax."

The NEA took a slightly different stance, however, when it came to smaller and medium-sized foundations. Stevens elaborated that NEA staff could recommend specific projects to smaller foundations because the NEA had more time and experience to carry out the "due diligence."[30] It is important to remember that in the 1960s and 1970s there were roughly 5,500 foundations with assets more than $500,000, giving at least $25,000 in annual grants.[31] The Foundation Center estimated that there were somewhere around 26,000 foundations in 1971, over 95% of which had been established since World War II.[32] By reference, there were only about three dozen foundations with assets over $100 million. In Stevens's mind, he tied this form of assistance with an appropriate role for public money. "I know the spirit of the law is that we should not be making grants where private groups can. And so we want, in every possible way, to encourage and increase the amount of giving by foundations to the arts and humanities."[33] Donald Engle at the Martha Baird Rockefeller Fund for Music wrote to Stevens that learning more about the aims and operations of the NEA and state arts agencies was useful for his own work as director.[34] Furthermore, he confided to Stevens that those involved in arts funding could "accomplish more on a personal basis among colleagues than a formal position among agencies," emphasizing the role of individual relationships.

Therefore, analyzing how individuals acted within both the constraints and freedoms of the field of cultural production demonstrated how close connections among foundation and government leaders reinforced already collegial communication. Going one step beyond the phone call, the lunch meeting, and the managerial assistance, however, was coordination in actual, monetary terms. In this regard, the NEA and Ford and Rockefeller Foundations concentrated the field further through their matching grants, even as they tried to promote cultural and funding pluralism in the United States.

Cultural Pluralism in Theory and Practice

> The importance of pluralism in support of the arts, a philosophy clearly articulated by the Congress when it established the Arts Endowment, is one to which the Endowment is deeply committed. When assistance is provided by widely diverse sectors of society ... the arts can only benefit. Domination from one source of funding does not exist; the arts are free to develop according to their own needs and goals. A full partnership effort helps ensure a healthy cultural environment.[35]
> —ANNUAL REPORT, NEA, 1970

> Foundations have a magnificent opportunity to maintain the richness of pluralism and heterodoxy which has strengthened our national life and to contribute heavily to social melioration if they have the wit and intellectual capacity to do it. If they don't, I really don't know exactly who will do it outside central government—and I, for one, am not prepared to settle for complete state control yet.[36]
> —ANNUAL REPORT, Rockefeller Foundation, 1972

As historian Robert Bremner has shown, the idea of "pluralism" has characterized U.S. philanthropy since the earliest European immigrants arrived in America.[37] In the early twenty-first century, common parlance has tended to define "pluralism" in relation to "cultural pluralism," but the term also had an entirely different meaning in the midcentury world of philanthropy. In Bremner's as well as the NEA's usage (as earlier), "pluralism" meant financial support from a diversity of contributors. Pluralism dominated not just in the arts, but other fields as well, such as the financing of higher education (a model that British and continental European universities have tried to emulate), social services, and other cultural support.

Similar to NEA chairman Roger Stevens, his successor Nancy Hanks also advocated pluralism of funding sources. In a memorandum from Hanks to the NEA's program directors, she spoke of her unwavering belief that "as government support [grew], the involvement of private support [was] even more important."[38] She continued, "this is a belief that we all have in our bones. ... [I]t is intuitive; it is also, of course, practical because the money is needed." Remember that before becoming chairman of the NEA, Hanks was vice chairman at the Rockefeller Brothers Fund and executive secretary to their report, "Performing Arts: Problems and Prospects." Among the report's recommendations was that "federal aid for arts organizations . . . can be most effectively provided through matching grants to meet the capital needs of arts organizations."[39]

Under Hanks, one of the Arts Endowment's key operating principles was an "Economy Through Cost Sharing."[40] The federal government intended funds to "supplement rather than replace resources available to arts institutions," as explicitly stated in the legislation establishing the NEA. For the Arts Endowment, matching funds supported its legitimacy as a government agency that was doubly and triply effective because for every dollar that it granted, it required its grantees to raise even more outside. According to its records, during the first four years of the NEA's existence, it had disbursed a total of $25.4 million ($190 million in 2017), while generating more than $48.7 million ($360 million) from other sources.[41] Therefore, it argued that its overall impact in the arts field was $74.1 ($25.4 + $48.7) million from 1965 to 1969.

Yet, there were also objections to the appropriateness and usefulness of matching funds. For instance, educator Frederick Bolman urged caution in the way foundations complied with matching grants allocated by the government.[42] His resistance was hardly concealable: "To match federal monies is not only financially unnecessary but a deflection of the private foundations from their proper role." According to Bolman, the private foundation's greatest strength was to "pay for real innovation," to find "new ideas not publicly recognized," and to provide the "sensitive explorer function of research and development in many areas of our culture." To Bolman, matching requirements issued by the federal government actually prevented foundations from exercising their special role as engines of creativity.

According to him, by falling into the trap of government requirements, foundations risked "the danger of political domination and a disastrous blurring of the distinction between public and private initiative in our society."[43] In his final damning critique, he warned that "the federal matching programs can bleed private foundations to virtual death" and that the functions of boards and staffs were reduced to "clipping coupons and mailing them to Washington." He feared that foundations fell into the trap of bankrolling government projects rather than cultivating their own initiatives.

In reality though, there was actually little overlap in grant projects (with a few exceptions in arts education) by the government, Ford, and Rockefeller. Bolman's fear—at least in the arts field—that foundations simply duplicated government funding of the same grantees did not materialize. Rather, they practiced a high degree of homogeneity in the *types* of organizations they funded, namely high arts performing institutions. From the perspective of cultural pluralism, the larger concern was the similitude of their funding, which the expert-designed skeleton built on dollar matches reinforced. The framework was wide-reaching and tightly knit because smaller foundations and individual patrons viewed the NEA and Ford and Rockefeller Foundations as leaders in the field. With the resources both to produce and to justify their expertise and decision making, their impacts were doubly (or triply, or more) significant. One specific example of how the matching grant was quadruply powerful was the NEA's Treasury Fund grant, a unique financial and structural incentive that encouraged the government and private contributors to coordinate their funding.

The NEA's Treasury Fund Grants

Originally called the "Unrestricted Gift Fund," Congress included this type of grant in the National Foundation on the Arts and the Humanities Act of 1965 to encourage gifts made to the NEA. Congress intended the government agency "to work <u>in partnership</u> with private and other non-federal sources of funding to further the development of the arts in the United States."[44] The act originally authorized up to $2.25 million ($18 million in 2017) annually to match unrestricted donations, but that amount steadily rose over the next decade and more.

Rather than the ratio of a $1 + 1 = 2$ match—that is, $1 of federal money for $1 of private money—Treasury Fund grants were matched at a $1 + 3 = 4$ ratio—that is, $1 of federal money for $3 of private money. Essentially, private donors gifted money to the federal government, with checks made out to the Department of the Treasury (hence the name), which the NEA held in a separate account and appropriated independently of other funds.[45] Contributors initially gave donations for unrestricted use, or for programs recommended by the chairman and the NCA. In 1968, the NEA opened up donations for designated use, such as for a specific nonprofit, tax-exempt arts organization. So, rather than an individual writing a blank check to the Treasury Department for some unspecified arts endeavor, he or she could stipulate the recipient of the donation. Once the agency approved the Treasury Fund grant, then the designated arts organization needed to find a second match of resources (hence, the $1 + (1 + 2) = 4$ ratio).

For example, an individual like Aaron Copland or a corporation like Exxon could propose to the NEA chairman a Treasury grant of $100,000 for the Boston Symphony Orchestra. If the NEA approved the grant, then the Boston Symphony Orchestra would need to match both Copland's/Exxon's $100,000 and the NEA Treasury grant of $100,000 with its own $200,000. The required match could be met from any combination of nonfederal and private contributions. The total amount raised by the Boston Symphony Orchestra would in sum be $400,000.

In 1969, the NEA's annual report began listing contributors to the fund, including individuals and organizations. That year, gifts came in from 55 individuals, foundations, nonprofit institutions, and corporations, totaling roughly $2.4 million ($16 million in 2017)—more than double the congressional appropriation of $1 million.[46] The following year, donations were sent from 109 communities in 32 states, ranging from $2.50 to $250,000; 201 individuals, 76 foundations, 51 corporations, and 34 other public and private sources including school districts, unions, and universities contributed $2 million. Hanks and Barnaby Kenney (chairman of the National Endowment for the Humanities) sent to Congress supplemental appropriation requests. The fact that these were "supplemental" indicated the program's success in bringing outside sources of funding.[47] In the letter, Hanks and Keeney mentioned two other reasons for an increase: first, a high ratio of private to public funding accorded with President Nixon's goals of greater private contribution, and second, "projects in the national interest could be supported with minimum expenditure of federal funds." In other words, Treasury Fund grants were in line with Nixon's Republican platform on arts support: they were cost-effective *and* high impact.

Hanks and Keeney argued that matching funds provided a way for "private views and judgments" to be represented in public decision making.[48] The funds were an "assurance" that individuals and private organizations were "heard and heeded throughout the process by which programs are established and funds allocated." They saw the inclusion of these viewpoints as "essential" in "fields in which the sensitive issues of academic and creative freedom" were constantly present. After Congress approved in 1968 an amendment to allow Treasury grants to be given for specific use (as mentioned, previously a gift to the fund was *carte blanche* for unrestricted use), then, according to Hanks and Keeney, a "dramatic increase in private giving ensued." They noted that "givers insisted on a voice in determining programs and applicants which were to be jointly supported, a voice which the 'unrestricted gift' provision of the Act denied them." That is, Aaron Copland wouldn't write a check to the Treasury Department for "music," but he would if it went specifically to the Boston Symphony Orchestra.

But despite the glowing stories of success and the large amounts of private money raised by Treasury Fund grants, another reality was ignored: the voices that spoke in this field of cultural production were those best positioned to give, and the voices that the Arts Endowment heard generally said the same thing. In other words, despite the rhetoric that some donations were as small as a few dollars, most were in the thousands, tens of thousands, or hundreds of thousands of dollars, and they were largely targeted at the same arts organizations: orchestras, opera companies, and conservatories. Therefore, the NEA, rather than promoting a diversity of grantees and bolstering the democratic voice of individual citizens through these grants, actually brought about the opposite result, homogenizing the arts field.

Table 3.1 provides records for the NEA's Treasury Fund grants beginning in 1970, the first year it made information available through its annual reports.[49] Of importance to note was that the NEA did *not* fund the vast majority of grants through the Treasury Fund method. Apart from those in the music division, the only others were grants to national ballet and contemporary dance tours.[50]

A few trends are immediately noticeable. First, only three jazz grants were made with the help of the Treasury Fund. The Jazzmobile Inc. received a grant in 1973, and Jazz for the New York Jazz Repertory Corporation obtained a grant in 1974 and another in 1975. By contrast, the NEA paid for, on average, over a third of grants to opera companies through the Treasury Fund, and the proportion was over two-thirds for orchestras. The ratio for major orchestras was much higher than for metropolitan orchestras (with only 10% supported in this way). Between 1974 and 1976, nearly all major orchestras received Treasury Fund grants; between 1972 and 1975, almost all music conservatories received Treasury Fund grants.

Looking deeper into 1970, the first year of available data, shows that the NEA funded none of the jazz programs through the Treasury Fund, nor programs in

TABLE 3.1

Treasury Fund Grants by Category, 1970–76

Year	Jazz	Opera	Major Orchestra	Metropolitan Orchestra	Chamber Orchestra	Conservatory
1970	0 of 11	7 of 8	11 of 15[a]	—	—	—
1971	0 of 26	6 of 8	9 of 29	3 of 39	—	—
1972	0 of 67	17 of 45	14 of 32	4 of 49	2 of 2	7 of 8
1973	1 of 85	15 of 37	12 of 28	6 of 58	2 of 7	11 of 11
1974	1 of 78	18 of 55	28 of 34	5 of 65	1 of 6	16 of 16
1975	1 of 62	17 of 49	31 of 33[b]	8 of 65	2 of 8	17 of 17
1976	0 of 71	16 of 40	31 of 31	13 of 69	—	6 of 15

[a]In 1970, there was only the "Orchestra" category; the following year the NEA divided orchestras into "Major" and "Metropolitan," categories determined by the American Symphony Orchestra League. Major orchestras ranged from the Boston Symphony Orchestra and the New York Philharmonic to the Honolulu Symphony Society and the Indianapolis Symphony. Metropolitan orchestras included the Greater Akron Musical Association, the Erie Philharmonic, and the Louisville Philharmonic Society.

[b]In 1975, the NEA changed the category for "Major Orchestra" to "Orchestras with Budgets over $750,000"; it changed the category for "Metropolitan Orchestra" to "Orchestras with Budgets between $100,000 and $750,000."

"Contemporary Music Performing Groups" or "Composer Assistance." By contrast, it made seven out of the eight grants to the opera program (the one exception was the Lake George Opera Festival). The $600,000 ($3.8 million in 2017) grant to the National Opera Institute, Washington, DC, was the largest of these grants. A slightly lower ratio was found in the orchestra program, but it was still a significant eleven out of fifteen grants, or more than two-thirds. Five six-figure grants were awarded to the Cincinnati Symphony Orchestra; the National Symphony Orchestra Association of Washington, DC; the Pittsburgh Symphony Society; the St. Louis Symphony Society; and the San Francisco Symphony Association. Among the contributors to the fund were composers Aaron Copland and Vladimir Ussachevsky, the Leonard Bernstein Foundation, the Ford Foundation, the Martha Baird Rockefeller Fund for Music, and the Save the Philharmonic Fund.

Such analysis demonstrates that while the NEA thought Treasury Fund grants ensured the voice of democracy in arts funding, they actually had the reverse effect: by trying to level the playing field, the NEA ended up giving more resources to those who were already playing, not to those who sat outside of institutional power structures. Private contributions to the Treasury Fund hardly supported jazz groups, or folk and other ethnic groups. This reality was true despite the expansion to roughly one thousand contributors to the fund in 1976, a 2000% growth from fifty contributors in 1969. The pursuit of pluralism in funding sources thus reinforced a conservative bias, bolstering the status quo. It did *not* come to represent a cultural pluralism in grant recipients.

Matching grants maintained by the NEA and the Ford and Rockefeller Foundations were significant and oft-used tools in the U.S. field of cultural production between the 1950s and 1970s. The NEA tried again in the mid-1970s with an essentially beefed-up version of its Treasury program, which it called "Challenge Grants"—supporting, once more, through multi-million-dollar awards, predominantly orchestras and opera companies. At the Ford Foundation, matching grants were of supreme importance with its endowment-building efforts for orchestras, conservatories, and art schools. Another example was Ford's $7.7 million ($38 million in 2017) Cash-Reserve program for civic opera companies and other nonprofit professional performing arts groups. Rather than supporting musicians' salaries—as had happened with the Symphony Orchestra Program—the cash-reserve grants focused on achieving financial self-sufficiency through eliminating "accumulated net current liabilities" (i.e., debt the organization owed) and establishing a reserve fund to help with liquidity, or cash flow problems.[51] The Rockefeller Foundation expected all of its university music center grants to be matched with increasing contributions from the hosting institutions.

Matching requirements were not the only way, however, that the government and private foundations homogenized the arts field after World War II. The shifting environmental contexts of postwar America also impacted and constrained them. Among the most significant political factors were laws that dictated foundation governance, as well as the fearmongering climate of the Cold War. The field was fraught with not only suspicions and public finger-pointing but also congressional investigations and legal constraints. Laws and the political environment incentivized foundations to act more conservatively and to cooperate to an even greater degree.

Congressional Investigations and the Social Role of Foundations

The need for foundations to provide a positive benefit to society was rooted in their status as tax-exempt organizations. As Joel Fleishman writes, "the risk that foundations could lose their tax-exempt status is not merely theoretical," but actually based in law.[52] Public concerns during the 1950s and 1960s grew with respect to their growing assets, the promotion of certain political ideologies, and allegations of excessive salaries paid to trustees and executives. Congress carried out close to two decades of investigation. Considering the tremendous amounts of money foundations wielded, as well as their influence as nonstate actors with significant soft powers, plenty was at stake given their nondemocratic structures.

Congressional investigations began in 1953, initiated by Representative Edward E. Cox (D-GA), and continued in 1954 with Representative Brazilla Carroll Reece (R-TN) and in 1961 with Representative Wright Patman (D-TX). In the end, the Tax Reform Act of 1969 imposed a 4% excise tax on foundations' net investment income to cover Internal Revenue Service (IRS) monitoring of their fiscal operations.[53] Additionally, Congress placed restrictions on their business operations, including grants to donors or their relatives. It demanded more disclosure, for example, through annual reports filed with the IRS (990-A forms). And foundations needed to spend at least 6% of net investment income annually. This expenditure requirement addressed the concern that foundations were growing too large and diverted too much money away from the economy. The Rockefeller Foundation saw little value in this measure, instead accusing Congress of punishing and making more difficult the work of private philanthropy.[54] Box 3.1 lists the five largest foundations in 1969, as well as their expenditures as a percentage of market value.

As a result of the greater public scrutiny, foundations responded by gathering and coordinating more frequently with each other. Ford Foundation officer Richard Magat noted to president McGeorge Bundy that after the Patman investigation, he began meeting regularly with his counterparts at Rockefeller, Carnegie, Sloan,

BOX 3.1

THE FIVE LARGEST FOUNDATIONS, MARKET VALUE ASSETS, AND
EXPENDITURES AS PERCENTAGE OF MARKET VALUE, 1969[a]

1. Ford Foundation: $2.9 billion ($19 billion in 2017), 9.7%
2. Lilly Endowment: $780 million, 1.0%
3. Rockefeller Foundation: $760 million, 5.1%
4. Duke Endowment: $510 million, 4.4%
5. Kresge Foundation: $430 million, 2.1%

[a]According to *Foundation Directory* records, in Cuninggim, *Private Money and Public Service*, 65–68.

Commonwealth, Russell Sage, and the Twentieth Century Fund.[55] He referred to them as "informal" sessions, usually taken over lunch, seven or eight times a year. They were "useful if not sensational," according to Magat, "as a means of trading bread-and-butter information about the media and particular writers," as well as projects in progress. The participants of the meetings, however, were concerned about "formalizing" the group and the public appearance of such gatherings.

The NEA also tried its best to facilitate communication and coordination with other funding entities within its policies and operations. Nancy Hanks even appointed a task force to study its role with private, corporate, and general foundations. The task force included Kenneth Dayton (an NCA member, a later trustee of the Rockefeller Foundation, and a large private donor) as well as Margaret Hickey and Harlow Heneman (both members of the Rockefeller Panel on the Performing Arts, which Hanks had organized as its secretary).[56] The report proposed strengthening communications with, and knowledge about, the programs of private foundations.[57] "Since a number of foundations already have programs in the fields of cultural development and the arts," the task force noted, "it would seem logical and practical for the Endowment to learn more about them and to have such information available for program direction and consideration." Furthermore, the task force experts recommended exchanging information regarding project areas where there was a common interest.

Ford and Rockefeller coordination throughout the period of investigations and the Cold War, as well as the NEA's own task force, indicated that arts grantmakers responded to greater public scrutiny by working even more closely together. For foundations, such cooperation was a markedly different way of operating, contrasting with their more secretive and independent decision making prior to the midcentury, and certainly before the NEA's establishment. As a final illustration, a key event took place in the field in the mid-1970s: the meeting between the most powerful actors and experts in arts funding, who determined the future of public and private relationships and the role of foundations in the system. Above all, such a meeting demonstrated how powerful institutions and the individuals who worked within them shaped the American music field.

"How Can Foundations Help the Arts?"

The Rockefeller Foundation's "How Can Foundations Help the Arts?" meeting in 1974 marked a point of reflection, signaling almost a decade after the establishment of the NEA and two decades after the two biggest foundations entered the cultural arena.[58] Participants debated many issues concerning leadership, forms of grantmaking, and pluralism; thus, the meeting served as a useful demonstration of how the government and foundations achieved working relationships on a practical level. It showed the government's genuine concern regarding the necessity of private funding, and the symbolic and financial threat that foundation withdrawal from the arts posed. Foundation leaders and government representatives discussed these issues on a deep and thoughtful level. Not only did the transcripts reveal their attitudes and arguments, but also their postmeeting reflections and correspondence articulated their shared understandings.

At the meeting were the top brass of the large philanthropic institutions, arts organizations, and federal and state government agencies (see Box 3.2).[59] Rockefeller Foundation president John H. Knowles led initial discussions.[60] Participants deliberated the "best role over the next decade for the private foundations" and the most effective way to coordinate sources of support from individuals, businesses, and public agencies. Knowles began by arguing that with the entry of government funding, foundations could not just "supply a steadily diminishing fraction" of arts organizations' total budgets. Their central problem was "recognizing the limitations of [their] relatively small money and small influence." He asked, "How can the Rockefeller Foundation with its annual $3,000,000, started at a time when there was zero support from the public sector, find its unique role now that there is almost $100,000,000 from the public sector? It certainly isn't by doing the same that we have been doing the last 10 years."

From the Ford perspective, of note was officers' extensive use of economic and market-driven vocabularies, which were apparent throughout the meeting, and their desire for informal political cooperation. Vice president Lowry advocated giving "working capital" to organizations at the beginning of fiscal years, as was done in "the business world." President Bundy referred to the "economics of the arts" and

BOX 3.2

ATTENDEES, "HOW CAN FOUNDATIONS HELP THE ARTS?"

- John H. Knowles (president, Rockefeller Foundation)
- McGeorge Bundy (president, Ford Foundation)
- W. McNeil Lowry (vice president of arts and the humanities, Ford Foundation)
- Amyas Ames (chairman of the board, Lincoln Center)
- Anthony Bliss (executive director, Metropolitan Opera)
- Douglas Dillon (chairman of the board, Rockefeller Foundation; president, Metropolitan Museum)
- Nancy Hanks (chairman, National Endowment for the Arts)
- Eric Larabee (executive director, New York State Council on the Arts)
- Goldwin McLellan (president, Business Committee for the Arts)
- Kenneth Dayton (trustee, Rockefeller Foundation; chief executive, Dayton-Hudson Corporation)
- Robert Sarnoff (chairman, RCA Corporation)

the management of nonprofit organizations. Economist experts had already played a decisive role in steering Ford's emphasis on endowment building and financing in music. Additionally, Bundy acknowledged the "quiet relationships" professional staff had with the political process. "We're not supposed to lobby," he spoke, "but I find that in the field of the arts, as Nancy Hanks says, that the friends of the arts in Congress do not regard it as lobbying to have visits from their friends in private foundations." Perhaps Bundy wanted to have his cake and eat it too—he wanted foundations to have power derived from networks of professional and personal connection, while avoiding any criticisms of collusion, favor, or privilege.

The arts organizations clamored for much larger sums of money and were loud campaigners for increased public funding. Amyas Ames, chairman of the board of Lincoln Center, argued that increasing federal aid had not kept pace with market inflation and that arts organizations were experiencing another crisis.[61] He argued that arts institutions were worse off than they were a few years previous and he proposed a massive increase in government funding for the arts to more than $500 million a year ($2.5 billion in 2017). In 1974, the NEA's budget was $60 million, so this suggestion represented an increase by almost 900%. Not even Nancy Hanks supported such a dramatic jump in the NEA's budget in so short a time period. She and others stated that a sudden influx of money would overwhelm staff and that they could not maintain a high quality of grant recipients.

Hanks, the sole representative of the federal government and the only woman, was a convincing and elucidating voice both before and after the meeting. Two weeks prior to the gathering, Hanks had already sent a letter to Knowles expressing how "distressed" she was about the possibility of Rockefeller ending its arts program.[62] "I do not wish to write in superlatives, but I view this as tragic and only hope that I can in some way persuade you and the trustees to change your minds." She continued, "I deeply believe that it will be a sad day indeed when (and if) government monies start to replace private monies in the arts. And, I will do everything I can to prevent this happening." At the meeting, she argued in support of the "absolutely essential quality of private leadership in the cultural development of this country," stating that foundations not only possessed large sums of money but also exhibited, along with the NEA, a "leadership factor" that influenced other donors.

At the event, Hanks also noted that foundations' "professional staff" were important because they played an "essential" role in guiding the grantmaking and development of public programs. "We call on them all the time," Hanks said. In a similar vein, she noted that other foundations used the NEA itself for guidance and direction. "We think," spoke Hanks, "this is a very important two-way relationship." Eric Larabee of the New York State Arts Council agreed with Hanks's point on the significance of professional staff, who he argued were critical in supporting small foundations that lacked personnel and otherwise exhibited a "very herd-like mentality." Executive director of the Metropolitan Opera Anthony Bliss also agreed. "Many arts organizations," Bliss said, "have so little money that their own staffs are very thin, very unsophisticated, and in many cases, ill-trained." In 1972, only 20% of foundations had any paid staff at all, including secretaries, and only 5% had any full-time paid staff.[63] The NEA and large foundations provided leadership and technical assistance, helping smaller foundations to operate more efficiently and effectively.

In the end, neither the Rockefeller nor the Ford Foundation disbanded its arts program. Instead, those programs became incorporated into more interdisciplinary goals set by the two institutions: the newly established "Arts, Humanities, and Contemporary Values" division of the Rockefeller Foundation in 1974, and Ford's "Education and Public Policy" division in 1980. The only major grant the Rockefeller Foundation made in the field of the arts until the 1980s, however, was its funding of the Recorded Anthology of American Music. Through the end of the 1970s, the division lacked clear direction. The same was true of Ford's program, which experienced a significant loss in leadership after W. McNeil Lowry's retirement in 1974.

Taking a step back and examining the individuals present at the "How Can Foundations Help the Arts?" meeting, though, gives further room to reflect on what these large funding bodies considered worthy endeavors for help. The Rockefeller Foundation invited those who represented the largest, longest-standing arts institutions in New York City: Lincoln Center, the Metropolitan Opera, and the Metropolitan Museum. These institutions had also received the bulk of foundation and government support, some benefiting from tens of millions of dollars of funds from the NEA and Ford and Rockefeller Foundations. They further indicated a close and interlocking network of individuals. To name just a few examples, Lincoln Center was a central initiative of John D. Rockefeller III's that opened in 1962, and the Metropolitan Opera was one of its constituent entities. Douglas Dillon was both the chairman of the Rockefeller Foundation and the president of the Metropolitan Museum. And industrialist and philanthropist Kenneth Dayton was a Rockefeller trustee, while also just having served on the NCA and as a member of the NEA's task force on public–private cooperation.

Perhaps the smaller size of the meeting prevented the comprehensive inclusion of a wide range of variously sized arts organizations representing different geographic regions, aesthetic priorities, and social missions. Discussions could have become unwieldy, and some groups would always be left out. But by only inviting those experts who benefited the most from foundation activity in the arts and those who decided on the policies of arts funding to begin with, discussion limited the types of experiences that these men (and Hanks, the one and only exception) had at their artistic conglomerates.[64] Thus, by "the arts," what the Rockefeller Foundation, in particular, had in mind were the high arts of the Western European tradition, and those located primarily in New York. Whatever problems there were in arts funding were those that the largest performing arts institutions and museums decided. The greatest challenges to cultural pluralism in this field were thus, as has been a recurring theme, self-reinforcement and closure. The consequences of greater collaboration and cooperation were that funding institutions introduced change uneasily, winners stood the best chances of winning in the future, and losers were repeatedly left out of the system.

Conclusion

By the numbers, the Rockefeller Foundation, Ford Foundation, and NEA represented a small fraction of the total U.S. field of cultural production during this time period. The network of public and private sources of arts funding additionally included wealthy individuals, multinational corporations, local foundations, and state arts agencies. Yet, between the 1950s and 1970s, the two largest philanthropic foundations and the federal government composed a significantly oversized proportion of influence and impact. The system was overwhelmingly top-heavy, and the political, economic, and cultural elite were strongly interconnected in the fields of both power and cultural production. They stood at the center of arts grantmaking and their decisions carried tremendous legitimacy and weight.

Scholars like Joan Roelofs have pointed out the limits of pluralist interpretations of the United States, arguing that "the system is not, as it is claimed, open to all interests, for the powerless rarely organize."[65] They are deterred by lack of resources and time and a "hegemonic ideology that prevents them from even recognizing their grievances," leading to "a culture of passivity." Robert Arnove articulates a more damning critique, arguing that foundations, rather than promoting cultural pluralism in the fields of education and social science research, imposed ethnocentric values and engaged in cultural imperialism—"the use of political and economic power to exalt and spread the habits of a foreign culture at the expense of the native culture" (*The Harper Dictionary of Modern Thought*) and "the deliberate and calculated process of forcing a cultural minority to adopt the culture of the dominant group in a society" (*Dictionary of Social Science*).[66]

The reality in the arts field cannot be so severely characterized as Arnove's account of education and social science research, but his argument still holds some weight. Investigation of how foundations like Ford and Rockefeller worked in tandem with the federal government to establish the U.S. arts world has heretofore been limited, but this examination shows that despite striving for pluralism both of funding sources and of grant recipients, the vast majority of grantmaking went to Western European high art organizations. The NEA supported jazz and folk music, but those represented only a fraction of its overall budget.

As has been emphasized, the "fault" did not lie necessarily with any individuals—consultants, experts, and officers fought tooth and nail for the limited funds they could raise, and believed in the critical value of the art forms and genres they supported. But the field of cultural production was imbalanced. Some were decked in gear from head to toe, while others competed with hands tied behind their backs. The Ford and Rockefeller Foundations and the NEA laid down channels through which funds flowed with greater ease. The tool of matching grants, and Treasury Fund grants in particular, provided the illusion of democratic voice in arts grantmaking, when they actually allowed those with high levels of economic, social, and cultural capital to subsidize their own aesthetic priorities with the federal government's money. Tax-deductible contributions to nonprofit organizations operated in a similar fashion, directing billions of dollars outside of the federal government's control.

As sociologists Michael Grenfell and Cheryl Hardy point out, fields and capital operate through forms that are "misrecognized," rather than struggles that are open and explicit.[67] Individuals involved in the process are not conscious of their own biases and would either defend the objectivity of their decisions or deny the inordinate power and privilege that they possess. They "misrecognize" their possession of capital and the impacts that their decisions have in the field, determining which art is available and of value. Historians can investigate and analyze such misrecognitions and demonstrate the consequences they have on society. Indeed, the arts programs of the NEA and the major foundations have changed from what they were in the mid-twentieth century, yet one of the continuities in the system has been the roles of expertise, matching grants, and social capital in decision making.

Perhaps of all the forms of capital, social capital is the most important in this field of cultural production. Grenfell and Hardy reach the same conclusions through their examinations of the visual arts, photography, and painting. According to them, to do well in the field of photography, it was "almost essential to enter the field from the middle or upper classes." Access to valorized subjects and social circles determined success. The same was true in this examination of the roles of expert consultants and foundation and Arts Endowment staff and officers. Social capital in the form of first-degree connections among composers, performers, managers, directors, and boards of trustees mattered a tremendous amount in the voices they heard and the matching grants they specified. Social capital was a strong source of misrecognized power—misrecognized because it was overshadowed by discourses of expertise, objectivity, and professional management. The fields of power and of art were tightly woven and difficult to penetrate. These are important considerations to remember because unlike economic capital, *social capital is never taxed*.

Experts in Action

[The] lack of understanding of basic technique, and
accompanying tendency to ape mannerisms, is very
widespread in contemporary music—so widespread
that one can often detect, instantly, in the work
of younger composers, the superficial features of
something that might be called "the foundation
style," a dreary routine of academic formulas that
is guaranteed to win fellowships and prizes.[1]

—WINTHROP SARGEANT, 1958

4

THE ROCKEFELLER FOUNDATION, THE UNIVERSITY

NEW MUSIC CENTER, AND "FOUNDATION MUSIC"

FAMOUS *NEW YORKER* WRITER Winthrop Sargeant was a powerhouse in
twentieth-century classical music criticism. In his book, *Listening to Music*, Sargeant
lamented that "foundation music" embodied all the problems of an alienated, ivory
tower. For him, it existed—and persisted—only because private foundations supported it. As the general argument went: foundations recruited composers to serve as
experts on selection committees, who then chose other composers with whom they
were well connected, creating a closed loop that fed off of itself and produced music
of a similar kind. According to Sargeant, his idea of the "foundation style" was a
mixing of "twelve-tone scales" and influences of the "*Boulangerie*" (a reference to the
pupils who studied with famous French composer and teacher Nadia Boulanger).[2]
"Foundation style" was somewhere between serial and dissonant neoclassical.[3]

Foundation officers and their hired experts were well acquainted with the critique.
For instance, the Ford Foundation's report, *Sharps and Flats*, acknowledged that
"foundations have been criticized for allowing committees of composers to award
commissions . . . too often the composers anointed their friends and disciples, who
created what came to be known as 'foundation music.'"[4] Even today, music written in the "Ivory Tower" still tugs at suspicions of esotericism and elitism because
it conjures images of a privileged white male composer at an Ivy League university,
disconnected from the "real world," acting as an "expert" on behalf of grantmaking

Ask the Experts. Michael Sy Uy, Oxford University Press (2020). © Oxford University Press.
DOI: 10.1093/oso/9780197510445.001.0001.

institutions.[5] He decided what was "good" and what was "bad," based on his own aesthetic preferences.

The point to be made is *not* that foundations patronized a monolithic style of "foundation music," but that critiques against "foundation music" emerged because competition for musical and financial resources after World War II was fierce. Divisions between composers of different styles—tonal, atonal, and serial music—became entrenched. Which music and how foundations supported music was contentious. Moreover, Cold War anxiety, escalated by the Soviet Union's successful launching of Sputnik in 1957, pushed the nation to aggressively prioritize a scientism that seeped into the arts. Composers who rationalized and justified their work along lines of research, mathematics, and technology benefited. As musicologist and cultural historian Nadine Hubbs characterizes the era, "new musical 'laboratories' were erected by such institutions as Columbia and Princeton, arcane studios where learned men used the latest scientific equipment to create and manipulate electronic sounds."[6]

Perhaps no other issue concerning Western art music after World War II has been more controversial than the "serial tyranny"—or its myth. The tyranny's alleged pervasiveness and power compelled composers to write serialist music or be left out of the university and prize-awarding system. Serialism was (and is) a compositional practice based on organized and repeated patterns (rows or series) based on pitch, rhythm, or other musical elements. "Twelve-tone music"—also known as dodecaphonic music—is a form of serialism. In 1999, musicologist Joseph Straus ignited a flurry of responses concerning the power and influence of serial composers, and the role of the university and grantmaking institutions, by arguing that the serial tyranny was a myth.[7] He sought to set straight the misconception that serial composers had come to dominate prestigious music departments in the United States or that they controlled publications and awards committees.[8]

Serialism has been a useful punching bag for those criticizing the ivory tower and the academic composers who supposedly write irrelevant and alienated music. At the same time, serialism and electronic music have benefited from their symbolization of technological progress, aesthetics free from commercialism, and the pursuit of uninhibited artistic creativity. As Hubbs argues, serialism not only profited from its perceived connections with science but also accrued a "moral-political privilege" because serialists presented their music as an art form off-limits to Soviet artists.[9] It came to represent, par excellence, freedom and democracy—ideals quintessentially "American" during this period of anti-communism.[10] What is clearly missing in the debate surrounding "serial tyranny," though, is a better understanding of what exactly arts grantmaking institutions were funding, in terms of individual composers and performers, as well as new music centers, and attendant support of equipment and facilities.

At the Rockefeller Foundation, an incredible burst of funds and energy occurred during the period 1964–70, when its officers gave nineteen grants to twelve colleges and universities to build, or solidify, programs in new music composition or contemporary chamber music.[11] Notably, after the foundation established its first Music Advisory Committee in 1963, its officers targeted schools of higher education spread across the country with the hopes of forming regional centers of new music. The grants were often in the hundreds of thousands of dollars, which had an exceptional influence, especially for burgeoning music programs. In total, the foundation gave over $2 million (roughly $17.5 million in 2017) during these six years of frenzied activity, as shown in Figure 4.1 and Table 4.1, indicating the grant periods of Rockefeller funding. While $2 million spread over a decade was just a small fraction of Rockefeller's overall giving, for the schools and individuals who benefited from the grants, such an infusion was like a gushing pipe in a funding desert. It allowed composers to build state-of-the-art electronic studio oases and provided time to experiment, compose, and perform their works across the country.

Not only has this significant funding program been underexamined by scholars investigating the myth of serial tyranny, but also the concentrated network of composers and performers who capitalized on these grants has been left out as well. Members of this network served as crucial experts for Rockefeller in the way the foundation germinated and spread its project. One notable expert was Milton Babbitt, who had just made a large splash with his infamous article "Who Cares

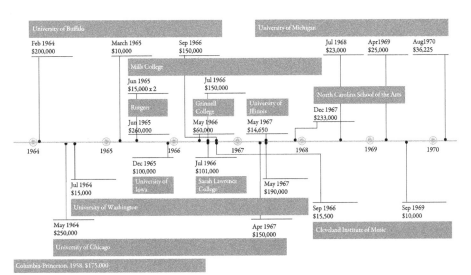

FIGURE 4.1 Periods of Rockefeller Foundation funding, university new music center grants, 1958–70. I thank Sarah Nam and Cheng Gao for their suggestions and help in improving Figures 4.1 and 4.2.

TABLE 4.1

Rockefeller Foundation University New Music Center Grants, 1958–70

Schools	Grant	Grant	Grant	Total
University of Chicago	$250,000 (1964)	$150,000 (1967)		$400,000
University of Buffalo	$200,000 (1964)	$10,000 (1965)	$150,000 (1966)	$360,000
Rutgers University	$265,000 (1965)			$265,000
North Carolina School of the Arts	$233,000 (1967)			$233,000
Mills College	$15,000 (1965)	$15,000 (1965)	$200,000 (1966)	$230,000
University of Washington	$15,000 (1964)	$190,000 (1967)		$205,000
Columbia–Princeton	$175,000 (1958)			$175,000
Sarah Lawrence College	$101,000 (1966)			$101,000
University of Iowa	$100,000 (1965)			$100,000
University of Michigan	$23,000 (1968)	$25,000 (1969)	$36,225 (1970)	$84,225
Grinnell College	$60,000 (1966)			$60,000
Cleveland Institute of Music	$15,500 (1966)	$10,000 (1969)		$25,500
University of Illinois	$14,650 (1967)			$14,650
Total				$2,253,375

If You Listen?" of 1958. But the foundation involved many others, such as Ralph Shapey, Lukas Foss, and Salvatore Martirano. They all served as experts while simultaneously benefiting from foundation grants and participation in the system.

Composers and performers clamored for foundation support in the name of science, and the foundation officers offered eager ears, already influenced by teleological worldviews and fears of Soviet advancement during the Cold War. The Rockefeller Foundation, in fact, had always carried the reputation of being the most "scientific." Frederick Taylor Gates, the Baptist clergyman who served as John D. Rockefeller's principal business and philanthropic adviser, believed in "systematic, scientific principles to cure the 'root causes' underlying both physical illness and social problems."[12] He termed these principles as "scientific giving." After World War II, many officers and trustees with scientific educational backgrounds reinforced this culture.

Rockefeller's support of these new music centers fit within its overall goals of bolstering universities, creative artists with impact and promise, and the development of regional hubs across the United States (see Figure 4.2). According to arts director Norman Lloyd, the foundation wanted to pair universities with new arts groups so that it could bring together creative and performing artists with educators and arts students. In his report, "The University as a Regional Arts Resource Center," he wrote further that through these arrangements, artists had an "institutional base where they are free to work," without commercial constraints.[13] They could experiment with new ideas while students and teachers benefited by having "in their midst a corps of dedicated professional artists who provide standards and open new vistas." In sum, Lloyd argued that with such a partnership, universities could perform "a social as well as a cultural service for their immediate and regional communities."

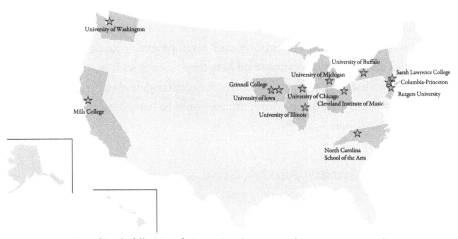

FIGURE 4.2 Map of Rockefeller Foundation university new music center grants, 1958–70.

The most prominent music composition facilities were at Columbia University (in partnership with Princeton University), the State University of New York at Buffalo, the University of Chicago, the University of Iowa, Rutgers University, and Mills College. All relied on Rockefeller money, and the leaders at each one— prominent composers who held administrative and faculty positions—maintained close ties with foundation officers. Columbia and Princeton were strongholds for serialist composers, especially Milton Babbitt, Roger Sessions, and Charles Wuorinen. Other composers like Elliott Carter and Ralph Shapey who did not self-identify as serialists but who wrote in atonal and highly modernist styles also benefited from the institutional prestige and facilities, even if Carter never held a university position.

Admittedly, there is a danger in, and an extreme difficulty of, pigeonholing any of these composers into a specific stylistic categorization, whether serial, experimental, tonal, or otherwise. Their compositional styles changed over time and for a number of reasons. Think of the long careers of Aaron Copland and Igor Stravinsky, who spanned the spectrum of tonality, atonality, and many things in between. How much harder it is to categorize individuals when the differences are more subtle and nuanced. In any case, as musicologist Emily Abrams Ansari and others point out, tonality and serialism are not mutually exclusive and there are ways to write music that is both serial and tonal, as well as music that is at times tonal and at other times atonal.[14]

Therefore,rather than a serial tyranny, the real supremacy lay in elitism and specialization, reliant on the fundamental separation between musical experts and nonexperts, on "true" appreciators of musical advancement and those laypeople listening to the works of the past, or popular and commercially successful music. In the words of Babbitt, composers were "specialists," and they needed to be funded and respected as such in a modernizing and technologically advancing world. Rockefeller's support of this ideology began in the late 1950s, with two prestigious Northeast schools. Tracing the history and development of Rockefeller's support at each new music center demonstrated how they set root within American higher education. Similarly, through its grants, Rockefeller fundamentally supported individual experts, and an analysis without them would be like a history of Los Alamos without Oppenheimer.

The Beginnings: Columbia–Princeton, Buffalo, and Rutgers

THE FIRST STEP: THE COLUMBIA–PRINCETON ELECTRONIC MUSIC CENTER

At the root of Rockefeller's investment in electronic music was a composer-expert system focused on laboratory science, technological advancement, and cross-Atlantic studio rivalry. The Columbia–Princeton program was unique because it was Rockefeller's first exploration into an electronic music studio. Its support of composers Otto Luening, Vladimir Ussachevsky, and, most importantly, Milton Babbitt, demonstrated its investment in key experts in action. It set the stage for all future Rockefeller grants to universities and new music.

The program began when Columbia professors and composers Luening and Ussachevsky requested in 1953 a small grant-in-aid ($3,240; $30,000 in 2017) for the purchase of equipment "exclusively for creative research in the field of electronic music."[15] With the grant, they bought tapes, recorders, a switchboard, and other materials. Ussachevsky explained to Rockefeller officer Charles B. Fahs why they needed the support:

So far all the electronic musical inventions have been snapped up by the popular field which has a way of riding any new horse to death before it ever achieves a full stride. Already a few popular arrangers are using some of the most obvious techniques of tape music, but with so little imagination that I am depressed over the effects they produce.[16]

Rockefeller aid was therefore needed to preserve the noncommercial use of, and research into, the new music. Further in the memorandum, Ussachevsky delved deeper into the scientific explanation describing how the tape recorder "transform[ed] the sounds it received, enabling the composer to treat sound as a substance, measurable in feet, inches, and seconds, that is plastic as clay for purposes of further manipulation." By this statement, Ussachevsky tried for no less than complete mastery and control over the sound medium, and he employed technical and rigorous language to describe his process. He argued that a "laboratory" attached to the university was indispensable "to carry out experiments."[17]

Around the same time, Princeton professor and composer Milton Babbitt also applied for funds from the foundation for his own work on electronic music. He too tied music composition with the fields of science and technology, and emphasized his background in mathematics. In a long letter to Rockefeller officer John Marshall, he reminded Marshall that he (Babbitt) was a "one-time member of the Princeton mathematics faculty," which meant that he possessed the "scientific background that has enabled [him] to keep abreast of the scientific literature in the electronic music field."[18] Babbitt emphasized that he had lectured to mathematicians and physicists of both Princeton and the Institute for Advanced Study on the mathematical and physical aspects of electronic music.

The composer eventually got down to business: the unavailability of equipment prevented him from producing more electronic music. There was, however, a solution: the latest RCA synthesizer. Babbitt argued that the synthesizer represented new technology that could eventually lead to a "shift in the balance of power" between U.S. and European electronic studios. Working with the synthesizer's developer, Dr. Harry Olson (director of the RCA Acoustical and Electromechanical Laboratory in Princeton), Babbitt contended that the synthesizer could be used to "produce music of genuinely contemporary significance, but only by composers whose musical orientation is as sophisticated and responsibly 'advanced' as the scientific orientation of the creators of the synthesizer." Marshall's memo indicated interest in Babbitt's proposal. He wrote, "while I suppose all of us have mixed feelings about electronic music we have heard, it does open up possibilities which undoubtedly deserve exploration."[19]

Despite some initial misunderstandings and disagreements, the composers at Columbia and Princeton developed a solid working relationship with one another by 1958. Ussachevsky and Babbitt reported to the foundation that they were permitted to work with the RCA synthesizer at Princeton for two days a week without charge.[20] The next stage of development was, at the initial suggestion of Marshall, to develop a field for the music, in cooperation with multiple universities. Ussachevsky proposed housing a main studio complex at Columbia, since there was already an electronic studio. That New York City was a leading center of music in the United States was also an advantage.[21]

The large grant request first needed Rockefeller board approval, so officers in the music division precirculated recordings of electronic music to the trustees and other directors.[22] Director for biological and medical research Robert S. Morison wrote in an amusing memo that he did not find one record that could be "unreservedly recommended as an enticement to the trustees" to approve the grant. On the other hand, he wrote that Ms. Morison suggested one "as ideal for playing on next Halloween to give the macabre thrill to the more aggressive of our tricks-and-treats guests."[23] Fortunately for Babbitt, Luening, and Ussachevsky, recommendations made by "distinguished composers," such as Roger Sessions and Darius Milhaud, convinced the trustees more than the director for biological and medical research and his wife did (although their objections foreshadowed officer skepticism in years to come).[24] Milhaud, for example, sent a positive telegram.

> To those who lament that there are no Beethovens working in the tape medium, I retort that even Beethoven could not have overcome the lack of music paper and quills—and we must have the electronic equivalents of these when another Beethoven comes along![25]

For Milhaud, musical genius needed adequate resources, equipment, and funding. Sessions's letter was resounding and urgent:

It is of great importance that the project should be carried on under non-commercial auspices, in a place where both competent musicians and competent scientists are available. This seems to me to make it clear that it should be carried on under university auspices. Finally, the project seems to me a necessity if we are to hold our own in a cultural sense, not only as regards Europe, but as regards the Soviet Union, as well.[26]

Sessions wanted the project to be "noncommercial" because RCA had previously used the synthesizer for popular and profitable music making, a concern that Ussachevsky had already brought up. But Sessions alluded to several other issues, among them the importance of the project's location at a university with both musicians and scientists, as well as the threat of cultural developments in Europe and the Soviet Union. Thus, Sessions, a Princeton professor, composer, *and* colleague of Babbitt, called to attention the Cold War threat to the officers and the cultural-moral imperative to support this music. Sessions's letter came within a year of the Soviet launching of Sputnik, the first artificial Earth satellite in 1957, and the resulting panic that the United States had fallen behind in science and faltered in the arts. Moreover, his mention of rivalry with European studios echoed Babbitt's letters to the foundation.

At the same time, Babbitt's "Who Cares If You Listen?" in *High Fidelity*, published February 1958, added further fuel to the music-science-university engine.[27] In the article—actually originally titled "The Composer as Specialist"—Babbitt's connections among serious, advanced, contemporary music and science, research, and specialization reached their zenith. The impact on the wider public's perception of academic or "foundation music" cannot be underestimated. Babbitt proposed "total, resolute, and voluntary withdrawal" by the composer into "private performance and electronic media, with its very possibility of complete elimination of the public and social aspects of musical composition." By doing so, "the composer would be free to pursue a private life of professional achievement, as opposed to a public life of unprofessional compromise and exhibitionism." The university was vital to provide sanctuary and resources for composers just as it did for scientists.

As a result of the article, Babbitt indeed became the composer-as-specialist par excellence. Through his position in academia and his forceful rhetoric, he was the spokesman for serious, advanced, contemporary music, while also serving as the arbiter for much music supported by the Rockefeller Foundation. A year later in 1959, Rockefeller officer Robert W. July met with Babbitt and asked him what he thought were the new directions in modern composition. Babbitt replied that "the main line for the moment derives from twelve-tone theory."[28] That same year, with the support of arts patron Paul Fromm, Babbitt established the Princeton Seminars in Advanced Musical Study, which lasted only two summers, but as musicologist Monica Hershberger argues, the seminars "paved the way for the journal *Perspectives of New Music* and the founding of the Ph.D. in music composition."[29] Over the next two decades and beyond, the foundation frequently consulted Babbitt for his recommendations. He was not just a specialist in the way he composed; he was also a specialist in the way Rockefeller entrusted him and other composers to make decisions based on their knowledge and experience.[30]

Thus, the Rockefeller trustees and officers approached these new music projects at university centers against the backdrop of Babbitt's influence as a figurehead for serial music, the specter of Soviet advancement, and the lofty visions of the university haven. The foundation agreed to $175,000 ($1.5 million in 2017) over five years for the Columbia–Princeton Electronic Music Center, with the understanding that the two universities would take over full support of the program after the end of the grant, an important requirement of self-sufficiency that the foundation enforced for all its grantees. It was the first grant to a new music center and became a point of reference for the foundation's future support to Buffalo and Rutgers.

THE SECOND STEP: THE STATE UNIVERSITY OF NEW YORK AT BUFFALO CREATIVE ASSOCIATES AND THE RUTGERS UNIVERSITY CONTEMPORARY CHAMBER ENSEMBLE

After its initial foray into new music, several years passed before the foundation again invested hundreds of thousands of dollars into university centers. Instead of a directly scientific or technological approach, however, the grants shifted focus toward the cutting-edge of aesthetics and repertoire, as well as a more direct relationship between the university and its surrounding community. Rockefeller's first set of new grants went to the State University of New York at Buffalo in 1964. The $200,000 grant ($1.6 million in 2017) paid for a center of performing and creative arts under the joint direction of Lukas Foss, composer and director of the Buffalo Philharmonic Orchestra, and Allen D. Sapp Jr., chairman of the department of music.[31] Foundation officers considered Buffalo a "strong and independent regional center," and they intended to develop further locations for the "future growth and strength of the musical scene in the United States." Rockefeller extended the project for another two years through 1968 with a grant of $150,000.[32]

Similar to Babbitt at Columbia–Princeton, Foss was the expert in action at Buffalo. In officer Gerald Freund's presentation to the trustees, he commented on Foss's leadership and character, citing that Leonard Bernstein thought of Foss as "an authentic American musical genius."[33] Freund wrote that the grant was "enthusiastically recommended by the Foundation's Advisory Committee on Music [established a year earlier, in 1963] and has been favorably commented upon by composers and instrumentalists." It helped that the advisory committee included Foss, Bernstein, and Copland, who were not just colleagues, but close friends, illustrating another tight circle of artist-experts. According to Nigel Simeone, editor of Bernstein's letters, the two shared a friendship that lasted fifty years, from their time at Tanglewood with Copland, through their studies at Curtis, until Bernstein's death in 1990 (Foss lived until 2009).[34] Copland was already experienced with Buffalo after holding one of its Slee composer professorships.

Importantly, Rockefeller considered Buffalo a regional center for the development and promotion of new music. The center and its associates immersed themselves in the community, performing regularly and often. They were both performers and neighbors to local residents, as noted by Renee Levine Packer, who documented the center's history after spending many years working there.[35] The city became a hotbed for "downtown" experimentalist composers—or artists who were active in downtown New York City, in contrast to the "uptown," "serious" composers at Columbia.[36] The Buffalo center set the stage for Rockefeller's further interest in establishing new music communities in Iowa, Michigan, and Washington. Even after the foundation ceased funding in 1968, the Buffalo center continued on for another twelve years. By the time it closed in 1980, more than a hundred creative associates had participated as fellows, and many of these artists had either come from or later went to the numerous other Rockefeller-funded havens.[37]

One of these new music sanctuaries was at Rutgers University. Its Contemporary Chamber Ensemble moved from New York City to the university in 1965 with a $265,000 ($2 million in 2017) grant from the foundation. Conductor and composer Arthur Weisberg directed the group, and he worked with composer Beatrice Witkin, leader of the Committee for International Composers Concerts. After entertaining various proposals to be in residence at Hunter College and New York University, the group finally agreed on Rutgers, when the university hired several of its members as faculty, made building space available, and agreed to on-campus concerts. Like many of its grants, Rockefeller tapered its giving, with the expectation that Rutgers would find other resources to continue the project.

Lukas Foss and Leonard Bernstein also endorsed the Rutgers ensemble as "perhaps one of the best performing groups of contemporary music."[38] Perhaps it is not a surprise, though, that the Rutgers Committee for International Composers included Bernstein and Copland as members. Additionally, Elliott Carter, Darius Milhaud, Edgard Varèse, Stefan Wolpe, and Pierre Boulez also served. The ensemble chose Carter to run the first weekly composers' workshops at the New Brunswick campus. Carter had already given "a very strong endorsement of the aims and forms of the program" at a press conference to announce the Rockefeller grant.[39] The first commission went to another committee member, Wolpe, an aspect that worried Rockefeller consultant Martin Bookspan: he expressed concern that Wolpe was already a member of the ensemble and was Witkin's composition teacher (as was Roger Sessions). Despite the range of stylistic differences, the Rutgers ensemble operated in ways that demonstrated once more the small number of individuals working closely together in the contemporary music field.

Consistent with almost all projects supported by the foundation, the ensemble approached Rockefeller music director Norman Lloyd again in 1967 regarding prospects for further funding.[40] Based on its tapering agreement, Rutgers should have fully supported the program by that point. Lloyd noted, however, that the project at Buffalo had also taken longer than initially expected to become financially self-sufficient, speculating that Rutgers might be in a similar situation. Officer Freund commented pessimistically that Rutgers was the one music group he would have dropped. After visiting the university in May 1968, officer Howard Klein wrote that the program did not fully succeed because it "was too ambitious a program for Rutgers at the time it was begun."[41]

Supporting Regional Centers of Music Composition and Performance

"One small lingering doubt ... Why Buffalo?" wrote Alan Rich music critic of the *New York Herald Tribune* to officer Freund when asked to evaluate the proposal.[42] Freund responded that he "fully agreed" on the question, but he countered by asking, "Why not Buffalo?"[43] Freund noted that the project was already an experimental one and needed to be tried *someplace*. When compared to the vibrant music scene of New York City, upstate New York indeed seemed like an unusually quiet and perhaps more conservative location to experiment with new bells and whistles. What would audience members think? Would there be an audience? While the industrial city on the shores of Lake Erie had some powerful modern art supporters at the Albright-Knox Art Gallery, the city's reputation did not scream "avant-garde." Nevertheless, Rockefeller officers took a chance on Buffalo, and they ventured into other schools across the country because they hoped to develop regional centers for new music. They wanted the centers to have a larger impact on the surrounding area by both drawing audiences to the university and serving as a launching pad for groups to tour on a state- or region-wide basis. The University of Washington, the University of Iowa, the University of Michigan, the Cleveland Institute of Music, and the North Carolina School of the Arts were all part of this vision.

THE UNIVERSITY OF WASHINGTON CONTEMPORARY PERFORMING GROUP

The University of Washington served, according to Rockefeller officers, as a cru-cial "regional center" for students from the Pacific Northwest, extending to Idaho, Wyoming, Colorado, and California.[44] The foundation began exploring the univer-sity's School of Music in July 1964, when it granted a modest $15,000 over three years toward a training program for students in music performance.[45] The foundation fol-lowed up its interest in the school with a much more substantial gift of $190,000 in May 1967 ($1.4 million in 2017), to expand its new Contemporary Performing Group. In the second grant, officers again elaborated on the need to build a strong school on the West Coast, so that students did not need "to attend a school in the Midwest or on the East Coast."[46]

Director and composer William Bergsma had come to the University of Washington from Juilliard, where he had been associate dean, appointed by William Schuman as one of Schuman's first acts as president. Musicologist Steve Swayne notes that Schuman hired three other composition faculty in this initial burst in the mid-1940s, including Vincent Persichetti, Peter Mennin, and Robert Ward. Bergsma, Mennin, and Ward all later became conservatory presidents.[47] While the foundation asked Schuman to evaluate the Washington proposal, Schuman declined owing to a "lack of objectivity" and time, although he wrote that any "local effort to develop quality programs on the West Coast [was] very much needed."[48]

The University of Washington had plans to build a $3.7 million ($27 million in 2017) performing arts building and had taken steps toward increasing its public pro-file in music, for example, by adding to its faculty the composer-performers William O. Smith and Robert Suderburg, soprano Elizabeth Suderburg, and members of the Philadelphia String Quartet. These seven faculty members formed the "nucleus" of the Contemporary Performing Group, supplemented by nine more performer-instructors, including a resident woodwind quintet. Rockefeller approved the $190,000 over a five-year period and covered the partial salaries of its group mem-bers, as well as the costs of visiting composers and rental and copying fees. The foundation expected the university to overmatch its grant, contributing $250,000, and similar to its other programs, it assumed the school would cover full support by the end of the grant. The officers began to see a wider network of new music centers across the country, and Washington's group constituted "an important link in the network." Robert Suderburg did not stay forever, though, as he moved to become chancellor of the North Carolina School of the Arts, another Rockefeller grant recipient.[49] Bergsma also left in 1972 to serve as a faculty visitor at Brooklyn College.[50]

THE UNIVERSITY OF IOWA COMPOSERS WORKSHOP AND CENTER
FOR NEW MUSIC

In the central Midwest, Rockefeller made a large investment into the University of Iowa, which represented an archetypical case of combining a strong regional center with a contemporary chamber group and, eventually, a laboratory for electronic and experimental music. A year after the foundation's grant to the University of Washington, officers visited the University of Iowa on a two-day trip in October 1965. Freund was amazed by the orchestra's concert of Stravinsky's *Petrouchka*, writing in his diary that "he had never heard a superior performance" and he was even "inspired . . . to see this crew of corn- and beef-fed Iowans play and respond on an artistic level that would make any European capital's citizenry proud."[51] Freund suggested that with this talent, Iowans "look in the corn fields and beat the bushes in the area generally," rather than turn to New York or California. The visits cemented their beliefs not just in the agricultural bounties of the region, but also the benefits of a traveling jury to scout the area rather than sending recruiters to the East or West Coasts.[52] Freund asked William Schuman, Gunther Schuller, Richard Franko Goldman, and Peter Mennin to evaluate the proposal.[53]

After positive reviews, the foundation approved its large $100,000 grant ($800,000 in 2017) to Iowa shortly thereafter in December 1965. Officers agreed that the university had "one of the strongest and liveliest music faculties at any major American institution," and that it served as a key regional hub for the "central United States."[54] Iowa declared that there was no university between the Mississippi River and the Pacific Coast with as long-standing a tradition of sponsoring the creative and performing arts as it had.[55] The grant provided "both a laboratory for the creative interaction of composers and outstanding instrumentalists and a performing group of the highest possible quality." At Iowa, therefore, all the pieces were assembled: the scientific sheen of experimentation and discovery, excellence, regional impact, and residence within a university. The key actors were composer and professor Richard B. Hervig, conductor and professor James Dixon, and director of the School of Music, professor Himie Voxman. The Chamber Players fluctuated between ten and thirteen instrumental and vocal performers. The foundation expected Iowa's contribution to the number of fellowships to grow over time, similar to the stipulations it made to Buffalo and other programs.

At the end of the first two years, Iowa sent a report to Rockefeller, counting fifteen regular concerts, which included seventy-six compositions by forty-six composers, thirty-two of whom were American.[56] Composers at the center represented a little over a fifth of those who performed (ten of the forty-six). Additionally, they held six symposiums, programmed two television specials, and performed twelve out-of-town concerts in the midwest region. Milton Babbitt was one of its visiting composers in 1966. The Center for New Music has continued to the present, living up to the foundation's expectations of self-sufficiency, having been "funded by the University through the School of Music."[57]

THE CLEVELAND INSTITUTE OF MUSIC UNIVERSITY CIRCLE CONTEMPORARY CHAMBER MUSIC ENSEMBLE

Six months after the grant to Iowa, the foundation kept pace and expanded to the Cleveland Institute of Music (CIM) in September 1966. The grant was unassumingly sized, but still represented Rockefeller's interest in regional support, specifically of the "rich musical culture of Cleveland and northern Ohio." The grant paid for six concerts of "modern and contemporary music, together with electronic music, modern dance, and experiments in film and visual projections."[58] Officer Boyd R. Compton had visited Cleveland in March and remarked that the proposed budget was "extremely modest," due to participants devoting considerable free time.[59]

Director Donald Erb was assistant professor of music at Cleveland on a Guggenheim fellowship and on leave from Bowling Green State University. In an attempt to join together the working power of schools from the surrounding area, Erb collaborated with Raymond Wilding-White of Case Institute of Technology to establish the University Circle Studio workshop for electronic music, visual arts, and dance. The center offered a regional base to CIM, Case Western Reserve, Bowling Green, and other schools.[60] Over the years, Erb continued to be a useful resource to the Rockefeller Foundation. Director Klein in 1969 noted that Erb's appointment as composer in residence with the Dallas Symphony was "one of the most successful stints" in the program's three-year history.[61] Klein effused that Erb was "enormously resourceful and dynamic" and that "this man [Erb] in any situation given a modicum of help results in changes for the good." Erb developed a later incarnation of the group as the CIM Contemporary Music Ensemble in 1973, and it is now the CIM New Music Ensemble.[62]

THE NORTH CAROLINA SCHOOL OF THE ARTS AND PIEDMONT CHAMBER PLAYERS

Compared to the Northeast, the southeastern region of the United States had a far smaller presence of conservatories or art schools. In 1965, Governor Terry Sanford established, with generous state and private funding, the North Carolina School of the Arts (NCSA) as one of his educational projects. It was the first "state-established and state-supported school for the performing arts in this country," and the legislature paid roughly half of the annual operating budget of $1.3 million.[63] Tuition and a $1.5 million matching grant from the Ford Foundation over five years covered the other half. In 1967, the Rockefeller Foundation stepped in with its own $233,000 ($1.7 million in 2017), tied with bringing the Piedmont Chamber Players in residence. The school was racially integrated at both the student and faculty level.

Composer Vittorio Giannini initially led the school and proposed building a "resident faculty of instrumentalists" to teach and offer "first-rate professional performances of a broad musical repertory."[64] This group, known as the Piedmont Chamber Players, was eventually made up of twenty-two professional instrumentalists, who also served as leaders of the string, woodwind, brass, and percussion sections of the Winston-Salem Symphony. The players taught at local colleges, gave chamber music concerts, toured the southeastern United States, and premiered new works from local composers. Rockefeller officers saw the grant's primary purpose as the "cultural development of a part of the United States that has hitherto been lacking in high-quality musical performance." Unfortunately, Giannini passed away within a year, but composer Robert Ward, best known for his Pulitzer Prize–winning opera *The Crucible*, and one of William Schuman's first faculty composition hires at Juilliard (along with Bergsma), advanced to the helm. Ward served for seven years, until 1973, after which Suderburg, who had come from the University of Washington, replaced him. Around the same time, the school also officially became part of the University of North Carolina system.

THE UNIVERSITY OF MICHIGAN CONTEMPORARY PERFORMANCE PROJECT

Michigan was known as a vibrant place for new music, with festivals like ONCE, organized beginning in 1961 by composers Robert Ashley, Roger Reynolds, Gordon Mumma, and others. Rockefeller chose the university as a final boost to the midwest region. The foundation gave three grants for its contemporary music performing group, from July 1968 to August 1970, totaling $84,225 ($550,000 in 2017).[65] The first established the new group of seventeen members, to "train young performers in the problems of contemporary music" and give "young composers an opportunity to be heard as well as an opportunity to conduct their own music." Rockefeller officers expected the Ann Arbor–based group to perform and give symposia at other campuses, thus acting as a regional center. By the second grant, Rockefeller officers noted that the University Extension Service had indeed committed funds toward the costs of touring and out-of-town engagements, including in Detroit and other colleges throughout the state.

After the success of the first two grants, the Rockefeller arts division proposed to the trustees a larger appropriation to support the Contemporary Performance

Project for a further two years. The foundation saw Michigan as "an outstanding example of the importance of the university as a point of contact between creative artists and the public at large." Following a visit, Rockefeller gave $36,225, which was a little over a third of the total budget ($100,625), indicating a larger commitment on the part of the university. By 1973, the university had assumed the program into its budget in the sense that it gave academic credit for participation in the Contemporary Directions Ensemble.[66] Just like Iowa's artist community participation and Buffalo's creative associates, Michigan's role as a center for contemporary music was an integral aspect of Rockefeller's vision.

Foundation officers from the beginning clearly thought highly of composer and professor Ross Lee Finney, the expert in action at Michigan, describing him as "probably [having] developed more outstanding young composers than any teacher in the United States."[67] Finney was composer in residence and head of composition at the School of Music, one of the few music schools in the United States with a doctoral program in composition. As officers observed, he had the strength to "freely instruct and guide his students without forcing them to fit into a mold. As a result, his student composers range in style from modern conservative to avant-garde experimental." Finney's students included Pulitzer Prize–winning composers George Crumb and Leslie Bassett (who became a professor at the university, as well as deputy director of the group), dean of the School of Performing Arts at the University of Southern California Grant Beglarian, and renowned composer Roger Reynolds, who later led the Rockefeller-funded University of California, San Diego electronic music studio. Rockefeller's support of Finney was consistent with its overall effort to support key artists and composer-experts with promising futures. The new music centers at Mills College, the University of Chicago, and the University of Illinois also evidenced such an objective.

Supporting Key Composers and Performers

In addition to building regional centers, Rockefeller officers paid careful attention to exceptional artists, hoping these artists had a larger impact and influence on the field. As Lloyd noted in his diary, Finney was "undoubtedly one of the youngest-thinking 63-year-olds around. He has the kind of enthusiasm and excitement about his work—be it teaching or composing—that one expects to find in a 30-year-old."[68] Therefore, "backing a man like Finney, who is outstanding as a creative teacher, seems to me to be consistent with the aims of the RF's program in the Arts. . . . The Foundation would be strengthening the work of a man who is himself a great teacher and a trainer of other potentially great teachers."[69] The foundation took the same approach to advancing the work and influence of expert-composers and teachers Lukas Foss (Buffalo) and Milton Babbitt (Princeton), as well as Morton Subotnick (Mills College) and Ralph Shapey (Chicago). The foundation justified its support again and again by tying expertise with "innovation," "experimentation," and "vision."

THE MILLS COLLEGE PERFORMING GROUP AND TAPE MUSIC CENTER

At the heart of the union between the Mills College Performing Group and the Tape Music Center in San Francisco was Morton Subotnick, teacher of theory and composition, and eventual leader of the ensemble. In addition to his work at Mills, he and composers Pauline Oliveros and Ramon Sender had founded the San Francisco Tape Music Center. Similar to Finney, the foundation was thoroughly enthusiastic about Subotnick. Officer Compton reported in his diary for 30 December 1965 that Subotnick was a "visionary." "He simply recognizes that the aesthetic potentiality of our era is quite enormous and there is a chance for as rich and intellectually relevant a life for us as Western man has enjoyed since the Middle Ages."[70] Compton praised Subotnick for his interest in the music of India and Japan, as well as being "a man of technology and a born tinkerer." Even in "envisioning" Rockefeller's own direction in music, the officer advised it "very worthwhile to know a lot about the personality and outlook of this new breed of artist." Elaborating further, "he is first of all a skilled professional musician. . . . [S]econdly, he is an unusual intellect and critic who has the strongest sense of the continuity of art and culture in Western life."

Rockefeller's initial grants to both Mills and the Tape Music Center began in 1965, with the launch of the Performing Group as a chamber music ensemble in residence.[71] The foundation gave $15,000 ($120,000 in 2017) because it saw the group as the "latest stage in the development of an unusually rich musical environment on the campus of this liberal arts college for women."[72] The foundation directed a similar grant of $15,000 to the Tape Music Center to "further its experimental work."[73] In the officers' words, the center served as "an excellent electronic laboratory . . . and studio where electronic compositions could be performed." A year later, the foundation gave $200,000 ($1.5 million in 2017) toward the merger of the Mills College Performing Group and the Tape Music Center.[74] Officers envisaged the grant to combine the "outstanding musical ensemble on the West Coast" with "a catalytic center of experimentation" into a "single, loosely-structured environment." The facilities consisted of two synthesizer studios, two mix and dubbing studios, one multitrack recording studio, and a small film studio.

Unfortunately, what happened during the following years revealed how tied the success of the center was to the original conceivers of the program, Subotnick,

Oliveros, and Sender. Mills music director Nathan Rubin wrote to the foundation in 1967 that Oliveros had left to take up a position at the University of California, San Diego.[75] To replace her was Jaap Spek, "considered by [Luciano] Berio and [Karlheinz] Stockhausen the leading European engineer and, until recently, Stockhausen's long-time technician." Rockefeller officer Boyd R. Compton left the foundation to administer precisely the *same* New York University intermedia program that Subotnick had left for.[76] Suffering another blow, Spek decided at the last minute not to join Mills, and the school chose Anthony Gnazzo as a replacement (previously a research associate at Simon Fraser University, Vancouver). Adding further turbulence to the situation, the new Mills president Robert Wert decided not to renew Gnazzo's contract two years later, citing complete disagreement between Gnazzo and the music faculty and performing group. Composer Robert Ashley then took over.[77] Reflecting on the overall grant to Mills, Rockefeller director Klein attributed the high turnover and instability to the original departure of Subotnick, who had been the most capable administrator and coordinator.

THE UNIVERSITY OF CHICAGO CONTEMPORARY CHAMBER PLAYERS

Rockefeller's interest in the University of Chicago's ensemble was connected to the leadership of Ralph Shapey, who codirected the group with Leonard Meyer. Rockefeller officers noted that under the "dynamic leadership" of its conductor, Shapey, the players had an unexpectedly "profound influence on musical performance in Chicago."[78] The Contemporary Chamber Players, a group formed through the first Rockefeller grant in 1964 of $250,000 ($2 million in 2017), was unique because it was composed of graduate and postgraduate students who served as performer-composers or performer-musicologists on fellowships.[79] Officers argued that the ensemble had improved the "spirit and atmosphere of music making" in Chicago, transforming a city "in the musical doldrums" to once again "take its place among the leading centers of music performance in the United States."[80] Additionally, Shapey became active as guest conductor with the Chicago Symphony Orchestra, exposing musical audiences in the city to "his great knowledge of contemporary musical literature." Rockefeller gave its second grant of $150,000 three years later in 1967, for the Contemporary Chamber Players.

In memoranda, letters, and discussions, the foundation explicitly tied the Chicago grant to its other grants to Buffalo, Princeton, and Columbia, and the musician-experts it consulted to evaluate the proposal *came from the same places*: Arthur Mendel (chairman of the Department of Music at Princeton), Allen Sapp (chairman of the Department of Music at Buffalo), and Lukas Foss (director of the Buffalo Philharmonic), along with Aaron Copland. While Foss's assessment was somewhat more critical, the foundation officers concluded that the proposal "looked very good . . . for the same reasons that the similar venture in Buffalo looked good."[81]

A review of the Contemporary Chamber Players concerts from this time period showed that Shapey chose to perform many of his own pieces while he led the group. For example, he performed his Concerto for Clarinet and Chamber Group (1954), *Dimensions* for Soprano and 23 Instruments (1960), String Quartet No. 6 (1963), *Songs of Ecstasy* (1967), and *Configurations* for Flute and Tape (1965) between 1967 and 1969. The University of Chicago commissioned his Partita for Violin and

---

BOX 4.1

PAUL FROMM (1906–87)

Paul Fromm was an influential patron of twentieth-century new music, with significant reach across many schools and people.[a] Fromm was born in Germany and moved to the United States in 1939 to escape the Nazi regime. He settled in Chicago and became a naturalized citizen in 1944, continuing the family business in wine. He established the Fromm Music Foundation in 1952 and over the decades, he commissioned close to two hundred pieces by more than 150 composers.[b] According to David Gable, long-time assistant to Fromm, an "enduring aspect of the foundation has been its personal and unbureaucratic nature" where Fromm gave commissions to composers, in part, based on the advice of other esteemed artists.[c] His four closest friends were Milton Babbitt, Elliott Carter, Ralph Shapey, and Gunther Schuller, the first three of whom wrote memorial tributes in the edited collection of his selected papers.[d] As Gable notes, "Fromm regularly turned to Babbitt for advice, particularly to solicit recommendations of promising young composers," as well as when "Babbitt recommended that Fromm commission Shapey, [and] Copland that Fromm commission Luciano Berio."[e]

Fromm's cultural support ranged from sponsoring festivals, such as the Festival of Contemporary Arts at the University of Illinois in 1957 (pre-dating Rockefeller support); to commissions, Fromm Fellowship Players, and the Tanglewood Festival of Contemporary Music (headed by Copland and then, in 1964, by Schuller); to the jointly sponsored Seminars in Advanced Musical Studies at Princeton, and *Perspectives of New Music* (until 1972). Thus, Fromm's reach overlapped with many of the projects supported by the Rockefeller Foundation.

---

[a]David Gable and Christoph Wolff, eds., *A Life for New Music: Selected Papers of Paul Fromm* (Cambridge, MA: Harvard University Press, 1988). I am grateful to Caitlin Schmid for sharing this source with me.

[b]The foundation moved to Harvard University in 1972.

[c]Gable and Wolff, *A Life for New Music*, x.

[d]Ibid., xvii.

[e]Ibid., x, xvii.

Thirteen Players (1966), which he later performed the following year. Shapey benefited from Rockefeller's partial payment of his faculty position through the grant to Chicago, as well as his relationship with other music patrons, such as Paul Fromm (see Box 4.1).

An annual Fromm-sponsored concert with Shapey's Contemporary Chamber Players began in 1967, and Shapey received three commissions from Fromm (*Dimensions* [1960], *Songs of Ecstasy* [1967], and his String Quartet No. 7 [1972]).[82] As Shapey remembered in his memorial tribute, Fromm came to all the concerts of the Contemporary Chamber Players before deciding to institute an annual concert series. "It was obvious that he had waited to see how good we were and what kind of programs we would put on," wrote Shapey.[83] Shapey moreover praised Fromm's philanthropic work, while illustrating his own close connections to the operation. "Everyone wanted a Fromm commission. It was and is a very prestigious commission," Shapey acclaimed. And as he wanted to make clear, "it was sufficient enough for me to phone Paul and ask him to commission someone." Shapey and Babbitt clearly felt quite close to Fromm, and they exerted an influence on him that had larger repercussions in the field.[84]

An examination of some of Fromm's commissions in conjunction with their performances at new music centers across the country uncovers, notably, a small circuit of chamber music works that toured the United States. Several pieces in particular had multiple performances across four or five universities within a two- to three-year time span. Composers flourished in this circuit and they capitalized on Rockefeller's interests in supporting regional centers as well as the artistic development of key individuals. They also succeeded in attracting the patronage of new music benefactors like Fromm. Other composers of a slightly older generation additionally went along for the ride: university centers consistently programmed repeat performances of works by Anton Webern, Arnold Schoenberg, and Edgard Varèse. All centers took part in the renewed interest of earlier modernist and serialist composers.

The Music Circuit

As an investigation of the many archived concert programs and reports sent to the foundation reveals, Rockefeller-funded electronic and new music centers kept the family relatively small. The music they performed was often written by composers who led other new music home institutions. The fact that the same experts moved freely throughout this closed system was no coincidence but a product of a tight and interlocking social and cultural network. Ralph Shapey was a phone call away from Paul Fromm; Fromm was a personal letter away from the Rockefeller arts director

Norman Lloyd; Lloyd was a train ride away from lunch with Milton Babbitt and Roger Sessions. Given such immediate connections, perhaps unsurprising is the fact that Shapey's and Babbitt's pieces were among those most performed across centers in the United States.

Furthermore, Rockefeller's primary focus on chamber-sized music ensembles translated to an incentive for composers in this circuit to write predominantly chamber music. Ensembles brought together various permutations of instrumentalists and vocalists—some of whom were composers themselves. They were trained in extended performance techniques and modernist aesthetics. Their flexibility to assemble small groups of different sizes meant that fewer composers wanted to write large-scale orchestral works. The economics would not have made sense. Groups composed of fewer musicians were also cheaper for the universities. Schools like Sarah Lawrence College, with smaller student bodies, and public schools like the University of Illinois, with fewer financial resources, got a lot of bang for their buck with new music chamber ensembles. In the contemporary music circuit, they also served as important stops for tours traversing East to West and places in between.

THE UNIVERSITY OF ILLINOIS WORKSHOPS FOR THE PERFORMANCE OF CONTEMPORARY MUSIC

Compared to Rockefeller's grants in the hundreds of thousands, its $14,650 ($108,000 in 2017) to the University of Illinois was relatively humble. The grant was, however, not an effort to sustain a multi-year-long center, but rather summer workshops on contemporary music. Moreover, these workshops served as an intensive training ground for the other new music centers across the region and country. Foundation staff noted that numerous participants had gone on from Illinois to become members of the Creative Associates program at Buffalo (two), the Center for New Music in Iowa (three), and the Contemporary Chamber Players in Chicago (two).[85] Rockefeller officer Lloyd saw the workshops as "a concentrated form of the Creative Associates [Buffalo] plan."[86] In fact, professor of music and director of Illinois's Experimental Music Studio Lejaren Hiller moved to Buffalo to become codirector with Foss in 1968. Hiller had founded the University of Illinois studio in 1958, after completing his bachelor's, master's, and doctoral work (in chemistry) at Princeton, studying under Babbitt and Sessions.[87]

The grant-in-aid to Illinois, given May 1967, additionally encouraged the work of one composer in particular, director Salvatore Martirano. Martirano invited musicians from around the country to participate in several weeks of rehearsals and concerts, giving them "a unique opportunity to familiarize themselves with contemporary performance techniques." Shapey specifically recommended Martirano to

Rockefeller's officers Lloyd and Freund.[88] Shapey had served as a visiting composer at Illinois in 1965–66 with Peter Westergaard, Roger Reynolds, and Eric Salzman.[89]

Martirano sent a report of the 1967 summer workshop upon its completion.[90] He shared that they performed forty-two compositions, twenty-eight of which were by U.S. composers, and fourteen by composers from nine other countries. Seven performances were premieres and the vast majority had been composed within the previous five years. While the summer workshops eventually ended, Martirano continued to teach at the university until his death and retirement in 1995. He was active in the Experimental Music Studio and used the school's ILLIAC supercomputer to design and construct an instrument called the SAL-MAR Construction.[91]

THE SARAH LAWRENCE COLLEGE AEOLIAN CHAMBER PLAYERS

Sarah Lawrence College was significant because it served as both a crucial port of call along the circuit and the temporary home of the Aeolian Chamber Players, a group known for its commissions and performances of new works. Located in Westchester County, New York (about fifteen miles outside of the city), the liberal arts college originally for women was founded in 1928.[92] Its list of music faculty over the years contained many prominent composers and administrators, including William Schuman, Norman Dello Joio, and none other than Rockefeller director Norman Lloyd (he taught there for twelve years until 1946, when he joined the music faculty at Juilliard as director of education, under Schuman). One reason the foundation took a special interest in Sarah Lawrence was its belief that smaller private liberal arts institutions fared poorly vis-à-vis larger universities. Officers saw one solution was to "attract to the campus a small group of professional performers" to serve as both faculty members and "musicians-at-large to the community."[93] In 1966, the foundation gave $101,000 ($760,000 in 2017) to establish a residency for the Aeolian Chamber Players, a professional contemporary group.

The players had extensive experience on several college campuses, such as Bowdoin College and the University of Virginia, and had performed at venues like New York's Town Hall and Carnegie Hall. They consisted of a violinist, cellist, flutist, clarinetist, and pianist under the direction of Lewis Kaplan. At Sarah Lawrence, they performed in five formal concerts each year, in addition to monthly seminars and open rehearsals. Shapey, Easley Blackwood, George Rochberg, and Morton Subotnick had all received commissions specifically for the Aeolian Chamber Players.

To review the grant application, Rockefeller officer Freund and consultant Martin Bookspan asked for three expert evaluations.[94] Bookspan reached out to Julius Bloom (executive director, Carnegie Hall Corporation), Eric Salzman (*New York Herald Tribune*), and Howard Klein (*New York Times*)—the same Klein who became Rockefeller arts director in a little over five years.[95] Bloom regretted that he could give "no first-hand information on the group."[96] Bookspan wrote to Freund that he only came across one person who could speak about the Aeolian Chamber Players, Ted Strongin, one of the music critics of the *Times*. Strongin gave a very positive review of the group, citing it as "one of the best ensembles for contemporary music."[97]

Sarah Lawrence president Esther Raushenbush recommended to the foundation several additional expert references, some of whom were composers who had received commissions from the college. She forwarded letters of recommendation from Gideon Waldrop (Juilliard), Rochberg, and Shapey, all of which were glowing.[98] Rochberg said that the players were "first-class interpreters of the twentieth century and earlier music," while also stimulating "an entirely new repertory of works by serious composers of high quality."[99] And Shapey effused his pleasure working with the chamber group. "Even at times when I was satisfied," Shapey recalled, "they felt it could be even better and they took it upon themselves to make it so."[100]

After the foundation gave the grant, Lloyd attended a concert of "Electronic Music and Mixed Media" by the players in 1968, noting a program of works by Mario Davidovsky, Kenneth Gaburo, Milton Babbitt, Morton Subotnick, and Salvatore Martirano.[101] (Gaburo was a colleague of Martirano's at Illinois.) Regrettably, Lloyd's evaluation was unflattering. "If only these people knew when to stop!" he noted. "There is a kind of permissiveness and amateurness that creeps into many of these experimental works to the point that one wishes to see some critical judging and editing exercised." Lloyd singled out Martirano as writing "superior works" and being "one of the most imaginative composers around," but also lamented that "it would be too bad if men like him were destroyed by giving them accolades for what amounts to adolescent-like self-indulgence." A month later, president Raushenbush wrote to Lloyd that Sarah Lawrence was not requesting a renewal of the Rockefeller grant. It envisioned instead "a more modest core group."[102]

TOURS AROUND THE CIRCUIT

In addition to the commissions offered by the Aeolian Chamber Players, Sarah Lawrence invited many composers to serve as guests on its campus with concerts that featured their music. Elliott Carter lectured in August 1965 and had a composer's seminar in March 1967; a year later Morton Subotnick came twice in September 1966 and November while he was still at Mills; George Crumb came in February and December 1967 after serving as a creative associate at Buffalo; Ralph Shapey, well into his time at Chicago, came in January 1967 and joined Crumb in February; and George Rochberg was invited twice in March and April 1967. Other seminars at Sarah Lawrence included those for Ross Lee Finney (Michigan), Stefan Wolpe, Luciano Berio, and Milton Babbitt (Princeton), *inter alia*.

Sarah Lawrence also invited Mario Davidovsky, the Argentinian-born composer living in New York City. Davidovsky had met Babbitt and Copland at the Tanglewood Music Center in 1958, and by 1960, Davidovsky was the associate director of the Columbia–Princeton Electronic Music Center. He later became a tenured professor of music at Columbia in 1981, after teaching at various places like the University of Michigan (1964) and the Instituto Torcuato di Tella in Buenos Aires (1965, also a Rockefeller-funded center).[103] Davidovsky's *Synchronisms (I,* 1963, for flute and tape) received performances at the most number of Rockefeller-funded centers, beginning at Sarah Lawrence (1965), then moving on to Buffalo (1966), Chicago (1968), Washington (1969), and Michigan (1970). *Synchronisms* eventually became a series of twelve compositions for solo/small ensemble and prerecorded tape. He composed the second in 1963 for flute, clarinet, violin, cello, and tape, and it was performed at Iowa (1968), Sarah Lawrence (1968), and Michigan (1969). The sixth won the Pulitzer Prize in 1971.

The University of Washington, the University of Iowa, and the University of Michigan were among the major stops on the musical circuit, performing many of the same pieces as other centers. Composers George Rochberg, Peter Westergaard, and Niccolò Castiglioni, just to name a few, found success in the circuit. Rochberg's Aeolian-commissioned *Contra Mortem et Tempus* (1965) was performed at four centers at least five times during the time period. Rochberg wrote the work (*Against Death and Time*) shortly after the passing away of his twenty-year-old son.[104] *Contra Mortem et Tempus* and *Music for the Magic Theatre* (also 1965, and a Fromm Foundation commission) marked the famous stylistic change in the composer's orientation from serialism to tonality.

Westergaard's Variations for Six Players (1963) was another popular piece that received four performances within a six-month period in 1966 at four universities: Chicago (May), Illinois (July), Rutgers (October), and Iowa (November). Composer George Crumb had analyzed it the year prior in an article for *Perspectives of New Music*, where Westergaard also joined the journal's board.[105] Crumb noted that the variations were based on a "source hexachord" made up of minor seconds and minor thirds, which to him also recalled many of Webern's rows. Several years later in 1968, Westergaard too officially joined the Princeton Music Department.

As a final example, Castiglioni's *Consonante* (1962) received its U.S. premiere at Rutgers (1964) and the piece was further performed at Mills (1967), Washington (1968), and Chicago (1969). During that time, Castiglioni was a creative associate at Buffalo (1966); visiting professor of composition at Michigan (1967); Regent Lecturer in composition at the University of California, San Diego (1968, where

Pauline Oliveros went after her time at Mills to help build its own electronic studio along with Roger Reynolds); and professor of music at Washington (1969). While Rochberg, Westergaard, and Castiglioni were, to a degree, exceptional cases in this music circuit, their career paths and that of their compositions showed how much overlap there was across the Rockefeller centers.

To balance out the performance of new music, the circuit revived several European and European-émigré composers' works, including those of Anton Webern and Alban Berg, as well as Edgard Varèse, Igor Stravinsky, and Arnold Schoenberg. For example, Varèse's *Density 21.5* was the most performed piece (Rutgers, 1964; Cleveland, 1966; Washington, 1967; Chicago, 1968; and Michigan, 1969). His *Octandre* was also played at Chicago twice (1964 and 1965) and once each at Washington (1966) and Iowa (1967). Webern's Concerto for Nine Instruments had performances at Chicago (1964), Washington (1966), and Michigan (1969). The new music centers programmed many other pieces of his, and several centers played Stravinsky's Three Songs from William Shakespeare (1953), his Balmont Songs (1954 rescoring), and Three Japanese Lyrics (1913).

Conclusion

In the grand scheme of foundation giving, $2 million may not seem like manna from the heavens. The Ford Foundation in one fell swoop gave $3.1 million to the Metropolitan Opera in 1963. The Rockefeller Foundation spent more than double that amount on the Recorded Anthology of American Music. And the National Endowment for the Arts's (NEA's) annual budget for orchestral spending alone was 300% of this figure. Two million dollars over several years was not going to break the bank for any of these funding institutions, but for the grant recipients, this money was a treasure chest of riches. It changed the game in a field that otherwise had few options. Composers and performers were unlikely to get support of this magnitude from their home universities without the initial seed funding from Rockefeller. Receiving hundreds of thousands of dollars (or the equivalent to millions of dollars in present value) was striking it rich. And the fact that multiple colleges and universities across the country benefited from Rockefeller support within the span of less than a decade was a gold rush for experimental and twentieth-century music.

The Rockefeller Foundation's support of new music university centers was a clear example of how experts worked in action to finance the composition of chamber works and to perform them on music circuits that crisscrossed the country. Regional centers spanned from coast to coast with several heavyweights in the Midwest. Composers, teachers, and directors of these centers exercised an outsized influence as godfathers of new music. Babbitt at Princeton, Martirano at Illinois, and Finney at Michigan taught many students who would go on to play important roles in this art world. Babbitt's *Ensembles for Synthesizer* (1964) was performed at least three times in the first half of 1966, at Rutgers, Iowa, and Illinois. The Iowa concert coincided with Babbitt's role as visiting composer over a three-day lecture, panel, and concert of chamber works. His *Philomel* (1964) was similarly performed several times at Chicago, Iowa, and Sarah Lawrence. The Ford Foundation commissioned the piece as a prize for Bethany Beardslee's selection in its Concert Artists competition.[106] Martirano's *Ballad* (1966) was played at Illinois, Buffalo, and Michigan. He also toured and gave lectures and presentations. And one of Finney's famous pupils included George Crumb, whose *Madrigals* and *Night Music* were frequently programmed.[107]

New and contemporary music experts did well in this system because of their ability to weld science, the university, and the grantmaker together. The prestige system of foundations' grantmaking buttressed Babbitt and serialism at the same time that Babbitt also declared the roles and rights of the "composer as specialist" within advanced university settings. The larger system of institutional support amplified and strengthened the position of experimental composers, serving as a megaphone for their claims. Many composers needed the academy, but avant-garde composers needed it more. While Elliott Carter was known to never have taken a university position, he still played the role of expert on the sidelines, benefiting from the feverish activity of new music.

Furthermore, the withdrawal of big foundation grants in music to university centers, organizations, and individual artists beginning in the late 1970s, and the subsequent decline in the prestige of serialism, demonstrated the dependence and interconnectedness of the music to this system.[108] (To note, other factors had an impact as well, such as Rochberg's defection, Stravinsky's death, the emergence of minimalism, and improved relations between the Soviet Union and the United States.) As the Rockefeller Foundation already understood in 1971:

> In retrospect, foundation-supported groups at universities such as Buffalo, Chicago, and Iowa helped the academically entrenched composers develop their own skills to a higher degree. . . . But wider audiences were not demonstrably created, nor did the new music find its way into the mainstream.[109]

Winthrop Sargeant lamented the prominence of "foundation music" the same year the Rockefeller Foundation gave its first six-figure grant to a university music program: the joint venture between Columbia and Princeton. The programs at Buffalo represented forays into more experimental music, Chicago and Rutgers continued more serial work, and Mills a further exploration of electronic and tape music. "Foundation music" was a pejorative blanket term for academic music ostensibly disconnected from society. Not all "foundation music" was serial or electronic, just like some, but not all electronic music was twelve-tone, and vice versa. Serialism was a compositional method, while electronic music was a compositional medium. What was common to all three, however, was intentional cultivation of professionalism and prestige within American higher education and a reliance on noncommercial sources of funding. The main problem, though, was how "foundation music" would survive without foundations. Rockefeller's false expectation that it only provided initial seed support and the centers would eventually become self-sufficient followed a pattern similar to Columbia–Princeton—that is, they didn't. For this reason, Rockefeller saw Rutgers as a failed project, while the other centers also never maintained the same large-scale operations as when they were recipients of the foundation's beneficence.[110]

Musicologist Michael Broyles rightly suggests that the serialists were "particularly adept at securing support" from places like the Rockefeller and Ford Foundations and that they "discovered academia and bent it to their purposes" with their rational and scientific orientations.[111] As Joseph Straus even admits, what his empirical analysis could not measure was prestige and that "certainly serialism in this period commanded an intellectual interest *out of proportion* to its actual measurable presence on the musical scene."[112] From their university positions, avant-garde composers derived tremendous legitimacy through academic credentials. They used these positions of power to influence the U.S. system of arts grantmaking after World War II, and they capitalized on the cachet of postwar scientism. Serialist and electronic composers persuaded foundation officials to pay for their equipment and facilities based on arguments of scientific and technological progress. The university composers—rather than foundation officials—pushed the rationale of postwar scientism and competition with European electronic studios. Once the officials witnessed the products of their philanthropy, they began to question the merits of the new music. As Ms. Morison and Dr. Morison, Rockefeller director for biological and medical research, already predicted in 1958, few university presidents could be persuaded to devote hundreds of thousands of dollars to music that sounded to many like a Halloween soundtrack.

William Vickrey [1962] put forth the hypothesis
that most donors direct their gifts not toward the
most disadvantaged in society but rather to those
only slightly below them on the income ladder.[1]

—CHARLES CLOTFELTER, 1992

5

THE FORD FOUNDATION, MATCHING GRANTS, AND

ENDOWMENT BUILDING

SYMPHONY ORCHESTRAS ARE large and expensive beasts in the performing
arts. For a society to sustain a professional orchestra, substantial costs, energy, and
time must be expended. Several dozen violinists, violists, cellists, and double bass-
ists; multiple stands of flutists, oboists, clarinetists, and other woodwind players; the
instrumentalists in the brass and percussion sections; they total fifty to one hundred
performers and a conductor. Professional orchestral musicians require immense
training, beginning in primary and secondary school, and continuing through universities and music conservatories. Orchestras require concert halls that can seat
hundreds, if not thousands, of people, which must also be maintained and designed
according to sophisticated acoustical principles. The bill runs high.

In 1970, orchestral musicians playing in the eleven largest orchestras in the United
States made on average $15,650 for a thirty-six-week season.[2] That is equivalent to
roughly $95,000 in 2017. (By comparison, the starting salary for a member of the
Los Angeles Symphony Orchestra in 2017 was roughly $150,000.[3]) Multiply that by
an eighty-member orchestra, a conductor, guest artists, and other fees, and the costs
escalated rapidly. According to a Ford Foundation study during this time, total salaries, fees, and fringe benefits accounted for more than three-quarters of an orchestral
budget, the highest among the performing arts.

Ask the Experts. Michael Sy Uy, Oxford University Press (2020). © Oxford University Press.
DOI: 10.1093/oso/9780197510445.001.0001.

The Ford Foundation's magisterial two-volume economic analysis from the 1970s, *The Finances of the Performing Arts,* was its attempt to understand what was happening in the professional worlds of music, theater, and dance. It was a four-hundred-page, small-font, head-scratching exercise calling upon economics and arts administration experts to parse through thousands of logs of accounting data. Importantly, *The Finances of the Performing Arts* built upon the path-breaking work begun by economists William Baumol and William Bowen a decade prior, and it called upon Baumol to serve as one of its key expert-consultants. Ford's own approach to the performing arts was to heed primarily the warnings of economist experts, already begun with reports and publications from the middle of the 1960s, including, "On the Performing Arts: The Anatomy of Their Economic Problems" (Baumol and Bowen, 1965); *The Performing Arts: Problems and Prospects* (Rockefeller Brothers Fund, 1965); and *Performing Arts: The Economic Dilemma* (Baumol, 1966).

At a cost of roughly $1.3 million ($6.4 million in 2017), the foundation collected financial records from an astounding 166 professional nonprofit performing arts groups, including twenty-seven resident theaters, thirty-one opera companies, ninety-one symphony orchestras, nine ballet troupes, and eight modern dance companies, each with a minimum budget of $100,000. The initial collection analyzed six seasons, from 1965–66 to 1970–71, plumbing the depths of costs and income, "with particular attention to the earnings gap."[4] This "gap" was the difference between how much an organization spent and how much it brought in through tickets or subscriptions. The gap needed to be filled with income from government subsidies or charitable donations.[5]

The foundation was trying to understand how effective (or ineffective) it had been in its unprecedented symphony program a few years prior. Giving $80 million in 1966 to over sixty orchestras was the equivalent to more than half a billion dollars in 2017. Influenced by the reports and advice of economists from the mid-1960s, the foundation most notably believed in the power of endowment building. Endowments were investments of money and property set aside by nonprofit organizations for the long term, which (usually) delivered annual incomes from interest payments and appreciation. If the Ford Foundation could stabilize the orchestra's finances and encourage sufficient matching sources to lay an endowment's solid basis, then the organization could rely on payments from the principal to help with costs. As long as the economy grew (and the orchestra's board managed the endowment wisely), the money would continue to come in, and hopefully, the orchestra never needed to touch it. In principle (and principal), the plan made sense for a prudent investor: rather than making annual donations, a lump-sum meant that the grantee never needed to knock on the foundation's door again, unless it had a special project in mind. In reality, though, Ford officers and their economist experts made too many assumptions about how the money would be raised, saved, and spent.

Supporting orchestras made up a substantial part of foundation and government funding in the arts. Not just the Ford Foundation, but also the Rockefeller Foundation and the National Endowment for the Arts (NEA) contributed significant sums of money to prop up Western art music. (By contrast and contrary to its name, the NEA was not actually an "endowment," nor did it have an endowment, but rather, it was, and is, a grant-making government agency that relies on an annual budget determined by the president and Congress.) As the Ford investigation noted, "The symphony orchestras were the first professional nonprofit arts groups in the United States to have patrons."[6] During the 1960s, the Rockefeller Foundation established orchestra composer-in-residence programs to expose performers to new music and to encourage composers to write in the orchestral idiom. The University-Symphony Orchestra Program also lengthened concert seasons, providing additional income to musicians in exchange for educational outreach to college communities and surrounding areas. The NEA's Symphony Orchestra Program, begun in 1969, gave hundreds of thousands of dollars, and eventually, millions of dollars, annually. Governmental matching Treasury Fund grants encouraged further support.

A second way these three institutions sustained orchestral music was through the training of classical musicians. The Rockefeller Foundation and NEA gave hefty sums of money to conservatories. In 1970, the Rockefeller Foundation announced grants of $895,000 ($5.7 million in 2017) to six conservatories over a three-year period for scholarship support as part of its "Plight of the Conservatories" program. Rockefeller noted that over the previous hundred years, conservatories had produced eminent concert artists, but few alumni became wealthy enough to donate to them, as compared to colleges and universities. The foundation wanted to tackle especially the large problem of scholarship aid to students in need. The NEA also gave annual grants to conservatories across the country in the tens of thousands of dollars.

As a measure of both dollars and influence, however, the Ford Foundation held the moneybag, and it buttressed orchestras and conservatories throughout the 1960s and 1970s (see Box 5.1). Ford officers hoped that by establishing robust endowments, it could through one fell swoop alter the course of history for professional performing ensembles and individual musicians. It believed that not only the largest symphonies in New York, Cleveland, and Los Angeles but also the smaller and medium-sized metropolitan orchestras in Honolulu, Kalamazoo, and Hartford benefited. To accomplish its goal, the Ford Foundation sought to extend its impact by calling on its networks of wealthy donors and funding bodies. Foundation officers

BOX 5.1

THE FORD FOUNDATION'S ACTIVITIES IN MUSIC AND OTHER ARTS,
1957–74

- 1957: Establishment of the humanities and the arts division
- 1963–64: Grants to independent arts and music schools for scholarships
- 1965–66: Symphony Orchestra Program
- 1970: Conservatory Endowment and Operating Support Program
- 1971–74: Cash Reserve Program
- 1974: Report, *The Finances of the Performing Arts*

used heaps of financial data coupled with expert economic analysis to convince other donors to match its six- and seven-figure grants. Expertise and social capital were—once again—essential components to its strategy, even if Ford did not explicitly articulate them in these ways.

Foundations and the NEA anticipated matching grants to democratize arts funding at the local and national levels. Diversification ensured stable long-term health, as well as citizen involvement in the country's arts and culture. Historical financial and accounting records, however, painted a different picture. In practice, during the 1960s and 1970s, boards of trustees solidified support for elite arts and music institutions by calling upon their personal networks and black-tie connections. Overlapping social circles of Ford trustees and board members of the Boston Symphony Orchestra and Juilliard School of Music, for example, provided their own kind of closed-loop, big-dollar fundraising, leaving out arts organizations that didn't have a ticket to the Met Gala. The Ford Foundation mobilized its arts management, interactional expertise to command economic capital through matching grants, and social capital provided the direct link for such resource mobilization. This fixation on endowment building through matching requirements was an example of Ford's expertise in action.

A Closer Look at Matching Grants and the Tax Reform Act of 1969

The Ford Foundation advocated matching grants for their "multiplier effect": depending on the ratio requirement, a small seed grant could grow with other sources of support, thereby having a larger impact. Moreover, not only did money double or triple, but also so too did the "commitment of interest and expertise" provided by additional contributors as they became stakeholders in the future development of the grantee.[7] Sometimes the restrictions were so severe that if the grantee didn't raise enough outside support, it risked losing the entire amount. The Ford Foundation periodically discussed these conditions, debating whether such rules actually pushed grantees to meet their demands or whether such high-stakes requirements resulted in damaging and unfortunate outcomes for everyone involved. That is, neither the foundation met its goal of disbursing its money to a worthy cause, nor did the grantee get the financial support it needed.

The Tax Reform Act of 1969 also impacted Ford's emphasis on matching rules. As scholar Mary Anna Culleton Colwell notes, the law actually decentivized foundations to serve as sole donors, or even majority donors, of grant organizations.[8] Under the new regulations, if a foundation provided more than a third of a grantee's budget, it took on "expenditure responsibility" for the organization, which, in practice, meant increased reporting requirements and legal liability for the organization's actions. Colwell argues that the fear of taking on expenditure responsibility encouraged foundation trustees to communicate with one another and, in some cases, actually resulted in a tit-for-tat support of certain grantees in return for support of others. "These reciprocal grant arrangements," writes Colwell, were "the results of personal conversations and not formal agreements."[9]

Former president of the Danforth Foundation and consultant to the Ford Foundation Merrimon Cuninggim also observed that after Congress passed the Tax Reform Act, there was "growing cooperation among foundations."[10] Whereas "foundations [had] customarily lived in isolation from one another," after the change in law, they began working together "in increasing numbers of ways and their cooperative organizations [were] being progressively strengthened." After 1969, the Council on Foundations played an especially important role in this cooperation, with many of the large foundations becoming active members. By 1971, it listed 499 members in its annual report. Ford relied on other foundations and organizations, as well as private individuals, to donate to its causes and match its grants.

The Ford Foundation's Junius Eddy calculated that between 1957 and 1970, the foundation raised over $93 million ($750 million in 2017) in outside, matching donations.[11] Among its matching grants were $2.1 million to sixteen civic opera companies, $3.1 million to the Metropolitan Opera and $1.4 million to the New York Philharmonic (to help them move to Lincoln Center), and $3.2 million to New York City Center (previously City Center of Music and Drama). Additionally, the foundation's humanities and arts division requested in 1967 a trustee grant of $9.8 million to "strengthen institutional resources."[12] It believed that by consolidating "highly selected groups and companies," greater improvements were made for "individual development on the part of the professional artist." The foundation's grants to music conservatories and symphony orchestras were its biggest splashes in the pool, and through these programs, officers and consultants keenly focused on the professionalization of Western art music.

Ford's Initial Interest in Conservatories: Scholarships for Low-Income Students

Ford began its investigation of conservatory support much like it did with other programs, by organizing a conference and inviting people it saw as administrative experts in the field. The foundation planned its meeting in April 1962, inviting Victor Babin (Cleveland Institute of Music), Efrem Zimbalist (Curtis Institute of Music), John Brownlee (Manhattan School of Music), Leopold Mannes (Mannes School of Music), Chester W. Williams (New England Conservatory), and Peter Mennin (Peabody Institute).[13] Initially, Ford wanted to discuss "the financial problems of young artists entering upon or engaged in professional training in the fields of the visual arts and music." They were interested at this time in providing scholarships to students in need, rather than beginning immediately with conservatory endowments.

Through the expert advice of these men, Ford came to understand that conservatories faced many problems, suffering financial losses and decreasing enrollment. Conservatories had limited resources, which rising maintenance and personnel costs in the years following World War II further corroded. Some conservatories tried to solve enrollment problems by working with local colleges or universities, only to be "swallowed up by the academic institutions . . . or forced to generalize and attenuate their curricula in the arts."[14] For example, foundation records contained correspondence and failed plans for a merger between the New England Conservatory and Boston University in 1970.[15]

Following the conference, Ford mailed surveys to sixty-three independent schools of art and music. (Officers were concerned not just with music conservatories, but also schools for the fine arts.) The foundation hired two consultants "to assist the Humanities and the Arts Program staff": Charles Kent, director of Peabody's Conservatory of Music, and Joseph McCullough, director of the Cleveland Institute of Art.[16] Both were, yet again, examples of a grantee recipient who also served as an expert consultant. After receiving back fifty sufficient responses, the staff proposed to the trustees a "three-part program" at an overall cost of $12.1 million ($98 million in 2017). In music, officers requested $2 million ($16.2 million in 2017) for scholarship funds.[17] Eight schools of music and twenty-eight schools of art received grants. Table 5.1 lists Ford's grants in descending order of size.

One might observe that funding from Rockefeller, Ford, and the NEA consistently left out a very important conservatory during this time period: the Curtis

TABLE 5.1

Ford Foundation Grants for Scholarships in Music, 1963–64

Juilliard School of Music	$170,000
Manhattan School of Music	$150,000
New England Conservatory	$75,000
Peabody Conservatory of Music	$65,000
Cleveland Institute of Music	$40,000
Mannes College of Music	$40,000
California Institute of the Arts (School of Music)	$20,000
San Francisco Conservatory of Music	$20,000

Institute of Music in Philadelphia. The foundations and government agency understood that Curtis was self-sufficient because its generous patron Mary Louise Curtis Bok had already established it with a $12 million endowment ($170 million in 2017).

Early on, the Ford Foundation also decided that the neediest training programs were those that "allowed the greatest degree of professional concentration and the use of the strictest professional standards."[18] In its opinion, these schools were the independent conservatories of music rather than universities. The foundation viewed university programs, on the whole, as a dilution of the quality of specialized training for professional musicians because students had to divide their time between performance and academic study. It alleged, in particular, that state universities like Michigan and Iowa had less stringent admissions policies, and that their curricula "tended to weaken and generalize professional criteria in the arts." Ford officers also believed that students studying music at these schools were more likely to teach than perform professionally. Its perspective on Michigan and Iowa, as well as performance versus composition in general, differed significantly from Rockefeller's.

Originally, Ford hoped that the grants would spark other private giving. "These schools are so infrequently benefited by organized philanthropy," the foundation wrote, that providing scholarship grants "could have an important leverage effect on their general fund raising."[19] Unfortunately, officer Oleg Lobanov in his later program review asked Peabody if Ford money had attracted other scholarship money, and Peabody said, "generally no," although funds had been helpful in overall fundraising.[20] Learning from this lesson, Ford thereafter prescribed matching ratios as a central feature of later conservatory projects. They were also the backbone of the grants to symphony orchestras.

The Symphony Orchestra Program

Ford vice president W. McNeil Lowry recalled in his oral history president Henry T. Heald's internal competitions to fund large projects during the 1960s. At the time, the foundation owned 90% of the Ford Motor Company's nonvoting shares (the Ford family retained the voting shares), and in an effort to diversify its own financial holdings, it had begun selling its shares to the public. The sale of the shares additionally translated to a deluge of funding that needed to be spent quickly. In its entry for the internal competition, the humanities and arts division decided between multi-million-dollar grants to help either orchestras or the country's leading arts museums. As Lowry remembered, "at any rate, both Mr. Heald and the Board showed a disposition about the orchestra as the oldest center of cultural activity spread geographically in the United States and in its cultural history."[21] Just as it did with its program for conservatories, the foundation organized a conference and invited experts including orchestral musicians and managers.[22]

Based on the participants' advice, the foundation acted swiftly to disburse the mega-million-dollar gifts in 1965. The program, Ford's largest grant to the arts, totaled $80.2 million ($620 million in 2017) to sixty-one orchestras in thirty-three states, the District of Columbia, and Puerto Rico. It was the brainchild of Lowry, who recommended to the board an "unprecedented act of philanthropy in the artistic and cultural life of a nation" that would help "the most universally established of cultural institutions."[23] No one challenged the "universality" of orchestras as basic historical fact. The foundation gave grants to twenty-five major and thirty-six metropolitan orchestras, ranging from $325,000 to $2.5 million.[24] Ford designated three-quarters of the funds for endowments, which the orchestras needed to match dollar for dollar (or better) within five years. The foundation classified the remaining funds as "free" or "expendable," and the orchestras could use them as income while they undertook fundraising campaigns. Ford set aside "developmental grants" totaling roughly $4 million for specific projects, particularly to orchestras seeking to employ additional musicians. Overall, the program

> sought to consolidate the nation's rich orchestral resources, advance the quality of orchestras by enabling more musicians to devote their major energies to orchestral performance, attract more young people of talent to professional careers in orchestras by raising the income and prestige of symphony musicians, and extend the range of orchestras' services to larger and more diversified audiences.[25]

As part of each orchestra's contract, it received payment in Ford Motor Company shares, which the foundation only distributed after a ten-year holding period, provided that the orchestra met its matching requirements. Some critics argued that this arrangement protected the Ford Motor Company share price and overall value through the 1970s, at the least, because the orchestras could not sell their stock during the fundraising years.

Ford's eligibility criteria included the "quality of performance and repertoire," musicians' training and professionalism, "the volume and scope of an orchestra's services to its community," the proximity to other orchestras, and "the qualities of vision and realism shown" in the orchestra's future plans.[26] The foundation emphasized, though, that the size of the grant was not a ranking of the orchestra's artistic standing. It hoped the grants improved the quality of music by increasing musicians' salaries, allowing them to devote more time to performance. Ford also wanted to increase access to symphonic music by lengthening seasons and giving concerts in schools and neighborhoods. In its evaluation a few years later, the foundation acknowledged that four orchestras had failed to meet the matches: the American Symphony Orchestra (New York), the Brooklyn Philharmonic, the Kansas City Philharmonic, and the Little Orchestra Society (New York).[27] A fifth recipient, the Festival Orchestra in New York City, had stopped operating altogether in 1969.[28]

Matching grants were a fundamental tool—"the critical factor"—in turning the symphony orchestra into "a community responsibility."[29] Not only did the requirement "provide maximum leverage with respect to immediate and short-range needs," but also it ensured that in the long run, the symphony broadened its financial support. At least, that was the aim. The foundation hadn't anticipated that the most crucial aspect of attaining matching grants was the role of social capital, and that networks among the most elite donors only extended so far. Trustee membership depended on wealth and status, as evident in the number of chairmen, presidents, and executives in financial, manufacturing, and natural resources corporations who served on boards. As just one example, take Baltimore Symphony Orchestra president Joseph Meyerhoff, who was one of the richest individuals in the city, making his fortune in construction and property development. Not only was he president of the board, but also the orchestra performed in the concert hall named after him. While orchestras expanded their bases to include a handful of wealthier donors, they never achieved broad-based support. Whether everyday citizens had less desire to attend symphony concerts or orchestras did an insufficient job in attracting other audiences, far-reaching enthusiasm for orchestral music in the United States never made up for the income gap. Annual reports sent to the foundation and evaluated by its officers like Oleg Lobanov (see Box 5.2) showed the true picture of who contributed and how much it totaled.

BOX 5.2
OLEG LOBANOV

Oleg Lobanov worked at the Ford Foundation from 1969 to 1974. Prior to his work at Ford, he had substantial experience in the orchestral field. He was the manager of the Hartford Symphony and he served as the president of the Managers of the Metropolitan Orchestras (elected in 1964).[a] Given this occupational background, his disposition was already configured to orchestral management, and especially that of midsized (i.e., "metropolitan") orchestras. Among foundation officers at the three institutions, Lobanov fit in with the Western classical mold, in addition to Rockefeller director Norman Lloyd (a composer and administrator who had taught at Juilliard) and NEA director Walter Anderson (a teacher and administrator at Oberlin and Antioch College). Lobanov was the son of Russian immigrants and graduated from the University of Michigan with a bachelor's degree in prelaw, having also studied business administration before deciding on a career in music. After his time at Ford, he continued a stint at the Oakleaf Foundation and the J. Paul Getty Trust, before returning to performing arts management at the National Symphony, the Ballet Chicago, the Detroit Symphony Orchestra, and Escondido's Center for the Arts.[b]

---

[a] Edward F. D'Arms to Records Center, 28 08 1964, Folder: Background (1964 to 10/22/65), Box 42, Series VI, FA640, FF, RAC.

[b] Jonathan Gaw, "Escondido's Arts Chief Left Last 2 Jobs Under Cloud," *Los Angeles Times*, October 12, 1991.

The foundation had completed a test run in orchestral giving with the Detroit Symphony Orchestra. As historical context, before the 1950s, Ford operated as primarily a local foundation in Detroit and broader Michigan, where the motor company's headquarters was based. Its first grant to the Detroit Symphony was in 1941. Nearly two decades later in 1964, the foundation gave an additional $2 million ($16 million in 2017) to lengthen musicians' seasons through summer concerts and a winter pop series. What made Detroit such an interesting case study was its unique means of meeting its matching requirement. As of 1972, the symphony reported it had raised only $350,000 of its needed $2 million, or just 17.5%.[30] It hoped to make up the remaining balance from a *single* contribution: the Robert H. Tannahill Foundation, the benefactor of which had died in 1969. The "residue of his estate" was left "in trust for the benefit of the Symphony and other named charities." Tannahill had allocated one-eighth the share of the trust's income indefinitely to the Detroit Symphony. Fifty years after his death (i.e., 2019), the "Foundation Committee" had the power to distribute to each beneficiary the share of the trust's principal. The donation fell in a gray area: it was slightly more formal than a pledge, but less formal than an outright gift. The Tannahill committee, after all, could choose not to distribute. Nevertheless, the Ford Foundation chose to accept the single contribution as fulfilling the matching requirements of the grant.

Of importance was not that the gift ultimately qualified as a matching contribution, but that a single donor met more than 80% of Detroit's match. Furthermore, the money was figuratively kept within the "family." Robert Hudson Tannahill (1893–1969) was a cousin of Eleanor Clay Ford, the wife of Edsel Ford. His mother came from the Hudson family of retail department stores, where his father eventually became a vice president. Robert was an avid art collector and the foundation still exists (valued at approximately $54 million in 2017), although its programming has expanded greatly.[31] While exceptional, the Detroit Symphony Orchestra's reliance on big donors, frequently connected through circles of economic and social capital, was a pattern followed by all of the orchestras that met their Ford matches. The following examples of two major and two metropolitan orchestras demonstrated how they accomplished their fundraising, as evidenced from annual internal reports they sent to the foundation.

BALTIMORE SYMPHONY ORCHESTRA (MAJOR ORCHESTRA)

> Specifics: a 1:1 match, with $1 million endowment, $250,000 for development, and $500,000 expendable dollars
> Achieved match: $1,008,489 (1966–71)

The Baltimore Symphony Orchestra's fundraising was an archetype that many other major orchestras fit. The analysis in 1966 by professional fundraising firm Tamblyn & Bowen Inc. showed that Baltimore targeted several "basic constituencies" for support: its own board of directors, large industry, local businesses, wealthy individuals, and local foundations.[32] The auditors noted especially that the Baltimore area had "many large banking, retail, insurance, and other commercial corporations," which already contributed to the annual operating funds of the orchestra. Tamblyn & Brown concluded that the symphony could reasonably expect to raise approximately $1 million over a period of five years.

Baltimore achieved its goal of $1 million, with roughly $40,000 gifts in cash, $950,000 in marketable securities, and the remaining in other investments.[33] As the consultants predicted, about one-third of the gifts came from businesses and corporations, about two-fifths from corporate and other foundations, and slightly over one-fifth from individuals. As was true with all orchestras across the country, many of the largest gifts had strong ties with trustees from the board. For example, Baltimore board member C. E. Utermohle Jr. was also chairman of the board and president of the Baltimore Gas and Electric Company, which gave $50,000. Baltimore board member James J. Jacobs was also vice president of the Chesapeake and Potomac Telephone Co., which gave $35,000. Mr. and Mrs. Randolph S. Rothschild, members of the Baltimore board of directors, gave an individual gift of $20,000, and the president of the Baltimore Symphony Orchestra Joseph Meyerhoff, the same individual whose name adorned the concert hall, gave the largest individual gift of $113,253.

HONOLULU SYMPHONY SOCIETY (METROPOLITAN ORCHESTRA)

Specifics: a 1:1 match, with $750,000 endowment, $100,000 for development, and $250,000 in expendable dollars
 Achieved match: $781,741 (1966–71)

As an archipelago in the middle of the Pacific Ocean and separated from the continental United States by distance and time zone, the Honolulu Symphony tapped into its local sources of elite funding perhaps more than any of the other orchestras in the program. A main core of the fundraising efforts focused on Hawaii's "Big Five," a group of corporations that began as sugarcane processing industries. They eventually came to wield great political power during the early twentieth century, when Hawaii was still a U.S. territory. The Big Five included Castle & Cooke, Alexander & Baldwin, C. Brewer & Co., American Factors (now AMFAC), and Theo H. Davies & Co. Four of the five of these conglomerates and their family descendants contributed to the Honolulu Symphony Society's campaign and served as board members (the exception was Davies & Co.). For instance, Samuel R. Caldwell and Boyd MacNaughton (Brewer & Co.) were both on the board of directors of the Honolulu Symphony; E. Laurence Gay fulfilled the same role at AMFAC; and Mitsuyoshi Fukuda and John F. Murphy were from Castle & Cooke Inc.[34] The Harold K. L. Castle Foundation made annual donations of $10,000, while the Samuel N. & Mary Castle Foundation gave $15,000 a year. Samuel Northup Castle (founder of the original general store in 1851) had ten children with his second wife, Mary, who later became known as "Mother Castle" for her support of education programs. The Castle family descendants established a foundation named after them as the Samuel N. and Mary Castle Foundation. The Honolulu Symphony Society achieved its $750,000 goal with a final push in the last year, raising close to half of its requirement in 1971 alone.

KALAMAZOO SYMPHONY SOCIETY (METROPOLITAN ORCHESTRA)

> Specifics: a 1:1 match, with $500,000 endowment and $100,000 in expendable dollars
>
> Achieved match: $758,850 (1966–71)

Compared to other orchestras, the Kalamazoo Symphony spent a significant amount of its time fundraising smaller, grassroots gifts in the range of $5 to $10 from a larger number of individuals. Some of the major symphonies did not even bother with such efforts, or only did so through their "friends of the orchestra"–type programs. Kalamazoo got assistance from its community foundation, which gave a substantial gift of $300,000 in its final fundraising year, helping it surpass its requirement.[35] The community foundation, began in 1921 by William E. and Carol Upjohn, was further evidence, nevertheless, of the local economic and social elite in Michigan. The symphony benefited greatly from connections with the Upjohn family, which derived its wealth from the pharmaceutical company founded in the late nineteenth century and known for its friable (i.e., easily crumbled) pills. The Upjohn Company gave roughly $10,000 a year to the symphony, and there were direct connections between its board (e.g., vice president Dr. David Weisblat) and the board of the symphony. Members of the Upjohn family also gave individual donations of about $10,000 including Dr. and Mrs. E. Gifford Upjohn and Mr. and Mrs. John Upjohn. Finally, other individuals like Dorothy U. Dalton, James S. Gilmore Jr., and Mr. and Mrs. Preston S. Parish preferred to donate gifts of Upjohn company stock, which were equivalent to tens of thousands of dollars.

MINNESOTA ORCHESTRAL ASSOCIATION (MAJOR ORCHESTRA)

> Specifics: a 2:1 match, with $2 million endowment and $500,000 in expendable dollars
>
> Match achieved: $7,924,814 (1966–71, the highest achieving of the major orchestras)

What made the Minnesota Orchestra distinctive was its success at raising close to double its goal, or $7.9 million, over five years.[36] It was the best performing of the major orchestras in the Ford program. By comparison, the second-best fundraising symphony was Cleveland, which brought in 163% of its requirement, and the third was San Francisco, at 137%, but the vast majority stopped after fulfilling their obligation. Apart from its initial year, Minnesota raised well over $1.5 million each year, with a maximum of $2 million in 1969. How did it achieve such noteworthy success? As Ford Foundation records and musicologist Ben Negley's research showed, the orchestra experienced a "dramatic upward trajectory" during the 1960s and 1970s, demonstrated in part by increased subscription sales from 8,377 in 1969–70 (in the middle of the Ford endowment campaign) to 17,609 in 1975–76.[37] Managing director Richard Cisek referred to the Ford grant as an "effective fundraising catalyst in an already active philanthropic local community" and that it gave the symphony "legitimacy for going for an endowment of substance."

What hasn't been mentioned, however, was the importance of certain members of the board in Minnesota's skyrocketing success. The Dayton family, and especially Kenneth N. Dayton, played an outsized role in the financial stability of the orchestra. Kenneth N. Dayton was a former chief executive of Dayton Hudson (the same Hudson family mentioned in the Tannahill money for the Detroit Symphony) and grandson of the company's founder.[38] The "Expect More. Pay Less" company remains the second-largest department store retailer in the United States, and readers may be more familiar with its current name: Target. Dayton had become president in 1969 and chief executive in 1970, after the company had already gone public in 1967. He and his wife, Judy, over their lifetimes, contributed more than $100 million to the Minnesota Orchestra, the Walker Art Center in Minneapolis, and other civic and social causes. The Kenneth N. Dayton Irrevocable Trust provided $199,500 per year to the orchestra, while the K. N. Dayton 1967 Charitable Trust gave $197,000 per year. Additionally, Dayton provided further annual contributions of well over $100,000, not to mention separate donations from the Dayton Company Foundation equaling $200,000 to $300,000 annually. Other Dayton family members (e.g., Douglas J. Dayton, Sally B. Dayton, and the Grace B. Dayton Estate) gave more modest gifts, but nonetheless in the tens of thousands of dollars. Kenneth Dayton also went on to serve as a member of the National Council on the Arts (1970–76) and a trustee of the Rockefeller Foundation (1974–87).

Minnesota benefited as well from the generosity of Mr. and Mrs. Leonard G. Carpenter, who in total gave over $400,000; the First National Bank of Minneapolis, which gave $50,000 annually (George H. Dixon was on the board of directors for the orchestra, in addition to being the president of the bank); the General Mills Foundation, which gave $50,000 a year (James P. McFarland was on the Minnesota Orchestra's board and was chairman of the board for the foundation); and the Minneapolis Star and Tribune Fund, which gave $125,000 annually. These names, however, only barely scraped the surface in terms of the Minnesota Orchestra's significant fundraising success.

* * *

Whether major orchestra or metropolitan orchestra, these examples show how all relied on limited networks of fundraising, often from local sources. The largest cities like Baltimore called on some of the country's richest business and political leaders, but even in Kalamazoo and Honolulu, orchestras drew heavily on the nearby economic and social elite. These numbers make evident the transfer of wealth in the capitalist economy of postwar America, where rich donors contributed in a currency unknown to most citizens: "marketable securities." The gifts involved the transfer of company stocks or bonds that could be either held for appreciation or sold immediately for cash. The Baltimore Symphony Orchestra, for example, achieved 95% of its match in marketable securities. It called upon fundraising consulting services such as Tamblyn & Brown to help them, while the Boston Symphony Orchestra estimated paying close to $250,000 ($1.9 million in 2017) to retain the local fundraising expert James V. Lavin Company.[39] Metropolitan orchestras lacked the resources to engage bespoke consultancies and they could not get away with relying solely on wealthy individuals, as demonstrated by the Kalamazoo Symphony's earnest efforts at raising grassroots gifts below $10. Nevertheless, even Kalamazoo cleared its bill of financial health by calling on the Upjohn Company and family for a large portion of its match. Lastly, across all the orchestras, boards of trustees and especially their chairmen played significant roles in corralling other board members to donate, as well as bringing outside wealthy individuals into the fold. They led by example, opening their own checkbooks to support the cause.

The Second Push into Conservatories: Endowment and Capital Funds

Amid Ford's orchestra endowment program, it continued to invest in conservatories, the training grounds for professional musicians. The foundation gave three further grants in 1965 and 1967 to the Peabody Institute ($500,000), the New England Conservatory (NEC) ($750,000), the North Carolina School of the Arts ($1.5 million), and the Manhattan School ($2 million). These golden bricks paved the way for Ford's second series of much larger grants in the 1970s, taking what it had done with orchestras and applying the same strategy to conservatories. Selecting five schools for their "ability to train professional musicians" and leverage new sources of funding, Ford aimed to "consolidate a few key conservatories of music in the United States" under this officially titled "Endowment and Operating Support" program.[40] The NEC again made the cut ($2.5 million) and was joined by the Cleveland Institute of Music ($1 million), Juilliard ($7,275,000), and the San Francisco Conservatory ($1 million). The Marlboro School of Music, founded in 1951 by pianist Rudolf Serkin, also received $675,000, but it was more of an annual festival that took place on the Marlboro College campus, rather than a music conservatory.

In the words of officer Lobanov, conservatories "are the beacon lights that the universities strive towards in the area of strict professional standards of training."[41] The majority of the country's top performing musicians were still educated in the "conservatory method," known for its "rigorous professional one-to-one training."[42] As Ford officers saw it, the way to aid conservatories was through endowment and capital funds. And as was hoped with orchestras, increasing endowment income provided longer-term stability "with minimum future implications for the Ford Foundation."[43] Lobanov recommended a limited number of schools: Juilliard because it produced "more first-rank concert artists than any other school—by a wide margin"; the NEC, as long as it "devised a workable plan for future existence"; the Cleveland Institute of Music because of its location in the Midwest and affiliation with the Cleveland Orchestra; and the San Francisco Conservatory of Music for its "future potential" as the "major conservatory on the West Coast."

Ford placed the same stipulations on all four conservatories, although the grant amounts and matching ratios were different, based on each school's capacity for fundraising. Similar to the requirements placed on the orchestra grants, all the conservatories needed to raise outside capital funds within a specified time period. Moreover, the funds needed to be retained in an "isolated endowment account" that could not be accessed until the end of the campaign.[44] Similarly, Ford paid its grant in the form of Ford Motor Company common stock, although the conservatories also had a limited cash option. For tax purposes, however, the foundation greatly preferred the stock disbursement.[45] To sweeten the deal, Ford guaranteed a certain rate of return on the endowment linked to dividends and growth of the company's stock (although as a reminder, the foundation and the Ford Motor Company were completely independent entities).

Unfortunately for the foundation, none of the conservatories met its deadline, and each requested an extension, which the foundation approved. All four cited in one way or another the "nation-wide problem of asking at a time when market conditions were very depressed resulting in an understandable reluctance [to give donations]."[46] Economic uncertainty, distrust of the stock market, high inflation, low growth, and unemployment (the combination of the last three also known as "stagflation") marked the entire decade of the 1970s: 1973–75 was officially a period of recession, including the 1973 oil crisis and the 1973–74 stock market crash where the Dow Jones Industrial Average lost over 45% of its value. Times were not exactly ripe for huge endowment campaigns, especially among conservatory trustee members who had earned their wealth predominantly from big business. Nevertheless, by the end of the decade, accompanied by a more stable economy, the conservatories finally met their requirements (only the NEC took until the beginning of the 1980s to finish its campaign).

Each conservatory sent annual progress reports to the foundation, and through these reports, a story emerged that was virtually the same as for the orchestras, with one key exception: the conservatories relied heavily on wealthy board members and their friends, but they also benefited greatly from *other foundations*. As an examination of the biggest gifts revealed, the largest matching contributor was another multi-billion-dollar foundation, the New York–based Mellon Foundation. The product of the merger between the Avalon Foundation and the Old Dominion Foundation in 1969—both of which were led by children of banker and industrialist Andrew W. Mellon—the Mellon Foundation contributed astonishing sums that perked many ears. Giving to the Cleveland Institute of Music $350,000 in 1972 ($2 million in 2017) and an additional $300,000 in 1978, Mellon provided *a third* of the Ford matching requirement. In absolute terms, however, its $1.5 million in 1972 and $400,000 in 1978 to Juilliard were the biggest (total, $11 million in 2017). The San Francisco Conservatory received $300,000 in 1972, or just under a sixth of its match, and the NEC obtained $500,000 in 1970 and $450,000 in 1978, similarly, just under a sixth of its Ford endowment amount.[47] The Mellon Foundation's significant overlap with Ford Foundation giving was one clear example of Cuninggim's assertion of "growing cooperation among foundations" and Colwell's claim of "reciprocal grant arrangements" after the Tax Reform Act of 1969.[48]

CLEVELAND INSTITUTE OF MUSIC

The Cleveland Institute of Music (CIM) was exceptional in its fundraising because it met more than half of its Ford match from essentially six sources of funding: three individuals and three foundations.[49] Ford's grant to the CIM was for $1 million ($6.7 million in 2017), to be matched at a rate of 2:1. Officers argued, though, that the effective match was actually 3:1 because Cleveland had already raised $1 million prior to its application to the foundation, as a demonstration of its fundraising ability. Founded in 1920, the conservatory had as its first director composer Ernest Bloch, who later went to the San Francisco Conservatory in 1925. Pianist Victor Babin became director in 1961, and throughout the 1960s he expanded the conservatory's studios and access to equipment. Ford's grant to the CIM began in 1970, coinciding with the conservatory's fiftieth anniversary. The Ford trustee docket (also known as a request for authorization) noted that 95% of students at Cleveland were studying to become professional performers (and so, not music teachers), in line with the foundation's interests in professionalization.

The CIM overshot its goal of $2 million, and after the Mellon Foundation, several big grants helped it achieve this outcome. Kelvin Smith, the son of a cofounder of Dow Chemical and founder himself of a Fortune 500 company, Lubrizol Corp., donated the largest sum of money—$205,000—between 1971 and 1974. He not only was a philanthropist of the CIM but also endowed a chair for the music director of the Cleveland Orchestra.[50] Mr. and Mrs. Leland Schubert gave $110,000 in Minnesota Mining stock to the CIM in 1974, Schubert also serving as trustee to the orchestra's Musical Arts Association.[51] And just under the Schuberts was Ralph S. Schmitt, who gave a total of $99,000 in Weyerhauser stock to the conservatory between 1972 and 1974. He and his wife, Dorothy Prentiss Schmitt, served on the board of the CIM as well as other Cleveland-based cultural and healthcare institutions.[52] The Louise H. and David S. Ingalls Foundation put in $100,000 in 1973 to the CIM, and the Louis D. Beaumont Foundation gave $75,000 to the school from 1971 to 1974. Across these five donors alone, several of which had longstanding commitments to the conservatory, it was able to raise close to $600,000, or a third of its needed Ford match. Combined with Mellon's grants, the six donors covered more than three-fifths of the $2 million.

JUILLIARD SCHOOL

In the history of American conservatories after World War II, Juilliard has often been *the* exceptional case. Officer Lobanov wrote in 1970, "the single most important fact that characterizes The Juilliard School . . . is that The Juilliard School has traditionally always had first choice among talented students. If Juilliard wants a student, it is unusual for the student to go elsewhere."[53] He attributed Juilliard's power to its excellence of training, historical tradition, location, and opportunities to be seen by management recruiters. While New York City was large enough to sustain two other conservatories (the Manhattan School of Music and Mannes School of Music), Juilliard was the eight-hundred-pound gorilla on the scene.

Founded initially as the Institute of Musical Art in 1905, the Juilliard School of Music came to be in 1926 through its merger with the Juilliard Graduate School. Juilliard appointed William Schuman president in 1945, succeeded by composer Peter Mennin in 1962, who himself came from the Peabody Institute. Schuman had resigned from Juilliard to become president of Lincoln Center, where Juilliard eventually relocated in 1969, and changed its name to the Juilliard School, to reflect its training of students not just in music, but also drama and dance.

Having just moved to Lincoln Center, the school had tremendously ambitious plans to raise $36 million ($240 million in 2017) in an aggressive endowment campaign over five years, essentially doubling its endowment.[54] Its goal was to boost income so that it could pay for the increasing costs of faculty salaries. The drive was the first time Juilliard sought funds publicly. The Ford Foundation agreed to give $7,275,000 over five years, with $7 million intended for endowment, as long as the school matched this amount at a ratio of 3:1. It earmarked the remaining $275,000 as an expendable grant for operations so the school could balance its budget and avoid invading its principal during a critical first year of fundraising. Juilliard's board of trustees agreed to pledge a minimum of $7 million to the endowment, providing the first step toward the high match. As one might observe, a 3:1 match of $7 million does not add up to Juilliard's proposed $36 million, but rather $28 million, which the foundation believed was a more feasible goal.[55] The foundation designated the funds specifically for music, and not dance or drama.

Despite Mellon's gilded $1.9 million grants, it came in bronze on the donor podium; first and second place were occupied by two relatively obscure organizations: the LAW Fund and the High Winds Foundation.[56] The LAW Fund gave steadily to Juilliard over the fundraising years, providing three grants of $1 million, two of $500,000, and one of $2 million, for a striking total of $6 million ($35 million in 2017).[57] Not a legal service, the fund was supported by Lila Acheson Wallace (hence the acronym). Lila and DeWitt Wallace were the cofounders of *Reader's Digest*, and the Wallace Funds were a group of four private charitable foundations, including the LAW Fund and High Winds. The High Winds Foundation also reliably filled Juilliard's sails, with three grants of $1 million and two grants of $500,000, for a total of $4 million. Both funds contributed to the conservatory until 1986. Thus, between these two organizations alone—under the umbrella of the Wallaces—Juilliard received $10 million, and when added with the Ford Foundation and Mellon Foundation gifts, the conservatory obtained close to $20 million in endowment from just *four* institutions. To top up the number, the Rockefeller Brothers Fund also gave half a million dollars, and the Booth Ferris Foundation, a quarter million dollars.

Juilliard's board of trustees indeed lived up to their end of the bargain, despite some setbacks and delays. The largest donations came from board chairman David M. Keiser, a sugar industry executive and former president and board chair of the New York Philharmonic, who gave over half a million dollars to the endowment campaign.[58] Unfortunately, Keiser passed away unexpectedly in November 1975, before the completion of the drive. Ford vice president Lowry had written to president Bundy the year prior that Keiser was "one of the best fundraising campaign chairmen in New York or the country at large."[59] Trustees Richard Rodgers, composer and collaborator with Oscar Hammerstein II of many famed American musicals, and Alice Tully, who had paid for the construction of a chamber music hall at Lincoln Center, named in her honor, but who otherwise often gave anonymously, both contributed over half a million dollars.

In 1974, Juilliard contacted the foundation asking for possible amendments to its grant, seeking both to extend the end date by two additional years and to lower the matching ratio to 2:1 for the next $3 million and 1:1 for the last $1 million, meaning that it had only raised $10 million of its $21 million in the original time frame. Juilliard guaranteed that its board had played an active part in its fundraising, contributing $6.3 million, in addition to a pledged bequest of $1 million on the part of one trustee (which it claimed was the largest deferred gift ever made to the school). After discussion, Ford allowed an extension but prohibited any change in the matching ratio, thinking that the "strict ratio of three-to-one is the right carrot to keep in front of this unique institution."[60] Despite the campaign being Juilliard's first time to solicit donations from the public, its progress in 1976 showed that the largest contributors were foundations and trustees (each at over $6 million at the time); there was then a dramatic drop in contributions, with "individuals" giving roughly $880,000, corporations $790,000, and bequests $750,000.

NEW ENGLAND CONSERVATORY

Of the four conservatories, the NEC was the slowest to complete its drive, but it also distinctly benefited from the gifts of a famous alumna. Founded in 1867, the NEC was the first private conservatory in the United States. It has maintained a close relationship with the Boston Symphony Orchestra (BSO), and many of the BSO's players taught at the conservatory. In 1967, Gunther Schuller became president, taking over an institution struggling out of World War II. Ford music program director Richard Sheldon effused that Schuller had taken "a moribund conservatory and revitalized it."[61] Immediately, the board sought to strengthen the NEC's endowment, but it also faced increased spending, particularly for faculty salaries. Ford's grant to the NEC was $2.5 million ($16 million in 2017), matched 3:1, of which it allocated four-fifths to the endowment campaign, and one-fifth to eliminate the NEC's carry-over deficit (matched, 1:1).[62]

One of the NEC's most important patrons was trustee and alumna Martha Baird Rockefeller (1895–1971). To help meet the Ford match, she donated $1 million, in addition to a bequest to the school. Baird Rockefeller was a famous pianist in her own right, and the second wife of John D. Rockefeller Jr. She had established the Martha Baird Rockefeller Fund for Music in 1957, which received a further infusion after John D. Rockefeller Jr. left $48 million to her upon his death in 1960.[63] Baird Rockefeller graduated from the NEC in 1917 with highest honors, also winning that year the school's annual piano competition, which came with a $1,200 grand piano prize. Her fund gave grants to many concert artists and even musicology doctoral students. Her will disclosed a $1 million bequest to the NEC, where she had also been a trustee. Other beneficiaries included the BSO ($500,000), the New York Philharmonic ($1 million), Lincoln Center ($10 million), the Metropolitan Opera

($5 million), and the Martha Baird Rockefeller Fund for Music ($5 million).[64] Half of Baird Rockefeller's bequest to the NEC went toward paying off operating expenses and the other half went toward the Ford Foundation's matching requirement.

As an illustration of the importance of close and personal relationships between institutions and their donors, the NEC's Presidential Report in 1975 disclosed much insight on the conservatory's fundraising.[65] Several attachments at the end of the report cited prospective foundations and individuals to approach. For example, it noted that the NEC trustee W. Nicholas Thorndike had an "excellent personal relationship with the [Fidelity] Foundation's managing trustee, Ross Sherbrooke." Another potential donor, Ethan Ayer, was "a member of an old and wealthy Boston Family," with "a long-standing relationship" with the NEC, several members of its faculty, and president Schuller. Ayer expressed his desire to Schuller to establish the Ayer Professorship in Voice with an endowment of $300,000. Charles Summer Bird was "a longtime friend and admirer" of former NEC president Harrison Keller and had already endowed a gift in support of the Harrison Keller String Quartet. And Alice Tully, patron of Juilliard and the New York music scene, was "a good friend" of several NEC faculty members and president Schuller.

Despite these wealthy foundations, trustees, and individuals, the NEC required multiple extensions to meet Ford's match and it was the last of the four conservatories to do so, going well into the 1980s. By June 1980, it had still over a third of its $6 million to raise, and it approached the foundation, asking if pledges could count toward the match (rather than an outright basis, which had been a requirement of the original grant).[66] The NEC blamed "extreme financial difficulties" in the early to mid-1970s and then the "large cumulative, unfunded deficit" after 1976.

SAN FRANCISCO CONSERVATORY

Ford approved the last of the four endowment grants to the San Francisco Conservatory in 1972, giving it $1 million ($6 million in 2017) to be matched 2:1. The conservatory followed a quintessential model of garnering support from its trustees and local business and social elites. The school was founded in 1917, first as a piano school, and then incorporated fully in 1922. Its first director was composer Ernest Bloch, who had just come from Cleveland. The Ford Foundation saw the conservatory as a major force for training students on the West Coast, including violinists Isaac Stern and Yehudi Menuhin, and the school grew especially under accomplished pianist and president Milton Salkind, who took over in 1966.[67] In Ford's eyes, San Francisco was "one of the six or so quality independent conservatories in the country," and the only "independent conservatory west of Ohio." Under Salkind, full-time enrollment more than tripled from 41 in 1966 to 125 in 1972.

Furthermore, the foundation acknowledged the conservatory's strong community involvement, such as performances in hospitals and senior citizen centers, and work with elementary school children in disadvantaged areas.

The conservatory's goal was to build an overall endowment of $3 million, in addition to cultivating business support to help pay for scholarships. By the time of its application, the conservatory had cash and pledges of more than $800,000 from trustees and their families alone, accounting for 40% of the needed match. The chairman of the board of directors was John Beckman, a former partner at an investment firm, who Ford noted was an "extremely successful fundraiser." Other trustees whom Beckman had brought in represented some of the West Coast's business and culture elite, including Reid W. Dennis, chairman of the American Express Investment Company, and Bill Graham, the famous rock music promoter.

Once the San Francisco Conservatory's fundraising campaign actually began, the largest contributors, again, came from foundations and conservatory trustees. The Mellon Foundation gave $300,000; trustee and vice president of Goldman Sachs James D. Robertson contributed $166,666; trustee Richard Gump, Asian art collector and president of a luxury furniture retailer, gave $86,000; and president, CEO, and chairman of Levi Strauss Walter A. Haas Jr. provided $100,000.[68] Among these four donors alone, plus the $800,000 raised by trustees before the launch of the campaign, the prominent conservatory on the West Coast raised almost three-quarters of its Ford endowment match. Clearly, a significant amount of California wealth was eager to play its part in cultivating Western art music. In May 1976, San Francisco asked for an extension, consistent with the other three conservatories. It completed its drive by 1978.

* * *

The few years between the beginnings of the Symphony Orchestra Program and the initiation of endowment grants to conservatories made a significant difference. The economic instability of the mid-1970s wreaked havoc on the schools of music and their fundraising capabilities: a three-year recession, an oil crisis, and a stock market crash that slashed the value of personal savings and retirement accounts in half. The rich felt the pinch and were reluctant to part with their wealth during times of uncertainty. It was less a problem for the deceased, who gave away hefty sums of money in their bequests. But these schools couldn't just rely on obituaries.

The primary way conservatories raised money to meet their matching requirements was through boards of trustees—mirroring the orchestras—and new grants from local and national foundations. The Ingalls and Beaumont Foundations in Cleveland and the LAW Fund and High Winds Foundation in New York gave millions of dollars. The Ford Foundation lauded chairman John Beckman at the San

Francisco Conservatory, and the death of chairman David M. Keiser at Juilliard displayed the importance of a talented networker with high-net-worth friends. Not only the chairman of the board but also each conservatory's president was critical. The NEC was fortunate to have the charismatic and well-connected composer Gunther Schuller as its president, who had "long-standing relationships" and was "good friends" with many of the school's donors. He also creatively established endowed professorships and ensembles, attracting patrons to leave indelible marks. Lastly, the most important actor in this scene was the Mellon Foundation, which gave millions of dollars to conservatories.

Conclusion

As long-serving Ford officer Marcia Thompson reflected in an oral history, if she had to do the Symphony Orchestra Program over, she "wouldn't start out with endowment because . . . endowment is only as good as the management of the endowment or the management of the institution." She didn't think "most symphony orchestras had disciplined themselves sufficiently."[69] She questioned orchestra boards' knowledge of investment opportunities and their ability to self-evaluate. When the interviewers asked Thompson if the problem was the money going to musicians' salary increases, she replied that they were due for a raise anyway, so she didn't think it was the main issue. The "perennial obligation to raise [orchestras'] annual maintenance funds," though, was as difficult and problematic several years after the program as it had been in 1965.[70]

The foundation confirmed years later in *The Finances of the Performing Arts*, its multi-million-dollar costing investigation, that the main invaders of endowment capital—to make up shortfalls—were indeed orchestras. By the 1970–71 season (just several years into the Ford fundraising), orchestras in total were already taking $2.5 million from their endowments to pay for net operating losses of $3.4 million.[71] Orchestras continually found themselves in precarious situations, knocking on many doors. Throughout the 1960s and 1970s, the challenges only got worse. Between 1965 and 1970, average operating expenditures for symphony orchestras grew more than average operating income. Thus, a deficit of $16,000 per orchestra expanded to $37,000 annually over six years.[72] Yet, *The Finances of the Performing Arts* concluded that the gap between earnings and expenditures was "not the result of poor, unbusinesslike management," but, according to economic theory, was "inevitable."

Fast forward forty years and orchestras have not found themselves in any better place. As Ben Negley notes, even the Philadelphia Orchestra declared Chapter 11 bankruptcy in 2011, signaling that "no orchestra in the United States was 'too big to fail.'"[73] The Minnesota Orchestra between October 2012 and February 2014 had no performances because of contractual disagreements between musicians and managers, despite winning a Grammy award in 2013. Economist Robert J. Flanagan corroborates that very little has changed since the Baumol, Bowen, and Ford investigations, except for even greater declines in audience interest, rising competition from alternative forms of leisure, and investment and endowment income having made up a larger portion of orchestral revenues (13% in 2005 versus 6% in 1987, although there persist "highly dispersed annual returns" across the orchestras).[74]

Although both the Ford Foundation and the Rockefeller Foundation had ambitious national approaches to their music grantmaking, the differences in the specifics resulted from the differences in their experts. Rockefeller focused on new music centers because its officers worked closely with composer-experts who taught at universities; moreover, Rockefeller's "scientific" proclivities fit hand in hand with the mathematics, technology, and electronics that the composer-experts were selling. At the same time, Rockefeller officers understood that there was a vacuum in university music programs because of the Ford Foundation's—in Rockefeller's words—"deliberate rejection of academia as a vehicle for arts development in the United States."[75] Ford chose to cultivate the performance pipeline, from conservatory training through employment in orchestras and opera companies, because it saw the problem facing the performing arts as one rooted in artistic professionalism and management finances. Economics and arts administration experts argued that endowments were long-term solutions to provide annual investment income in the nonprofit field and to even out boom-and-bust cycles.

In other words, Rockefeller called more upon contributory experts (composers and musicians *active in* their field), while Ford relied on interactional experts (economists and arts administrators *knowledgeable about* their field). Not only did Rockefeller officers engage with contributory experts, but also they chose ones that matched their scientific, modern(ist), and teleological worldviews—they were the avant-garde. By comparison, Ford's interactional experts were not only nonpractitioners but also conservative advocates of the status quo: hardly anything was more conservative—or a greater display of unwavering faith—than building a colossal endowment for an organization's operations in perpetuity.

Nonetheless, whether performers, composers, new music centers, or symphony orchestras, common to both the Rockefeller and Ford Foundation grantmaking was their almost exclusive support of Western art music, their reliance on overlapping social spheres of elites, and their employment of experts. Matching grants spread the load and encouraged local responsibility, but primarily for the professional Western performing arts. Rockefeller and Ford sustained classical music through multi-million-dollar grants at a scale never achieved by any other kinds of music.

* * *

Demonstrating that classical music relied on wealthy white donors, however, goes beyond a sky-is-blue assertion. These arguments might make intuitive sense, but to validate them, one must put faces to names and point to the primacy of individuals acting through demonstrable evidence. Lift the curtain to see the wizard, and understand how classical music achieved its cultural position in American society. Contrary to claims of objectivity, expertise in the arts was inherently value laden and was never free from cultural preferences and expressions of tastes. Symphony orchestra and music conservatory presidents, Ford Foundation officers, and musician-composers and performers exercised expertise in the 1960s and 1970s. They made active decisions regarding what was more important and what was less important, and to them, classical music was the most important.

Sociologists Paul DiMaggio and Michael Useem have examined the limited access and interest in classical music during the 1970s. Looking into the "unequal consumption of the arts in America," they argued that families of different social classes passed down cultural preferences and aesthetic tastes through processes of socialization.[76] The strong relationship between family social class and formal education reinforced cultural reproduction over generations, which perpetuated differential class consumption and the frequency of exposure to the high arts. As they found, the upper-middle and upper classes dominated arts audiences during this time period. DiMaggio and Francie Ostrower further explored arts audiences based on racial differences, through black and white participation rates.[77] They demonstrated that even with controls for age, occupation, and a number of other factors, black Americans participated at lower overall rates than whites in Western European art forms, and substantially higher rates than whites in historically African American art. DiMaggio and Ostrower theorized that high costs of participation and racism impeded "the ability of blacks to convert cultural capital into educational and occupational advancement, diminishing rewards to, and thus motivation for, such investments."[78]

During this time, journalist Tom Bethell contended that arts funding was "in practice an income-transfer program for the upper-middle class."[79] In this light, it could be viewed as a redistribution of wealth because attendance at classical music concerts was so interconnected with social and racial background. Federal income tax deductions for individuals and foundations took away money that otherwise went to the government, including redistributive social programs such as public education, healthcare, unemployment benefits, and other arts endeavors. By deciding that money was better placed toward the artistic and cultural interests held by select members of society, the national government provided a de facto subsidy to inegalitarian institutions, even if exceptionally professional and artistic. And by demanding matching requirements for its grants, the Ford Foundation magnified the dominance of Western art music institutions in the nonprofit field. The foundation wanted to work hand in hand with others—as determined by stipulations in the Tax Reform Act of 1969—but the heaviest hands were those already at the top.

Moral arguments against exclusion should be distinguished between social and artistic ones. Since professionalization and elitism promoted the highest artistic accomplishment and creativity in a practice, one could argue that specialization needed to be nondemocratic to separate the amateur from the genius. But another person could ask, what social purpose did art serve if it was divorced from the general public and only a few could be the "true" appreciators? At the same time, it would be difficult to justify artistic genius confined by race, which was, at the least, an unintended consequence of the system. If classical music, then why not jazz or other genres of music? The National Endowment for the Arts's Bicentennial programs were examples of ways that folk and ethnic musicians and organizations could also be supported. The government agency, accountable to elected officials and the voting citizenry, needed to ensure that "nonprofit status" in the arts was a privilege that extended beyond the white upper-middle class.

THE NATIONAL ENDOWMENT FOR THE ARTS, THE U.S.

BICENTENNIAL, AND THE EXPANSION ARTS AND JAZZ/FOLK/

ETHNIC PROGRAMS

IN HIS THREE-DAY "outsider" observations on the National Council on the Arts (NCA), Lawrence H. Horwitz, an MBA candidate at Harvard Business School, former executive director of the Arts Council of Ohio River Valley, and a guest of chairman Nancy Hanks, pondered the various ways artistic expertise "fundamentally shaped" the music and arts styles the National Endowment for the Arts (NEA) funded. In his letter to Hanks, he asked, "Is it possible that the exclusive use of expertise (on the staff, panels, and the Council) tends to stifle support of popular mass-art forms, and creates an imbalance in the Endowment's concern for the arts consumer?"[1] Writing further, he observed, "emphasis was placed on the development or perpetuation of the arts from the viewpoint of the expert-artist," and that NCA members gave little consideration to "the person who has to listen or see what is created—the consumer." He pondered if this misbalance was perhaps "caused by the abundance of experts throughout the processes of grant application and review," and concluded that "frankly, the artist-experts seem concerned exclusively with their art forms and not at all with the audience." Horwitz suggested the NEA include panelists with "no vested interests as artists or devotees of particular art forms," and that "students and blue-collar workers" might also serve as useful panelists.

Ask the Experts. Michael Sy Uy, Oxford University Press (2020). © Oxford University Press.
DOI: 10.1093/oso/9780197510445.001.0001.

Who was the "arts consumer"? The question was as important as asking, who was the artist-expert? For the NEA, arts consumers were all Americans, black, white, brown, and everything in between, men and women, rich and poor, of all religions and creeds, from coast to coast. Private citizens and elected officials in Congress, as well as the president of the United States, held the NEA responsible to principles of both excellence *and* inclusion. President Richard Nixon tied his budget increase in 1971, for example, with the NCA's commitment to broad dissemination and availability of "arts of the highest quality across the country."[2] The NEA operated under close scrutiny, in a way the Rockefeller and Ford Foundations did not. Its turn toward the arts consumer—correlated with Horwitz's observations—led to several areas of distinctive funding. These new ventures were also the result of fervent debates surrounding elitism, cultural practice, and social inclusion among the NEA's experts in action during this time.

While Horwitz did not specify race or class in his observations, one could not ignore the developments in the black arts movement, the growing popularity of folk arts, and greater concerns for cultural pluralism during the 1960s and 1970s. Political disenfranchisement and deepening social and economic frustrations infused art making, especially at the community level. The Vietnam War, the civil rights movement, second-wave feminism, the Stonewall riots: each impacted the political and social environment—or, the field of cultural production—in which composers wrote music and musicians performed it. Forces for a new populism fought with defenders of elitism—while some, including NEA staff, asked, why not both? Women and racial minorities demanded more equitable representation in the very institutions that impacted their lives, including in government, schools and universities, and entertainment and media. These groups and communities, already fighting an uphill battle for organizational and financial resources and economic, social, and cultural capital, needed to find ways of penetrating the system to break it down. During a period of fervent political-social activity and creative cultural practice, expert-artists working with the NEA decided who received financial resources to embark on their artistic work.

In practice, the Arts Endowment was more vulnerable to sways in public opinion than the Ford or Rockefeller Foundations. Its operations were in clear view: every grant, every decision, every panelist, every NCA member, every expert. It published all of this information in its annual reports, which, in turn, congresspeople, arts organizations, and artists closely reviewed. Either as a response to the scrutiny or as a product of its greater racial and gender representation to begin with, the NCA and NEA were particularly conscious of expert membership. NEA staff kept profiles on all its panelists, categorizing each by geography, art form, profession, gender, and race.[3] Staff carefully forecasted who would remain, who would retire, and which areas needed to be filled. Dean of the School of Music at Howard University Warner Lawson was a member of the inaugural council from 1965 to 1968. Chairman Roger Stevens invited Marian Anderson onto the NCA in 1967. She became the first African American woman musician on the council. Duke Ellington, the first jazz musician, joined her a year later (although in reality, he rarely attended meetings). And in 1973, Billy Taylor became a vocal and passionate member.

Compared to the trustees of the Rockefeller and Ford Foundations, members of the NCA were predominantly practicing artists and arts administrators. Put another way, they provided direct contributory expertise based on their personal and professional experiences within the field. Given the much larger presence of artists on the NEA's "board," a larger range of knowledge about art was present, providing the opportunity for more diverse viewpoints and aesthetic tastes, compared to the private foundations. Inclusive representation on the NCA and among expert-panelists produced broader and more comprehensive arts grantmaking that was conscious of factors such as race, gender, and geography. At the same time, the NEA was distributing more than ten times the money in the arts field as Ford and Rockefeller by the late 1970s.

The NEA's approach was incremental and decentralized. Rather than a grand design envisioned and executed by its officers and panelists, the NEA's actions responded to the wider political, cultural, and social pressures. Its support of vernacular music outside the standard Western music canon, as shown in Box 4.1, manifested in four central ways: (1) the jazz program, (2) the Expansion Arts division, (3) the Bicentennial fellowships for folk and ethnic musicians, and (4) the Folk Arts division.[4] The jazz program began within the music division in 1968 with a panel led by radio announcer and producer Willis Conover. The NEA established its Expansion Arts program in 1971 after extensive discussion with community arts leaders across the country. The new division's goal was to support the myriad organizations in urban, suburban, and rural areas that had not traditionally been applicants. The "jazz/folk/ethnic" Bicentennial grants begun in 1973 were one-year artist fellowships or funds for organizations. And the Folk Arts program, started within "Special Projects" in the early 1970s, gained independence with its own staff and budget by 1977, and solidified under the leadership of Bess Lomax Hawes.

While the presence of Leonard Bernstein, Isaac Stern, Anthony Bliss (Metropolitan Opera president), and Herman David Kenin (American Federation of Musicians president) on the NCA indicated an initial focus on Western European musical practices, by the beginning of chairman Hanks's and music director Walter Anderson's tenure, discussions about proposals from "ethnic groups" moved to the forefront. From the NEA's own report on "Minorities and Women in the Arts," it defined minorities as "persons from four major ethnic or racial groups: blacks,

Spanish American, American Indian, and Asian American."[5] In analyzing the 1970 national census, the NEA determined that minority artists made up roughly 9% of artists in the labor force, compared to an overall labor force participation rate of 15%.[6] Hanks, Anderson, and many other experts debated perennially how applications from underrepresented minority artists should be evaluated, frequently citing arguments regarding "quality."

For example, as a response to a potential conference for black artists at the Kennedy Center, Anderson recommended to Hanks a firm policy where "decisions on support of projects identified by ethnic origin" needed to be determined "according to the same rigorous criteria which pertain to artistic potential and merit that are used in evaluating all other proposals."[7] Perhaps unsurprisingly, Anderson's suggestion did not pass without caution. Literature director Carolyn Kizer argued that "professional standards" needed to be weighed against "unequal opportunity to obtain those standards."[8] Kizer suggested that one way around the issue was to fund training workshops that maintained "thoroughly professional standards in staffing and instruction," even if the results were "still tentative by strict standards of quality." As arts advocate and strategist Holly Sidford eloquently articulates today, artistic quality "is an essential criterion in funding decisions, but what is deemed 'quality' may differ from community to community."[9]

While there existed many challenges and obstacles beyond its control, the NEA was, nevertheless, still an imperfect equalizer in a contentious cultural and social environment. Without a doubt, its support of orchestras, opera companies—what NCA member Billy Taylor and others called the "sacred cows"—and other organizations predominantly focused on Western classical music made up more than 90% of the music budget. The NEA and NCA wrestled internally with these decisions and attempted to think consciously about ways that its policies reinforced cultural and social exclusion, as mentioned by Horwitz at the beginning of this chapter.

Yet, there were hardly easy decisions to be made, and grantmaking necessitated choices, even among areas and styles that benefited otherwise underrepresented and minoritized communities. For instance, even if the NEA could allocate funding in proportion to racial, gender, or geographic demographics, *inter alia*, many other problems persisted. For instance, within jazz, there were many disagreements between advocates for the avant-garde (the "new thing") and those invested in more traditional and conservative styles. Commercialism and anti-commercialism were persistent themes, as well as the role and presence of white jazz musicians in a world rife with discrimination, segregation, and exploitation. Jazz musicians were strategic players in the funding system, and some factions organized more effectively than others in garnering support.[10] The challenges were vast and complex

BOX 6.1
A TIMELINE OF NEA EVENTS, 1965–82

- 1965: Establishment of the NEA
- 1967: Establishment of the NEA's first Music Advisory Panel
- 1968: First jazz panel
- 1969: First award in jazz to George Russell
- 1970: Full jazz program within the music division
- 1971: Expansion Arts division established
- 1973: Jazz/folk/ethnic Bicentennial Fellowships program
- 1977: Folk and Traditional Arts division established
- 1982: Jazz Masters Fellowships and National Heritage Fellowships

in distinguishing among the many ethnic, cultural, and musical practices of artists across the United States, representing many traditions. There were also some merits to Anderson's reluctance to relinquish the "same rigorous criteria" to evaluate quality—critics could argue that a non-Western artist only received a grant because of his or her race or gender.

Given these complexities, the NEA's investments in jazz, the Expansion Arts program, Bicentennial fellowships, and the Folk Arts program were even more remarkable endeavors that opened the field of music grantmaking in the late 1960s and 1970s. With these grants, the separation between Western high art and non-Western and indigenous music began to break down. The NEA slowly shifted from a structure that had predominantly supported composers writing only in serious forms of classical music into one that included more noninstitutionalized groups and artists, namely those performing jazz, folk, and music from a wide range of ethnic traditions. This result was not just a random occurrence, but the work of socially conscious experts in action.

The Jazz Program: Finding Expertise Outside of Classical Music

As famous poet (and later arts administrator) A. B. Spellman originally wrote in *Four Lives in the Bebop Business*, "jazz is a great American art, yet it is treated as a cultural stepchild."[11] Critiquing the Rockefeller Brothers Report on the Performing Arts (1965), Spellman noted that their attempt to survey "the entire situation of the performing artist in America . . . made no mention whatever of jazz."[12] Such absence was "characteristic of the American establishment's attitude." Spellman reinforced his point by citing Cecil Taylor:

I've known Negro musicians who've gotten grants, but it's very interesting that no Negro *jazz* musician has ever gotten a grant. If you're a black pianist who wants to learn to play Beethoven, you have a pretty good chance of getting a grant. That's that fucked-up liberal idea of uplifting the black man by destroying his culture. But if you want to enlarge on culture, forget it; your money will have to come from bars and that cutthroat record industry.[13]

Despite this initial frustration, Taylor eventually received a grant from the Rockefeller Foundation for a residence program at Antioch College, but his accusation against foundations in general rang true.[14] Ford and Rockefeller, compared to the NEA, gave only minimal amounts to non-Western or nonclassical music. Ford's contribution to jazz during the 1960s and early 1970s amounted to only three grants totaling $156,000 ($1 million in 2017): one to the jazz archives of Tulane University, and two to the New York Jazz Museum for performances and educational programs.[15] Initially, Rockefeller turned down jazz applications, including one from the Historical Institute of Jazz at Rutgers University to conduct interviews with important figures. Officers Norman Lloyd and Boyd Compton stated that if the foundation "were ever to become involved in this large field of folk and jazz music, we would need to survey the field in depth—something that cannot be done, considering the small amount of staff time available."[16] For the two officers, the problem was that they were already supporting Western art, their area of expertise; they did not have enough resources or staff to support much else.[17]

More generally, Ford and Rockefeller's approach to assist black or nonwhite musicians was to increase their number within high art fields (e.g., Taylor's statement about a black musician learning Beethoven) or providing "arts exposure" for students to orchestras and chamber groups. The Ford Foundation focused on scholarships to "qualified Negro instrumentalists" at thirty-six independent art schools and conservatories, or internships for black instrumentalists to join major orchestras. The foundation also gave funds for the special training of six black musicians with the New World Symphony, a racially integrated orchestra.

Yet even some of Ford's own staff questioned, albeit rarely, a one-sided Western high art approach. Staff member Junius Eddy—already distinguished from others at the foundation by virtue of his skin color—argued that "one does not have to deny the true richness of the Western cultural tradition to point out the presumptuousness, arrogance, and racism inherent in this simplistic approach to the culturally different person in our pluralistic society."[18] Eddy suggested that an obvious alternative was to invest more into the "arts groups and activities established and run by ghetto artist-leaders themselves."

Eddy was a member of a strengthening black arts movement during the 1960s. For instance, Amiri Baraka's Black Arts Repertory Theater/School (BARTS) in Harlem, founded after Malcolm X's assassination in 1965, was a cultural center and performance venue for black theater, music, and art.[19] Baraka built it as a "source of group identity and an antidote to political division" for African Americans. Leaders of the movement, including Baraka, essayist Larry Neal, A. B. Spellman, and saxophonists Archie Shepp and Marion Brown, closely aligned free jazz, or "the new thing," with the black arts movement, as well as a "defiance of European aesthetic discipline and a rejection of integrationist ideology."[20] At the same time, free jazz musicians were, nevertheless, consciously or unconsciously influenced by developments in Western musical modernism, including serialism and chance music. They saw themselves in a romanticized way as true artists, distinguished from the everyday and the common man.[21] And as jazz scholar Iain Anderson notes, Baraka, Neal, and Spellman "provided an intellectual basis for viewing jazz as a uniquely African American form, and their emphasis on the music's racial distinctiveness appealed to top-level policy-makers."[22]

These policymakers included those at the NEA, and in 1968, the government agency established its first jazz panel, made up of pianist and multi-instrumentalist Jaki Byard, trumpeter and bandleader Dizzy Gillespie, composer and horn player Gunther Schuller, jazz producer and radio announcer Willis Conover, critic and editor of *Downbeat* Dan Morgenstern, and vice president of BMI Russell Sanjek. Their first award went to pianist George Russell in 1969, a fellowship of $5,500 ($35,000 in 2017).[23] By 1970, the NEA had established not just a panel, but a full jazz program, which offered fellowships to jazz composers and arrangers for new commissions, as well as small scholarships to jazz students. The NEA gave matching grants of $1,000 to colleges, schools of music, and elementary and secondary schools to present workshops and concerts.

From its beginning, chairman Willis Conover was concerned about a broad representation of the jazz field, given the many competing styles. According to a memo from assistant music director Marjory Hanson to Nancy Hanks, Conover recommended reconstituting the jazz panel to keep Dan Morgenstern and Russell Sanjek (an "extremely good committee member"); to retire Jaki Byard, Dizzy Gillespie, and Gunther Schuller; and to add John G. Gensel (a "good member because he works with social activities" and "has a number of good ideas"), Milton Hinton (a "well-respected Negro bassist"), and Bill Evans (a "well-respected jazz pianist").[24] Hanson wrote that Conover thought that there were "so many different viewpoints to be polled" and that jazz was "a volatile subject." Hinton and Morgenstern went on to serve as cochairmen of the later established jazz/folk/ethnic section.

A review of the panel's meeting in December 1969 indicated that it agreed "after extended discussion" on several short-range and long-range needs in the field: first, the completion of works in progress through individual grants; second, composer-arranger college residencies, as well as travel-study internships with performing groups for gifted students; third, pilot educational programs at elementary and secondary schools; and fourth, educational television on jazz by the Corporation for Public Broadcasting.[25] The following year, the NEA reported grants totaling $50,325 ($318,000 in 2017) in jazz to twenty-six individuals and twenty-five organizations for new arrangements, workshops, seminars, and performances in schools and churches.[26]

While jazz always made up a small percentage of the music budget, reflected in both the size and number of grants, it grew steadily, in proportion to the increasing size of the NEA (see Table 6.1). By 1972, the jazz panel processed a significantly higher number of applications, as well as approved a larger number of grants. It gave thirty-three fellowships to American jazz composers for commissioning new works or supporting works in progress ($31,600; $185,000 in 2017); twenty-two jazz concerts in schools ($28,140); fifty-seven short-term residencies ($83,005); eighteen special projects ($86,420); and thirty-five travel-study fellowships ($15,760). That was a total of 165 grants. Furthermore, panelists and council members kept in mind the wide range of jazz aesthetics, just as Conover had advocated earlier. Council member Billy Taylor, for example, argued that there should be as much funding for the experimental in jazz as there was of older, traditional styles.[27] With both Taylor and Ellington on the council, there was a strong presence of the classical jazz idioms popular during the 1950s and 1960s. At the same time, there was no exclusion of "the new thing." In Iain Anderson's account of the later Bicentennial jazz fellowships, he notes that over twenty free jazz players received grants in the first five years.[28]

In addition to the field of jazz, the NEA began to broaden its support of other underserved arts groups and communities through its initiation of the Developing Arts program. Eventually titled "Expansion Arts," the program was the NEA's primary way of supporting noninstitutionalized, community arts that had a strong emphasis on addressing social and cultural inequalities within society. The key figures in the origins of the Developing Arts program were NEA chairman Hanks, deputy chairman Straight, director of music Anderson, director of education John Hoare Kerr, the Smithsonian Institution's special assistant Julian Euell, and the Ford Foundation's Junius Eddy.

TABLE 6.1

NEA Funding for Jazz, Orchestra, and Opera, Within the Total Music Budget, 1969–77

Year	Jazz	Orchestra	Opera	Music Total	Jazz as %	Orchestra %	Opera %
1969	$5,500	—	—	$861,620	0.64%	—	—
1970	$20,050	$931,600	$836,000	$2,525,195	0.79%	36.89%	33.11%
1971	$50,325	$3,761,031	$598,250	$5,188,383	0.97%	72.49%	11.53%
1972	$244,925	$5,307,260	$2,591,122	$9,745,797	2.51%	54.46%	26.59%
1973	$227,238	$4,760,085	$3,461,469	$10,382,210	2.19%	45.85%	33.34%
1974[a]	$419,298	$7,173,444	$5,343,679	$16,116,310	2.60%	44.51%	33.16%
1975	$671,208	$7,279,669	$3,108,364	$14,894,833	4.51%	48.87%	20.87%
1976	$1,059,864	$8,645,979	$4,512,246	$17,249,296	6.14%	50.12%	26.16%
1977[b]	$843,092	$6,335,450	$3,093,129	$17,332,202	4.86%	36.55%	17.85%

[a]From 1974 to 1977, with the Jazz/Folk/Ethnic Program, the NEA included other indigenous and vernacular forms of music.
[b]This table does not include the 1977 Challenge Grants, which the NEA gave in addition to the Music Budget. It was a further $5,915,000 for orchestras and $2,750,000 for operas.

Expansion Arts: Aiding Art in the Local Community

Ford officer Junius Eddy, at the forefront of community arts advocacy and the black arts movement, had initially envisioned a Developing Arts partnership between the NEA and the Ford Foundation, modeled after the American Film Institute, an already successful NEA–Ford cooperation. In his article for *Public Administrative Review*, Eddy had intimated an "initial federal grant to establish a national ghetto arts institute or center, with minority-group arts leaders in principal advisory and administrative roles."[29] The NEA further quoted Eddy in its annual report:

> As the blacks, the Puerto Ricans, and the Mexican-Americans, particularly, began to seek out the roots of an ethnic or racial heritage which the dominant society had systematically ignored or denigrated, the nature of the community-based arts movement began to change. The arts became an obvious and powerful vehicle in this cultural renaissance, a vehicle through which minority-group artist-leaders could begin to voice the social and economic concerns . . . and to reflect the new sense of ethnic pride and awareness they believe is essential to their survival in white America.[30]

The national center would have consolidated activities, served as an "informational clearinghouse," provided technical assistance, and carried out research and training. NEA's director of education John Hoare Kerr agreed that such an "Institute for Developing Arts" might have "strong ethnic representation."[31] Although the NEA–Ford idea never panned out, it sparked discussions and meetings about potential support for minority arts groups.

The first such gathering took place in January 1971, when invited experts shared their hopes and expectations with the NEA, as well as their frustrations and criticisms.[32] Topper Carew, founder of the New Thing Art and Architecture Center in Washington, DC, made the point that funding to minorities should be allocated according to their percentage of the population. He noted distrust and polarization among minority groups with the government, which they felt had discriminated against black people in the arts.[33] Julian Euell from the Smithsonian criticized the NEA's jazz program as "all out of proportion to other programs in music and was in fact practically nil in regard to symphony orchestras." Vantile Whitfield, a leading arts director from Los Angeles, hoped that the new division could be named "Community Cultural Development Program" and would support "arts and cultural programs initiated and based in underdeveloped and/or racial minority communities." Chairman Hanks took all of these suggestions into consideration and, at the end, advocated a pilot program of $1 million ($6 million in 2017), emphasizing the need for a good panel and full-time director.

Later that year, Whitfield (see Box 6.2) became the key candidate for director of the program. Kerr wrote to Hanks that he was amazed the NEA could even recruit Whitfield, and recommended that they "try to give him as high a [government] grade 15" as possible, with "as high a title as we can," that is, "full director" rather than "assistant program director."[34] Hanks announced Whitfield as its director in April 1971. One of his first acts was to change the name of the program from "Developing"—which

---

BOX 6.2

VANTILE WHITFIELD (1930–2005)

Vantile Whitfield graduated from Howard University in 1957 with a BA in Drama and Design, and from the University of California, Los Angeles, with an MA in Theatre Arts and Motion Picture in 1967. He was the artistic director of the Performing Arts Society of Los Angeles, which was a hundred-seat theater he built using his own money, and he was the founder and general manager for the American Theatre of Being.[a] He had served in the U.S. Air Force in Korea as a radio operator until 1952.[b] Among his other experiences and interests, he was a playwright; he designed the sets, lights, and costumes for James Baldwin's "The Amen Corner" in 1965; and he worked as a licensed cosmetologist in his mother's beauty shop during college.

Whitfield had been on the NEA's radar as a key leader in the field, having left a favorable impression while running panels on black leaders in education for the American Council for the Arts in St. Louis and San Francisco. As NEA education director John Hoare Kerr referred to him, he was a "mover" and "shaker" who had credibility among "blacks and establishment ties," while receiving "a lot of support from business."[c] Known also as "Motojicho" and a "dean of black theater," Whitfield made more than $25 million ($146 million in 2017) in grants through the Expansion Arts program to Native American, Latino, black, Asian, and white Appalachian communities.[d]

As a playwright, he wrote many significant works for the black theater repertoire, including *Changes, The Creeps, Don't Leave Go My Hand, East of Eden, In Sickness and in Health*, and *Wanted*. In 1969, he received the National Association for the Advancement of Colored People Image Award, and in 1970 the Los Angeles Drama Critics' Circle Award.

---

[a] Anthony D. Hill and Douglas Q. Barnett, *Historical Dictionary of African American Theater* (Lanham, MD: Scarecrow Press, 2008).

[b] Resume Vantile E. Whitfield, Folder: Developing Arts, Box 13, A1 Entry 2, RG288, Archives II.

[c] From John Hoare Kerr to For the Records, 12 11 1970, ibid.

[d] Yvonne Shinhoster Lamb, "Arts Administrator, Playwright Vantile Whitfield Dies," *Washington Post*, January 23, 2005.

was "demeaning" and "an affront . . . especially [to] those who 'developed' some of the greatest art forms we have in this country"—to Expansion Arts.

The NEA and Whitfield set their first guidelines for fiscal years 1971 and 1972. The first year they estimated a budget of $200,000, which they quickly increased the following year to $1 million ($6 million in 2017).[35] The program outlined its general purpose "to strengthen community-based arts organizations" for teaching and training in the arts, to "enable communities to express themselves through the arts," and to "produce original and promising works of art." It restricted eligibility to organizations with "professional leadership in their communities" that were tax exempt and had operated for at least a year. The NEA gave high priority to organizations that "generate artistic expression among groups which have lacked this expression in the past." It gave low priority to organizations that emphasized "maintaining traditional art forms rather than developing creativity" and those that were "primarily political rather than artistic in intent." Of interest, the guidelines noted that the program was open to groups "working with and for migrants, inmates of prisons, reformatories, and other institutions, and other culturally disadvantaged Americans." As a matter of tempering a possibly inherent politicization of arts from community-based and marginalized groups, the guidelines wrote that while

> indigenous art generated from within urban communities and minority groups may be expressive of the anger, resentment, and militancy which is present in the nation . . . at the same time, the panel which is named to help select grantees will be asked to keep in mind that the funds expended are derived from taxes paid by all citizens, and should not be given to support projects which are plainly contrary to the public interest.

The NEA did not define the "public interest," but it evidently tried to avoid diving head first into political controversy. As a government agency founded upon both the principles of "excellence" in the arts and "accessibility" to the arts, it needed to balance competing social and cultural forces. While all artistic practice and all arts institutions pursued social goals of some sort, the 1960s and 1970s were a time rife for seeing cultural movements outside the Western high art tradition as "social" projects. The guidelines balanced the fine line of stressing artistic quality, while not shying away from the interconnectedness between community art and activism. Programs for the incarcerated and disenfranchised were evidence of this mission.

The program also underscored that artists and organizations worthy of funding were not only located in the cultural centers of New York, Washington, DC, Chicago, and San Francisco. Even though it restricted itself initially to grants to "urban" communities, the program quickly specified that it existed for arts organizations from "rural" and "suburban" areas as well. By doing so, it took a stand that cultural marginalization and unequal access were not isolated to large cities. Its main areas of focus were community cultural centers, neighborhood activities, arts exposure programs, summer projects, regional tours and festivals, and instruction and training. In its first year, among the projects Expansion Arts supported were the Community Music School in St. Louis, Missouri ($7,000; $40,000 in 2017), the Harlem School of the Arts in New York City ($50,700), and the Performing Arts Society of Los Angeles ($40,000), the organization that Whitfield had led.

The Expansion Arts division swiftly became a backbone of the NEA and a widely regarded force for the arts across the country (see Table 6.2). "It seems to many of us that Expansion Arts," wrote Bicentennial Committee chairman Robert Wise to Hanks, "represents most directly so much of what the Endowment was set up for—to get the most of the Arts to the most of the people and especially the disadvantaged and the minorities."[36] Wise made this argument in light of the NEA's proposed budget cut to the program in September 1973. He and others cited that the Expansion Arts signified and symbolized equality and access within the Arts Endowment: it funded groups and artists from all of the arts, including music, dance, theater, and literature; it was an "omnibus category" that was defined more by the populations it served rather than the art forms. Wise was one of several individuals at the NEA who continually and consistently championed the program.

Three additional defenders were NCA member and jazz artist Billy Taylor (see Box 6.3), NEA consultant and panelist Stephen Benedict, and deputy director Michael Straight. Taylor and Benedict, for instance, pointed out that, contrary to

TABLE 6.2

NEA Expenditures of the Expansion Arts and Music Programs by Comparison, 1972–77

Year	Expansion Arts	Music	NEA Total	Music and Expansion Arts as % of NEA
1972	$1,137,088	$9,745,797	$36,321,887	29%/3%
1973	$2,524,556	$10,382,210	$45,286,183	25%/6%
1974	$4,098,629	$16,116,310	$71,817,984	24%/6%
1975	$5,697,759	$14,894,833	$86,946,671	18%/7%
1976	$5,373,972	$17,249,296	$95,617,421	19%/6%
Transition	$1,101,464	$9,724,680	$37,644,209	27%/3%
1977	$6,310,363	$17,332,202	$114,451,507	22%/6%

general opinion, stipulating matching grant requirements might exclude otherwise qualified and excellent applicants. According to the NEA's rules, it could not fund more than half of a project's budget, or more than a quarter of an organization's total budget.[37] At one NCA meeting, council member and arts philanthropist Kenneth Dayton encouraged the NEA to hold firmly to this principle of matching, "as he felt that a relaxation would bring a run of requests potentially damaging to the field." He urged grant recipients to continue cultivating new funds from outside sources. Council member Taylor, however, cautioned that the NEA "should not pay attention only to those organizations successful in fund raising," and that the NEA "might be more lenient toward Expansion Arts groups, for example, which are often the first to be cut by other funding sources."

At the same meeting, the Expansion Arts advisory panel made a strong argument that the NEA needed to "advocate" for community arts projects because they only received a quarter of total NEA funding, "a pitifully small portion for a large and underdeveloped body."[38] Instead, 75% of funds allocated to the arts went to "the large, expensive, highly visible institutions." Changing priorities among foundations made the "matching crisis" even worse for smaller groups. The panel argued that there had always been a "reluctant show of interest in minority groups on the part of most foundations," but "even those foundations whose sympathies we could always expect are now lessening or withdrawing from their support." In the end, the panel advocated educating the private, public, and corporate sectors "to the unique problems confronting community arts organizations."

In another setting, NEA consultant Stephen Benedict (also executive director of the Council on Foundations) cautioned a colleague at a state arts agency (with carbon copies to NEA staff) against overly prescribing matching rules.[39] While some strict requirements provided "the grantee more fund-raising leverage," in the Expansion Arts area, "by and large these groups simply do not have the social apparatus of a strong and affluent board and constituency nor, in many cases, is there any chance of developing along these lines, given the non- or anti-mainstream ideas and objectives that properly and understandably motivate many of them." If the NEA demanded a match, the "provision should be extremely flexible and discretionary." The NEA's more open approach to matching requirements in the Expansion Arts contrasted with their Treasury Fund grants to orchestras and opera companies. Those grants, however, continued to provide significant fundraising leverage and resource mobilization for Western music organizations.

Deputy director Straight's advocacy occurred in his close work with Whitfield and the recruitment of diverse panelists. Straight connected a broad geographical, racial, and social representation of grant recipients with an equally diverse membership among panelists. For instance, he recommended three years into the division's

BOX 6.3

WILLIAM EDWARD (BILLY) TAYLOR (1921–2010)

Billy Taylor, composer, lyricist, pianist, conductor, and arranger, was born in Greenville, North Carolina.[a] He graduated from Virginia State College in 1942 and earned a Doctorate of Music from the University of Massachusetts in Amherst in 1975 (his dissertation, "The History and Development of Jazz Piano: A New Perspective for Educators").[b] He taught jazz courses at Long Island University and the Manhattan School of Music.[c] He served on New York City's Cultural Council, beginning in 1968 with Leonard Bernstein and Richard Rodgers, among others. "Dr. Taylor," as he was known, served on the NCA from 1972 to 1978, and was a member of the NEA's Bicentennial Committee under chairman Robert Wise.

Taylor was an accomplished jazz pianist and in 1951 formed his own trio that recorded numerous albums, as well as performed regularly in nightclubs in New York and around the country. He had a regular presence on radio and television as a popular host, disc jockey, and program director. He was passionate about education and broad access to jazz. In 1964, he and the Harlem Cultural Council founded Jazzmobile, a transportable performing stage (initially a flat-bed trailer) that gave live jazz concerts on the streets of New York City and the schools of Harlem, Bedford-Stuyvesant, the South Bronx, and Westchester County. It traveled to cities in New Jersey, Maryland, and Washington, DC, as well as many others. Later in his career, he received the NEA's Jazz Masters Award in 1988 and the National Medal of Arts in 1992. From 1994 to 2002, he introduced live performances and conducted interviews with performers on "Billy Taylor's Jazz at the Kennedy Center."

---

[a]ASCAP Press Release, 24 10 1975, "Billy Taylor Named to ASCAP Board," Folder: Council Members—Correspondence 1973 and 1974, Box 11, A1 Entry 2, RG288, Archives II.

[b]Bill Bennett, "Taylor, Billy," New Grove, Oxford Music Online, published online January 31, 2014.

[c]Peter Keepnews, "Billy Taylor, Jazz Pianist, Dies at 89," *New York Times*, December 29, 2010.

existence that Whitfield search for panelists especially in California, as well as the "industrial Midwest, where I feel we are particularly weak, among urban, blue-collar workers" (groups already highlighted by Horwitz after his NCA visit).[40] Straight also suggested reviewing "areas which have been poorly served because (in part) they lack representation on our panels, and also in areas (such as East St. Louis) where strong projects may be found." Not only could panelists from the targeted region provide complimentary expertise, but also they could encourage potential grant recipients who otherwise might not have applied.

One of Whitfield's memoranda captured the annual process of reviewing panelists and demonstrated the ways he and Straight recruited a diverse group.[41] The memo listed each panelist by name, race (e.g., "Black," "Caucasian," "Puerto Rican," "Chicano," "Asian"), profession and affiliation, and a reason for retiring or staying. It cited various explanations for discontinuing a panelist, such as "personal career does not allow enough time," "has had problems being objective in review process" (but they "should be considered occasionally for on-site visits"), or "career making increasing demands, making it difficult to attend meetings without hardship." A. B. Spellman, who later became director, began by serving three years on the Expansion Arts panel, as well as the literature panel. In this memorandum, Hanks agreed with the recommendation that Spellman be put up for the NCA. Expansion Arts also cited several positive reviews, for instance, "possesses a strong knowledge of political procedures . . . [and] able to identify and facilitate technical assistance needs" for William (Bill) Strickland Jr., director of the Manchester Craftsmen Guild in Pennsylvania, who became the panel chairman. The division noted that Diego Navarrette Jr., dean of student services at Pima College in Arizona, would be "spiritually and articulately valuable as Vice-Chairman," and he represented his "racial and regional constituency well."

The division recommended new panelist appointments for several reasons, such as bringing "expertise of community museum programming to the panel," being a "well-respected dynamic community arts project director and fighter," and "an administrative-development type that is active in community arts activity and has been helpful to the program in the past."[42] Others were direct recommendations by former panelists. There was a clear concern for "better racial and regional balance," especially for Native Americans. Whitfield commented that the proposed panel for 1976 had a "very satisfactory" gender and racial balance, with nine men and eight women, and eight "Caucasians," five "Blacks," one "Chicano," one "Indian," one "Asian," and one "Puerto Rican." Lastly, a practice distinct for the division was its strategy of converting panelists into consultants. "All of our past panelists have deep moral concerns in relation to the program," as the memorandum indicated, "and would be extremely instrumental" as a "network of dedicated and reliable consultants."

Overall, the impact of Expansion Arts in the field may have been most powerful in its recognition of a group, rather than in purely financial terms. Even Whitfield noted at one of the NCA meetings that its "recognition support" allowed community arts projects to more easily "obtain local support and stimulate public interest."[43] Such support, however, could be a double-edged sword, as there was some evidence that recipients viewed a grant from Expansion Arts as a marker of lower artistic merit (echoing music director Anderson's earlier caution). As the theater panel chairman indicated, Expansion Arts funded some groups that then applied to other programs "perhaps looking for the 'professional stamp of approval.'"[44]

Whitfield attempted to clarify that the division directed potential grantees to other divisions if they did not fall within its "training workshops and similar projects."

At the same time, Whitfield shared panelists' concerns that the program had become "something of a 'dumping ground'" for other departments.[45] Panelists felt that other directors transferred numerous applications to Expansion Arts that they did not want to reject, which also led to confusion among applicants. In response, Straight convened special meetings among panel chairmen and program directors to increase communication among departments and to invite panelists from different areas to sit in as representatives for discussions. Eventually, some organizations came to receive support from both Expansion Arts (for workshop and training activities) and other NEA programs (for performances).[46] The NCA also developed greater clarity by developing a manual to "disseminate information on the program more effectively."

The Expansion Arts program was one crucial way the NEA widened its impact in music and the arts beyond the large "elite" performing arts groups. It was a unique area of support in a field otherwise dominated by Western art music and had no counterpart within the Ford Foundation or the Rockefeller Foundation. Experts and representatives among its officers and panelists, NEA staff in other divisions, and NCA members played crucial roles, articulating the importance and necessity of the division within the artistic field. The program laid groundwork for the development of nationwide community arts and worked in cooperation with other areas of music development, including the already existing jazz program, and the soon-to-be established jazz/folk/ethnic Bicentennial fellowships.

Celebrating Diversity: The Bicentennial Jazz/Folk/Ethnic Grants and Fellowships

The 1970s were a period of growing cultural awareness and self-advocacy, especially among racially and socially marginalized groups. In addition to the Expansion Arts division and its focus on community arts organizations was the NEA's development and cultivation of other vernacular and non-Western traditions *within* the music program. Director Anderson noted to chairman Hanks, for example, that with the jazz program and panel, "some other minority groups in this country with a cultural contribution" also justifiably petitioned for NEA support.[47] In the years leading up to the two-hundredth birthday of the United States, he proposed convening a joint jazz and folk music panel to include "Indians, Chicanos, American-Japanese, and so on."

The U.S. Bicentennial celebrations were an opportune time to prescribe and discuss quintessential American values and identity, yet consensus was not easily found.

Planning began with the American Revolution Bicentennial Commission, established by Congress on 4 July 1966, but years of debate and quarrel led to its demise. In December 1973, Congress tried again with the American Revolution Bicentennial Administration. The NEA had its own Bicentennial Committee chaired by Robert Wise, the motion picture producer and director. It recommended grants totaling approximately $13 million ($56 million in 2017) for Bicentennial-related projects for artists and cultural organizations.[48] Americana was on full blast: parades, fireworks, tall-mast ships, the Freedom Trail, the Bicentennial Quarter. Beneath the red, white, and blue, however, were still prevailing discontent and alienation. A *Washington Post* writer noted that Nixon's Bicentennial planning panel was largely made up of "white, middle-aged conservative Republicans and staunch supporters of the President," and many groups complained of the lack of events "of specific importance to blacks, youth, women, [and] American Indians."[49] To say the least, the United States was still engaged in the Vietnam War, and the Watergate Scandal led to Nixon's resignation in August 1974, followed by his pardon less than a month later by President Ford.

Just as the Rockefeller Foundation capitalized on the Bicentennial with its Recorded Anthology of American Music, the NEA established three central Bicentennial music programs: the first, individual grants for composers writing in a predominantly Western art tradition; the second, orchestral commissions; and the third, individual grants for composers and performers in a new "Jazz/Folk/Ethnic" category. In the first, from 1974 to 1977, the NEA provided over $1.7 million ($7.5 million in 2017) to 545 composer fellowships for new works. It was, up until this time, the NEA's largest foray into music commissions. The program funded a large variety of composers within tonal and atonal Western high art traditions. Many composers discussed in previous chapters were grant recipients, including Lukas Foss, Otto Luening, Salvatore Martirano, Steve Reich (his "Music for 18 Musicians"), George Rochberg, and Charles Wuorinen.[50]

In the second program, the NEA commissioned fifteen composers to write for thirty-one orchestras, which it divided into three groups: the "Top Six" (Boston, Chicago, Los Angeles, New York, Cleveland, and Philadelphia), the "Heavenly Seven" (Cincinnati, Detroit, Minnesota, National, Pittsburgh, St. Louis, and San Francisco), and a group of eighteen metropolitan orchestras in the Southeast.[51] Each group received one new work by an American composer, which the constituent orchestras performed. For example, orchestras of the Top Six commissioned John Cage (*Renga with Apartment House 1776*), Elliott Carter (*A Symphony for Three Orchestras*), and Morton Subotnick (*Before the Butterfly*). The southeastern group, including Birmingham, Jacksonville, and Winston-Salem, among others, jointly commissioned two new works by Norman Dello Joio and African American composer Ulysses Kay. The major orchestras received $70,000 ($300,000 in 2017) for the commission and the metropolitan orchestras received $40,000. Total performances of these new works numbered over three hundred.

In its last Bicentennial effort, the Arts Endowment embarked on a new program of artist fellowships and organization grants in folk, non-Western, and jazz musics. Hanks, Anderson, and members of the NCA sought in the "jazz/folk/ethnic" grants to broaden its grantmaking to more Americans and promote a fuller picture of musical practices in the country. Seeds sown with the NEA's first jazz grants in the late 1960s and the Expansion Arts division finally began to sprout. And while the Arts Endowment gave more money and a greater number of awards to its com- posers/librettists' fellowships and to special orchestra commissions, the jazz/folk/ ethnic grants indicated parity and inclusion through the strong resemblance with their Western art counterparts.

The NEA began this program in 1975, opening up for the first time the applica- tion for grants to artists of America's "indigenous music" and "varied folk/ethnic cultures."[52] As stated in its guidelines, the general purpose was "the creation of a broad artistic climate in the United States in which its indigenous musical arts will thrive with distinction through artistic, educational, and archival programs." The jazz/folk/ethnic panel chose individuals according to their "exceptional creative or performing talent and accomplishment" and organizations for their "high quality in performance and management."

The NEA made grants to jazz in four categories. The first two were nonmatch- ing fellowships of up to $5,000 ($23,000 in 2017) for composers/arrangers and per- formers. The third consisted of $1,000 nonmatching travel-study awards for young musicians to tour with professional artists or ensembles, or to participate in short- term instruction. Finally, matching grants to organizations were available for con- certs, educational programs, short-term residencies, or festivals and tours. Grants for folk/ethnic artists roughly mirrored the categories for jazz, with a greater emphasis on organizations. In the first category groups could apply for matching grants of up to $25,000 for festivals, tours, or community presentations. The second category was for those involved in the preservation of "living musical traditions," up to $15,000. Third, nonmatching fellowships of up to $1,000 were available for master appren- ticeships. And lastly, the panel set up a new "pilot" for individuals and organiza- tions that did not fit in any of the other categories. As context, the panel noted that the pilot was open "to provide flexibility for the program to offer a limited number of grants."[53] The category demonstrated its willingness to be adaptable within the funding structure.

As with any new program, its naming proved to be a topic of vigorous debate, and many voiced their opinion on the cumbersome title. Panelists and staff, including

Anderson, recommended changing its name to "American Musical Heritage," which they hoped conveyed "the breadth of the program without being prejudicial."[54] Others like director of programs and planning Larry Reger, objected that the name in this form was not "easily identifiable by the field," even verging on sounding "somewhat pompous," and that "it implied too broad a focus." Rather, "Jazz/Folk/Ethnic" should be maintained as the title and "American Musical Heritage" the subtitle. Panel cochair David Rockefeller Jr. noted that "some ethnic music might not be strictly considered part of the American heritage," and so the new title would be too "narrowly construed." In the end, Reger's suggestion won out and the NEA designated "American Musical Heritage" the subtitle in parentheses.

Another debate concerned the relative position of jazz, folk, and ethnic artists in the larger battle between purportedly high and low art genres. The contestations showed how panelists and council members thought carefully about NEA funding across the music division. NCA members discussed the issue at great length, for instance, during their thirty-eighth meeting when a member referred to the orchestras, opera companies, and professional theaters as the NEA's "sacred cows."[55] Council member Billy Taylor voiced his further objection that the Arts Endowment continued "to direct major monies to the main institutional programs at the expense of musical artists in areas such as jazz/folk/ethnic." As a counterargument, assistant music director Ralph Rizzolo argued that the NEA's contribution to major orchestras was less than 4% of their total operating budgets.[56] Other council members brought up the Ford Foundation study, *The Finances of the Performing Arts*, and the economic crisis facing the largest groups, hoping that even more money be directed to orchestras, opera companies, and theater groups.

The NCA continued the dispute over several further meetings. One major proposal advised increasing the maximum grant to jazz organizations from $15,000 to $40,000.[57] Hanks felt, though, that to raise the ceiling "without the anticipation of increased funds [the expected budget from the president of the United States, and congressional appropriation] was unrealistic." Most significantly, she added that this suggestion raised "the maximum for jazz organizations above that for metropolitan orchestras." Taylor disagreed with the comparison with orchestras and noted that jazz groups faced a number of difficulties that metropolitan orchestras did not. Council member and actor Clint Eastwood agreed and elaborated that even good jazz organizations had a bad and ugly time raising money from private sources since they were not as established as other groups. Council member and attorney Charles McWhorter felt proposing such a high ceiling, though, was irresponsible given the NEA "would not have sufficient monies to fund any jazz groups at this level." Instead, he proposed $35,000 for the largest groups and $15,000 for the smaller ones. The NCA voted and passed McWhorter's proposal, with Taylor voting against it.

While the Jazz/Folk/Ethnic program did not get all of the budget increases it hoped for, it nevertheless grew significantly in the years leading up to the Bicentennial. From 165 grants totaling $227,000 in 1973 ($1.2 million in 2017), the program distributed over $650,000 in 1975 ($3.1 million) to 194 beneficiaries, and $1 million in 1976 ($4.2 million) to 288 grantees. Examples of grants in 1975 were to Rev. Frederick Douglass Kirkpatrick ($3,500) "to compose ballads about the achievements and contributions of uncelebrated Black heroes"; a grant to the American Society for Eastern Arts ($6,500) to present programs in schools performed by musicians and artists of traditions from India, Bali, Java, and Sunda; and to Kamal Abdul-Akim ($1,000) "to compose and perform works for community and college performances by the ensemble, The Sound Revolution."[58] Panelists paid attention not just to racial and ethnic balance, but also to gender: between 1975 and 1976, the number of women applicants to the Jazz/Folk/Ethnic program more than doubled from twenty-three to fifty-six, and the number of grants to women more than quadrupled from four to nineteen, which showed an acceptance rate of 34% (just slightly under the overall rate of 38%).

The council approved two of the first grants to folk musicians in 1974, one to John H. Diercks Jr. of Hollins College, Virginia ($1,000), "to compose a festival cantata which utilizes folk materials of the settlers of the Shenandoah Valley," and the other to Earl H. Robinson of Los Angeles, California ($2,000), "to compose a work for symphony orchestra and ballad singer-narrator based on the folk and ethnic music and story of the State of Washington."[59] The NCA also gave six grants totaling $9,500 to individuals in the "ethnic" category including one to Alvin Batiste of Baton Rouge, Louisiana ($2,000), "to compose a Concerto for Traditional African Instruments and Orchestra"; one to Edward Boatner of New York, New York ($2,000), for an "Afro-American spiritual opera"; and another to Aristeo Brito of Tucson, Arizona ($2,000), for "musical arrangements for corridos and Chicano children's songs with historical narrative introductions in poetic form," *inter alia*. While Western art traditions clearly influenced several of these grants (i.e., orchestral works, cantatas, and concertos), there also existed a range of ethnic and cultural backgrounds, in addition to a geographical spread. Several of the music organizations funded in the ethnic category were the El Paso Community College, the North Jersey Cultural Council, and the Organizations of People Engaged in the Neighborhood.

Racial and gender diversity among the grant recipients was correlated to diversity among the panelists, as shown in Figure 6.1 and Table 6.3. African American composer, performer, and educator David Baker was chairman of the jazz section and folk singer Jean Ritchie and folk musician and folklorist Bess Lomax Hawes were chairs of the folk/ethnic section in 1975 and 1976, respectively. Baker, a student of George Russell (the first jazz musician to receive an NEA grant), also served on the

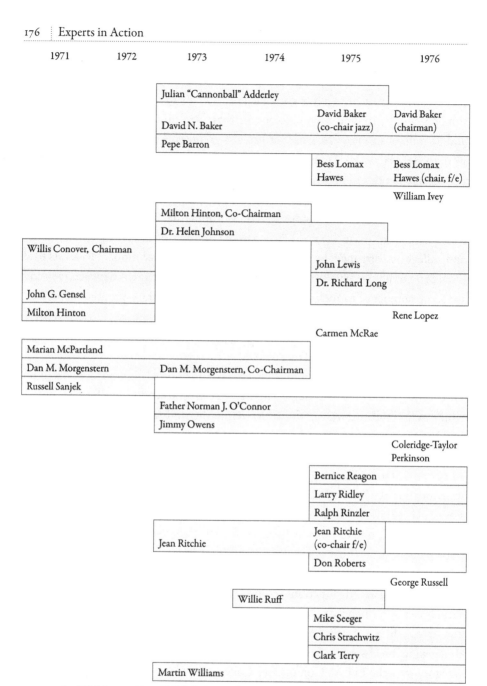

FIGURE 6.1 NEA jazz and jazz/folk/ethnic panelists, 1971–76.

editorial committee of Rockefeller's recorded anthology. Hawes later became director of the NEA's Folk and Traditional Arts program from 1977 to 1992. Other panelists included jazz artist Julian "Cannonball" Adderley and Pepe Barron (director of
the Programs for Spanish-Speaking Americans). See Table 6.3.

TABLE 6.3

NEA Jazz and Jazz/Folk/Ethnic Panelists, 1971–76, Affiliations Indicated by NEA (Beginning 1974)

- Julian "Cannonball" Adderley (jazz artist)
- David N. Baker (composer, professor of music, and director, Institute of Jazz Studies, Indiana University)
- Pepe Barron (director, Programs for Spanish-Speaking Americans)
- Willis Conover (radio broadcaster)
- John G. Gensel (jazz minister)
- Bess Lomax Hawes (associate professor, California State University, Northridge, and vice president, American Folklore Society)
- Milton Hinton (jazz artist)
- William Ivey (director, Country Music Foundation)
- Dr. Helen Johnson (professor of English at York College)
- John Lewis (composer, artist in residence, Davis Center, City College of New York)
- Dr. Richard Long (director, Center for African and African-American Studies, Atlanta University)
- Rene Lopez (salsa musician)
- Marian McPartland (jazz artist)
- Carmen McRae (jazz artist)
- Dan M. Morgenstern (critic, editor of *Downbeat*)
- Father Norman J. O'Connor (Paulist Fathers, Oak Ridge)
- Jimmy Owens (jazz artist)
- Coleridge-Taylor Perkinson (composer, cofounder of Symphony of the New World)
- Bernice Reagon (professor of history at Howard University)
- Larry Ridley (chairman, Music Department at Livingston College of Rutgers University)
- Ralph Rinzler (director, Festival of American Folklife, Smithsonian Institution)
- Jean Ritchie (folk singer, writer, folklorist)
- Don Roberts (head music librarian, Northwestern University)
- Willie Ruff (associate professor of music, Yale University)
- George Russell (jazz artist)
- Russell Sanjek (vice president of BMI Records)
- Mike Seeger (folksinger)
- Chris Strachwitz (president, Arhoolie Records)
- Clark Terry (jazz artist)
- Martin Williams (director of the Jazz Program, Smithsonian Institution)

The jazz/folk/ethnic grants during this period were a revealing complement to the Western high art genres that the NEA otherwise supported through its composers and librettists grants, as well as its very large sums of money to orchestras and opera companies. As with the Expansion Arts program, they also stood in contrast to the lack of such grantmaking devoted to diverse cultural and musical practices at the Ford and Rockefeller Foundations. While only representing a small part of the NEA's budget, they were important symbolic recognitions of the contributions of underrepresented communities. As the NEA noted in its retrospective on the program, there was still much to be done "to combat the notion that federal arts projects are an 'elitist activity.' "[60] The program's growth "ultimately required larger financial resources," and members of the Music Policy Conference argued for "reasonable parity in meeting the needs of indigenous musics comparable to support provided to the established musical arts." One final approach the NEA undertook was its Folk Arts program, which grew out of both the jazz/folk/ethnic grants and Expansion Arts. Hanks, Anderson, Whitfield, and Taylor continued to be advocates for such music, each in their own individualized ways, based on their own experiences and expertise.

Establishing Independence: The Folk Arts Program

The development of the distinct and independent NEA Folk Arts program was the result of pressures exerted by members of Congress, folklorists, and, to a lesser degree, folk artists themselves. Congressman Lucien Nedzi (D-MI) had initially introduced a bill to establish the American Folklife Center within the Library of Congress in June 1973.[61] Long-time arts advocates Frank Thompson Jr. and John Brademas joined in sponsoring the bill. Nedzi cited that a principal reason for the bill was the "failure of the Archive of Folk Song, established in 1928 in the Library of Congress, to generate substantial activities" and "the failure of the Endowment to give substantial support," despite its legislation including "folk art" among its responsibilities. In a pointed critique, the bill's reporting committee noted that "to date, the Endowment shows little inclination to make a genuine commitment in this area, preferring instead to focus on 'high culture.' " Hanks and other staff members were concerned about the development of a separate government agency that would encroach upon its grantmaking capabilities and acted quickly to maintain the area within its purview.

Hanks began planning for the Folk Arts program with an initial meeting of experts in December 1973, several months after Congressman Nedzi introduced his bill.[62] The invited consultants consisted of folklorists, representatives from the

Smithsonian and Library of Congress, state arts agency directors, and members of the Expansion Arts panel. The NEA particularly tied its interest in the folk arts with the upcoming Bicentennial. Several consultants expressed skepticism toward the NEA's commitment, wondering if it was just a "passing fancy." The Arts Endowment tried to assure them that it "launched programs only after careful consultation with the field" and hoped to have "sufficient resources to have an effective program." The resulting report showed that the NEA made most of its grants to the folk arts through the Expansion Arts division, followed by museums, and a scattering from visual arts, public media, music, and architecture and environmental arts.

While a definition of folk arts was generally hard to come by, there was "general agreement" that the arts field needed "to find a means of maintaining our cultural alternatives in the midst of a 'superculture,'" referencing the dominance of already institutionalized high art.[63] The consultants also agreed that existing molds did not fit in developing "critical faculties for evaluating folk arts" and that there was a need to "develop audience receptivity." Alan Lomax, a vocal participant in the discussions, and brother of Bess Lomax Hawes, mentioned more than once that the NEA "had not lived up to its stated objective of preserving our cultural heritage." Instead, it had "devoted itself to the preservation of middle European culture." Archie Green, president of the American Folklore Society, also agreed that the NEA had primarily "put down folk arts" to "reinforce European culture." He argued that folk arts groups had a harder time meeting matching grant requirements, and that many of them were not even registered as tax-exempt organizations. Green advocated a separate "vernacular music" panel, with membership of a "full-fledged Folklorist scholar, i.e., one with PhD credentials." He argued that the NEA had "shortchanged the field" and had provided "inadequate funding and inadequate representation on the staff and advisory panels."[64] The demand for PhD credentials revealed the field's own internal debate concerning the role of academia in legitimizing the objective study and preservation of "authentic" folk musics. The fact that the American Folklore Society criticized Jean Ritchie's appointment on the music panel (they were allegedly "outraged") because she did not have "the academic background or general prominence as a personality to compete with the big jazz names on the panel" also pointed to a troubling misogyny and degradation of women's work within the field.[65]

Following the meeting and report, the NEA hired as its director of folk arts Alan Jabbour in April 1974, former head of the Archive of Folk Song at the Library of Congress. Another meeting of experts occurred in July and they agreed upon two broad missions: first, "to assist Americans of various cultural backgrounds in participating in, celebrating, regarding and understanding their own traditional culture and its expressive forms," and second, "to help Americans of all backgrounds better to understand and appreciate the cultural expression of traditions other than their own."[66] Similar to the previous meeting, the consultants prioritized finding American folk art and artists through fieldwork; documenting them through film, video, and recording; encouraging performances through festivals; disseminating media widely; and educating students. Rather than individual support, they focused on organizations with a long-term vision, although they did not rule out the possibility of "direct support to certain folk artists . . . where it may prove useful."

After a few years, Jabbour returned to the Library of Congress as the head of its Folklife Center and Bess Lomax Hawes took over in 1977. Hawes had served as chair of the folk/ethnic section of the music panel the year prior, as well as organized the Smithsonian's Bicentennial Festival of Traditional Folk Arts. She already had an established academic career as a professor of anthropology at California State University, Northridge. Once at the NEA, her first plans were to build greater independence for the division. As she knew from serving as chair of the folk/ethnic panel, there existed a large overlap between the music program and the folk program, which generated confusion among grantees. Anderson agreed and recommended to Hanks that the folk arts should have its own full-time staff and funding.[67] After Hanks's retirement, the new NEA chairman Livingston Biddle approved the transfer of music funds and panel responsibilities in the area of folk arts to the division, beginning an increase in its budget from $1.6 million in 1978 ($6.1 million in 2017) to $2.4 million in 1979 and 1980 ($8.1 million in 2017). In its earliest years, the Folk Arts division made the bulk of its grants to music and dance, including festivals, films and documentaries, and master apprenticeships.[68] Hawes steered the helm until 1992.

Conclusion

> The audience for the Jazz/Folk/Ethnic Program is not only large, it represents a segment of the population not normally reached by cultural programming. It has an enormous effect when federal funds are employed to support grassroots, indigenous art forms and combats the notion that arts funding is solely for elitist forms of art music. Funding both the Metropolitan Opera and Jazzmobile recognizes that one is every bit as valid as the other.[69]

As the United States celebrated its two-hundredth birthday, Hanks sent this excerpt to Congress to champion its grantmaking and to advocate for greater budget appropriations in the future. In this statement, the NEA proudly declared the diversity and inclusiveness of its programs while it simultaneously tried to convince an important constituency—publicly elected officials—of its work. These congresspeople oversaw the NEA and determined how many government dollars were spent. The pronouncement was aspirational and symbolic, even as it was incomplete. For every dollar the NEA gave to the Metropolitan Opera, it still gave less than a penny to Jazzmobile. But the NEA did offer a helping hand to "grassroots" and "indigenous" music in ways almost no other funding institutions were doing. Some of those individuals most conscious about the plight of minority and community arts had direct experience working in the field, such as Expansion Arts directors Vantile Whitfield and A. B. Spellman, council member Billy Taylor, and music director Walter Anderson. These four people also made up the few minorities—specifically, African Americans—who worked at the Arts Endowment and NCA.

How best to cultivate excellence and simultaneously broaden access and resources to Americans amid cultural clashes, political upheavals, and growing socioeconomic inequalities was an unenviable dilemma. It did not stop, but continued through the end of the 1970s, and into the 1980s and 1990s. Efforts to change the cumbersome and problematic name of "Jazz/Folk/Ethnic" began again in its advisory panel in 1978 and passed approval by the music planning section.[70] The panel recommended dropping "ethnic" from the title in line with the fact that "Folk encompasses traditional music of all ethnic groups," while "ethnic" was "neither a satisfactory musicological term nor a popular one for describing a kind of music."[71] The panel cited that "folk" was "a term recognized and accepted by both professional and laymen."

In 1982, the NEA began its Jazz Masters Fellowship as a lifetime achievement award, a project that assistant music director Aida Chapman had conceived two years prior. Its first recipients were Roy Eldridge, Sun Ra, and Dizzy Gillespie. The same year, the NEA also started its National Heritage Fellowships to master folk and traditional artists "recognizing individual artistic excellence" and the conservation of America's many cultures for future generations. In its first year, it recognized fifteen artists including Cajun fiddler Dewey Balfa, blues guitarist Brownie McGhee, and Mexican American singer Lydia Mendoza. Both of these fellowships represented a continuation of the earlier jazz/folk/ethnic grants to individuals and provided a national platform to celebrate the important contributions of these artists. Around the same time, fifteen jazz leaders formed the National Jazz Service Organization in 1984, including long-time consultant and eventual NCA member David Baker, as its first president.[72] The NEA gave the organization a grant, a year later, to help it solidify its operations.

Unfortunately, the Expansion Arts division came to an end in 1995 when the NEA devolved the division's grantmaking to other areas, thus ending a twenty-five-year program specifically devoted to community-based arts organizations across the country. After Whitfield stepped down in 1977, long-time panelist and chair A. B. Spellman took the reins from 1978 to 1991. The popular and influential division helped many grantees who later became nationally renowned for their work with urban, rural, and tribal communities, including Appalshop in Kentucky,

Arte Público Press in Texas, the Institute of Alaska Native Arts, and the Japanese Community and Cultural Center in California.[73] As Spellman recalled in 2005, "we were responsible along with folk arts for . . . expanding the cultural portfolio of the Arts Endowment."[74] Thanks to Expansion Arts, the NEA broadened "the base of citizen participation in the arts" to "blacks, Spanish-speaking persons, and other ethnic minorities concentrated in urban neighborhoods, as well as residents of the more remote Appalachian, Indian, and rural American communities."[75] The Folk Arts program continues to this day. After Hawes's long service until 1992, another ethnomusicologist and folklorist, Daniel Sheehy, succeeded her.

For community arts organizations, folk musicians, jazz artists, and many others, a grant from the NEA was rarely just about the money, although financial resources undoubtedly helped. NEA staff, panelists, and consultants provided additional technical assistance to groups that were not ready to make applications. They were, in a way, providing an "expertise deluxe," not just passing judgment, but also applying other areas of their interactional expertise to enact social and cultural change in the field, aiding those who might otherwise be excluded. Moreover, for those that were successful, a grant from the federal government was an important national recognition that carried with it prestige and validation. The NEA intended its funding to be one piece of the puzzle, encouraging local sources to make their own contributions. It could not afford to ignore the "sacred cows"—the symphony orchestras, opera companies, and ballet troupes—because Western high art institutions were so well connected politically, socially, and culturally. But the NEA could also pay respects to other equally deserving artists, composers, and performers. Therefore, experts working toward an inclusive federal arts policy moved beyond legacy admission to increase diversity through their own affirmative action. The NEA found excellence across the United States, among myriad cultural and national practices, making an exceptional impact distinguished from the largest philanthropic institutions.

Neither philanthropy nor Kickstarter is sufficient
to support the arts in America—and we shouldn't
want them to be. Because while private donors
support elite and mostly urban institutions—
and while crowdfunding favors those projects
that can be marketed online—government
investment in the arts has a much broader
reach, a deeper and more profound impact.[1]

—DARREN WALKER, The Nancy Hanks
Lecture on Arts and Public Policy, 2017

EPILOGUE

AS I HAVE ARGUED in *Ask the Experts,* the decades of the 1950s, 1960s, and
1970s were an explosion in arts and music funding, especially by the Rockefeller
Foundation, Ford Foundation, and National Endowment for the Arts (NEA).
Expertise was crucial to this system of arts grantmaking. Consultants and panelists
made evaluations, formed advisory committees, and developed policy. Program
directors, chairmen, and boards of trustees exercised substantial discretion in
recruiting and employing expert opinion. Through the power of their institutions,
they changed the entire musical landscape in the United States. They drew, however, from a limited pool of individuals, relying on a tight network of connections that relied significantly on elite institutional affiliation and social capital.
Tax policies and congressional investigations on private foundations influenced
relationships among the funding institutions and the government, pushing toward
greater cooperation and conservatism. Additionally, matching requirements reinforced grantmaking targeted at arts organizations that already received funds, in
particular, symphony orchestras and university new music centers. By comparison, funding for minority and other underrepresented music groups relied on programs established by the NEA, such as the Expansion Arts division, Folk Arts, and
jazz projects.

Ask the Experts. Michael Sy Uy, Oxford University Press (2020). © Oxford University Press.
DOI: 10.1093/oso/9780197510445.001.0001.

Much has happened since the U.S. Bicentennial. Foundations, the government, and individuals have approached music and arts giving in ways both different from and similar to a half century ago. One significant impact has been growing economic and civic inequality in American society. According to Thomas Piketty, since the 1970s, wealth disparities have greatly widened the gap between the middle class and the "0.1%."[2] In another vein, political scientist Robert Putnam warns of declining bonding and bridging social capital, which can lead to greater tensions across class and ethnicity.[3] Sociologist Theda Skocpol cautions against diminishing civic engagement and the dangerous bypassing of citizens in political decision making.[4] Fewer people participate in traditional social organizations—like bowling leagues—and moreover, the United States lacks mechanisms to ensure greater social mixing, like a compulsory national service (e.g., as during the Vietnam War, although there were still critical exceptions).

Given these changes in the fields of power, a series of questions relevant to this study can be investigated in the realm of cultural production: Has there been a democratization or concentration of arts funding? Does the U.S. tax-deductible charitable contribution—in effect, a government subsidy for (the wealthiest) citizens to express their preferences—lead to greater or lesser cultural pluralism and access to the arts? What role do experts play in our society in how individuals and institutions give, how much they give, and to whom they give?

Darren Walker, quoted in the epigraph and current Ford Foundation president, is one manifestation of how times have both changed and yet remained the same. From his appointment, Walker was already cast of a different mold compared to other foundation executives: he was the first out, gay president of the foundation and the second African American president, after Franklin Thomas (1979–96); he was born in a charity hospital in Lafayette, Louisiana, and raised by a single mother; and he did not attend an Ivy League school. Instead, he graduated from the University of Texas at Austin for both his undergraduate degree and law degree.[5] He had, however, plenty of experience in the philanthropic field, having served as vice president at the Rockefeller Foundation for global and domestic programs.

Two years after becoming Ford president, Walker sparked much debate when he published "Toward a New Gospel of Wealth," referencing Andrew Carnegie's famous manifesto from a century past.[6] In the blog post, Walker threw some punches. Challenging the system of which he was also part, he wrote, "we need to interrogate the fundamental root causes of inequality, even, and especially, when it means that we ourselves will be implicated." Leaving no room for misinterpretation, he called out the ways "cultural norms and structures" are "deeply rooted" in "racial, gender, ethnic, and class biases."

In essence, Walker's concerns about present-day philanthropy mirror postcolonial critiques of late-stage capitalism: vast inequalities of access and wealth are sometimes ignored by those with even the best of intentions, and those who possess money to give away must educate themselves about their own blind spots. Walker has indeed overseen the racial, gender, and occupational diversification of Ford's board membership during his presidency, adding, for example, a CEO of a disability service and advocacy organization, Marca Bristo; a Nigerian lawyer, Gbenga Oyebode; an author and labor activist, Ai-jen Poo; and a public interest lawyer, Bryan Stevenson. Following the renovation of the organization's headquarters, Walker announced in late 2018 that its new name was the Ford Foundation Center for Social Justice.[7]

Yet while the Ford Foundation may serve as a source of inspiration for those who believe in the importance of social justice and equity, it is just one piece of a vastly complicated and exponentially growing field of philanthropic work. As arts consultant and researcher Holly Sidford cites, roughly 11% of foundations' giving goes to nonprofit arts and cultural institutions every year, but this distribution is "demonstrably out of balance with our evolving cultural landscape and with the changing demographics of our communities."[8] As was the case throughout *Ask the Experts,* the biggest recipients continue to be large and formalized arts organizations focused on Western European art forms; with their multi-million-dollar budgets they serve predominantly white and upper middle-income audiences. They receive over 50% of the sector's total revenue, yet, by number, make up less than 2% of the total field.[9] As Sidford notes, only 10% of foundation dollars to the arts go to "lower-income populations, communities of color, and other disadvantaged groups," and less than 4% go to projects with social justice goals.

While Walker and the Ford Foundation are trying to shift their priorities, they are only one of over ninety thousand foundations in existence in the United States. Ford is the second largest in the country in terms of assets, with $12 billion. The Rockefeller Foundation is thirteenth, with $4 billion.[10] Ford gives away roughly $500 million a year, and Rockefeller, roughly $170 million a year. The Bill and Melinda Gates Foundation dwarfs both with total assets of $40 billion (more than Ford and Rockefeller combined and doubled) and total annual giving of $3.9 billion (almost eight times what Ford gives and twenty times Rockefeller).

With a new age of supercharged eleemosynary activity by the likes of Mark Zuckerberg, Priscilla Chan, Bill and Melinda Gates, and Warren Buffet, scholars and journalists are more invested too in examining the practices of present-day philanthropy. Stanford University established its Center on Philanthropy and Civil Society in 2006 and Duke University its Center for Strategic Philanthropy and Civil Society in 2008. Investigative work has explored as well the potentially negative effects of private charitable giving, such as the displacement of democratic and public governance. In *Winner Takes All*, Anand Giridharadas suggested that "an ascendant power elite that is defined by the concurrent drives to do well and do good . . . [has] changed the world while also profiting from the status quo."[11] Codirector of the Stanford center Rob Reich has critiqued the way the U.S. government has subsidized private giving through tax policies in troublingly unequal ways.

No one, however, has looked at great length into the way philanthropists have given to arts and culture. These scholars argue that the expression of private interests should not be blithely celebrated, but carefully scrutinized, in light of alternative social and political structures. Private giving is susceptible to capture by vested interests—for good and bad—and there is a lack of transparency and participation by ordinary citizens in decision making that can have a large impact on them. What scholars have not argued, however, is that arts funding is perhaps the greatest embodiment of tastes and preferences. As it was during the cultural boom half a century ago, arts patronage is a conspicuous manifestation of givers' values.

So not just private giving but also the role of government funding in the arts is worthy of reconsideration. If society believes there is a public benefit to broad access and excellence in the arts, the government has a role in its support. The NEA continues to receive a miniscule proportion of the federal budget, 0.004%, yet its financial resources have significant impacts especially in underfunded rural and suburban areas and supporting the music of marginalized ethnic and traditional communities. While the NEA experienced a golden age in the 1970s under Nancy Hanks—and even President Richard Nixon—it did not fare well amid the controversies and culture wars of the late 1980s and 1990s. Paleoconservatives and neoconservatives attacked it throughout the last decade of the century and into the new millennium.[12]

During his presidency, Donald Trump threatened to eliminate both the NEA and its counterpart, the National Endowment for the Humanities. He and other Republicans have disparaged the NEA for its allegedly elitist favoritisms, but the reality is that the NEA and state arts agencies (which the NEA partially funds) are the few sources of financial help that sustain diversity in, and broad access to, the arts. As arts advocate Pam Breaux argues, only 10% of America's largest one thousand foundations award more than half of their grant dollars to underserved communities. By comparison, the majority of state arts agency grants go toward "low-income areas," and 40% overall of NEA grants take place in "high-poverty neighborhoods."[13]

In some respects, like the emergence of a new social elite and expanding income inequality, the field of cultural production in the United States has changed since the 1960s and 1970s. In other respects, like the concentration of wealth in big cities and states like California and New York, and the almost exclusive patronage of Western music institutions by foundations and wealthy individuals, the field has not changed much. The role of experts and expertise continues to profoundly shape how society and the government impart value and meaning to everything from science, to economics, to arts and culture. In light of growing social, political, economic, and technological changes, an ethics of expertise is necessary. In a world that is both intensely globalized and intensely local, where there is increased competition for attention, for recognition, and for resources, perhaps now more than ever how society chooses to allocate symbolic and cultural capital will impact individual and national identity.

Legacies of the Past: A Trickle-Down Theory of Arts Funding

More than five decades have passed since the establishment of the NEA, yet discussions surrounding the exceptionality of Western art music as the pinnacle of artistic excellence persist. Americans still commonly refer to music and art as "highbrow" or "lowbrow," and treat the former as more significant, more serious, more important than the latter. As historian Lawrence Levine noted in his influential study on American culture, the origin of the terms were not just rooted in the ethics of artistic appreciation, but also in a nineteenth-century racial theory based on bad science.[14] The terms came from popular "scientific" theories of phrenology, with the "high-browed" Caucasian from northern Europe contrasted with the "lowbrowed" non-Caucasian, exemplified in the "Cannibal New Zealand Chief."[15] Some sociologists like Richard Peterson have more recently found growing evidence of "omnivorous" consumption of both "highbrow" and "lowbrow" art and music among wealthier Americans, but the distinction remains entrenched in public and private funding patterns (not to mention the lack of such omnivorous behavior among less wealthy Americans). While the origins of this cultural ideology derive from over a century ago, Ford, Rockefeller, and the NEA reinforced their authority through their grants and the rhetoric they used to justify their grants.

For example, beginning in 1966, with the fourth meeting of the National Council on the Arts (NCA), esteemed violinist and NCA member Isaac Stern stated that "as professional standards became stronger and more safely entrenched [among symphony orchestras], they radiated downward their influence into the quasi-professionals, the amateur, and the entire [music] field."[16] Stern argued that the government should focus on the "powerful buttressing . . . of the present professional apparatus," which "by its strength . . . led and pulled everything up." His logic followed that if institutions like the NEA and Ford—both places where Stern served as an expert—supported artistic work of the highest merit, professionalism, and excellence, then eventually "artistic standards" made their way to "lower" art forms. In essence, Stern advocated a trickle-down theory of arts funding and quality.

This theory of excellence, however, was predicated on closed systems of expertise and elitism. As was the common theme in U.S. music funding after World War II, a relatively small number of experts decided the merits and priorities of grantmaking institutions. Their experiences, education, and socialization were heavily immersed and indebted to the discourse of elitism in the professional performing arts, most specifically in "highbrow" classical music. Little criticism can be leveled against striving for excellence and standards of professionalism; these goals pushed artists to pursue mastery of skill and human expression in a particular art form. Yet what this single-minded ambition translated to in practice was also an issue of equity and democracy. Experts after the war devoted inordinate resources to the value system of European concert music—at the expense of other genres and styles. Thus, rather than a trickle down of excellence from the top, more accurately, the system siphoned up resources from the many to the few.

To describe the system of arts grantmaking and expertise another way, it was—and continues to be—structurally "aristocratic," an idea philosopher Gloria Origgi discusses in her book *Reputation*.[17] Simply stated, in an aristocracy, the wealthy get wealthier. Origgi references academic citation networks as an illustrative example of a system that is "aristocratic": the more citations authors receive, the more they'll receive in the future. The unfathomable quantity of texts written every year means that reading or listening to everything is impossible. Instead, citation or reference networks identify and privilege a limited number of works, which readers are expected to know, even if the "work" (or concept the work represents) serves only as part of a much larger field or discourse.[18]

The same applied to arts grantmaking and arts expertise. Once an artist began to garner grants, he (male pronouns most often applied) was more likely to receive further support; once he was recruited as an expert, he was more likely to be sought after as an expert in the future. The power and legitimacy of his expertise grew. Sociologist Robert Merton made a similar argument in his theory of the "Matthew effect": to everyone who has, more will be given in abundance.[19] In the words of scholar James English, the competitive paradigm of the industry was "winner-take-all."[20] Or, as business sociologist Cheng Gao has argued, expertise was a "meta-resource" that contributed to a "positive feedback loop."[21] In this music history, those at the top—experts representing elite symphony orchestras, opera companies, and university music centers especially—accumulated higher levels of prestige and cultural capital than musicians of popular and minority art forms. The winner-take-all character of the system actually meant that little trickled down. These experts were (understandably) reluctant to relinquish assets or capital (who would want to?), and so arts grantmaking self-perpetuated in a closed and exclusionary cycle.

As a perhaps unintended result of this approach and funding structure, orchestras, opera companies, and universities became *doubly advantaged*, and jazz ensembles, folk musicians, and mariachi groups, among others, became *doubly disadvantaged*. The former received funding from the government and large philanthropic foundations, in addition to the benefits of recognized excellence that these grantmaking institutions bestowed. Ford, Rockefeller, and the NEA provided their stamps of approval, while the requirements for matching grants brought in even more funding at the state level, from smaller foundations and from wealthy individuals. At the other end of the spectrum, however, community music programs received little federal support and practically nothing from foundations, and they furthermore lacked the recognition these grants provided. Under this system, orchestras and universities were doubly advantaged from *both* public funds and private funds, and from *both* grants and honor. Those at the top of the arts world remained at the top, while those at the bottom languished at the bottom. The structural bias in favor of Western high art and supporting "quality" and "excellence" was at the expense of the equally laudable goal of cultural pluralism, for instance. These problems are not, though, just those of the past. The trickle-down theory of arts funding has persisted even through the congressional challenges and culture wars to open up (or destroy) the NEA in the last two decades of the century.

The Culture Wars of the 1980s and 1990s

The status of arts funding after the U.S. Bicentennial was tumultuous and perilous: financial resources from the Rockefeller and Ford Foundations shrank to fractions of what they had been, and although the NEA was not "zeroed out," as suggested by President Ronald Reagan's Office of Management and Budget, it suffered its first cut in 1982. The NEA limped along at roughly the same level until 1995 when Congress slashed its budget by nearly half. Several controversial art exhibitions sparked the "culture wars" of the late 1980s and 1990s, including Andres Serrano's "Piss Christ," a photograph of a crucifix submerged in the artist's urine, and Robert Mapplethorpe's "The Perfect Moment," a retrospective of the artist's photographs, some of which were considered homoerotic, sadomasochistic, and pornographic. It was the NEA's grant recipients rather than the NEA itself that selected both showcases; nonetheless, the Religious Right, including commentator and politician Pat Buchanan and Senator Jesse Helms (R-NC), attacked the government agency for funding allegedly offensive art.

As a response to political pressures, NEA chairman John Frohnmayer added a decency clause to NEA grant rules, which artists quickly criticized as a "loyalty oath" and an attack on freedom of expression. The clause ensured that the NEA took into consideration "general standards of decency and respect for the diverse beliefs and values of the American people." The "NEA Four"—made up of performance artists Karen Finley, John Fleck, Holly Hughes, and Tim Miller—sued the NEA after Frohnmayer denied their grants despite recommendation by the NEA theater panel. They also alleged that the decency clause violated their First Amendment rights. While the NEA Four found favor at the district court and U.S. court of appeals levels, the U.S. Supreme Court overturned these decisions, deciding that the clause didn't interfere with the right to free expression.[22]

At the same time, from the opposite side of the culture wars attacks came a congressionally mandated NEA Independent Commission.[23] Among the twelve-member body's recommendations was a system of differentiated criteria to evaluate publicly (versus privately) funded art. In addition to artistic excellence, they wrote that "publicly funded art must not ignore the conditions traditionally governing the uses of public money."[24] That is, the NEA should select grants that reflected "the cultures of minority, inner-city, rural, and tribal communities" and the advisory panels needed to be "broader and more representative in terms of aesthetic and philosophical views." The grants had to meet "professional standards of authenticity" while also encouraging "artists to achieve wider distribution of their works."

Unfortunately, the NEA could not expand its programming to implement these suggestions because Congress cut its budget in 1995 from $162 million to $99 million the following year. In fact, the government agency had to implement structural changes that counteracted the commission's advisement. Chairman Jane Alexander had the difficult and painful tasks of closing down the Expansion Arts division, integrating its work into other areas, and eliminating all individual artist grants, except in literature.

While the NEA invested more in minorities and low-income geographic areas than the Rockefeller and Ford Foundations, there was still room to grow. Sociologist Samuel Gilmore's analysis of NEA grantmaking during this period demonstrates the ways government funding was still imbalanced and inegalitarian. Specifically, grants to minorities (defined according to racial or ethnic U.S. census statuses as African Americans, Asian Americans, Latino Americans, and Native Americans) were lower in number, due to either lack of awareness about grants or lack of technical expertise to apply successfully for grants.[25] His data show

> the percentage of grants that directly support minority artists and minority-run arts organizations is decreasing as a percentage of the minority arts category, while minority outreach and minority programming by non-minority

organizations [i.e., Western high art groups] are an increasing portion of the minority arts pie.[26]

Gilmore's analysis indicates that while the overall level of funding for minority populations improved slightly across the NEA during the 1980s and early 1990s, grants to minority individuals decreased relative to nonminorities. Rather than providing more resources to minority artists themselves, the NEA supported the outreach programs of professional Western arts groups.[27]

There were, however, also some glimmers of change, including greater participation of minorities on NEA panels. For instance, Gilmore argues that when there were more minorities serving as panelists, the NEA gave a greater number of grants to minority artists and groups. While there may have been a number of factors involved that suggest caution in drawing a direct relationship, including the fact that minority panelists tended to be selected for programs that already had a significant number of minority applicants, nevertheless, "by simply displaying a culturally diverse panel, programs at the endowment communicated a positive predisposition for culturally eclectic work."[28] Moreover, an ethnically diverse panel facilitated the inclusion of wide-ranging expertise and experience in evaluating both traditional and nontraditional artistic activity.

The United States has only grown more ethnically diverse since the beginning of the new millennium, and minority representation is crucial if society chooses to value cultural pluralism and diversity. How institutions structure their selection process, mission, and decision making cannot rely on simplistic notions of expertise as conflated with academic credentials or social connections. Private sources of funding for the arts continue to grow larger and larger compared to relative giving by the government. Rather than honeybees pollinating a vast field, though, foundations have behaved more like moths drawn to flame on a late summer evening, returning again and again to the halo emitted by the concert hall.

Foundation Giving to Music and the Arts in the Present

Sociologist Lauren Rivera reveals in her book *Pedigree* how seemingly meritocratic systems of selection can be tipped by hidden scales of bias.[29] As Rivera found in the hiring practices of elite firms, anyone could in theory apply for a position, but in practice, only those with preexisting social connections or legitimized educational pedigrees (demonstrated through affiliation with prestigious universities) got jobs. Rather than a "contest system" of open competition, in which victory of the few prizes was claimed through individual effort and skill, firms relied on a "sponsored system" of existing elites choosing the winners.[30] Firms linked exclusivity with "practicality"—that is, there were only so many recruiters and so many hours in the day to conduct due diligence, but a decision had to be made. By analogy, the same was—and continues to be—true for arts grants made by the largest foundations. The system is not purely meritocratic, but highly dependent upon social and cultural capital.

The most recent data from the Foundation Center, a nonprofit organization that has gathered and analyzed information since the 1950s, provide evidence of the ways the wealthiest foundations remain firmly committed to venerated Western art institutions.[31] The data show that from 2006 to 2015, in the area of "music," over 15,000 funders gave roughly $4.7 billion to a little under 10,000 recipients. Of this $4.7 billion, more than a third, or $1.8 billion, was given to "orchestral music." A little under a quarter, or $1.1 billion, was given to "opera music," composed of 790 recipients. Paling in comparison, "folk and indigenous music" received $38.6 million, or just 2% of what orchestras were awarded; 1,611 orchestras received funding from 8,710 donors, while only 221 folk and indigenous organizations benefited from 482 donors.[32]

The largest funder in music was the Andrew W. Mellon Foundation, which has continued its strong interest in the arts and higher education since the midcentury, already evidenced in its substantial matching grants with Ford's music conservatories program (see Box E.1). In the decade between 2006 and 2015, Mellon gave multi-million-dollar gifts to several New York City–based cultural establishments: Brooklyn Academy of Music ($5 million in 2007), Metropolitan Opera Association ($4.8 million in 2008), Jazz at Lincoln Center ($3 million in 2011), and Carnegie Hall Society ($4 million in 2012). It also awarded $3.5 million in 2006 to the Anthology of Recorded Music, the

---

BOX E.1

THE TOP TEN FOUNDATION DONORS TO MUSIC, 2006–15

- Andrew W. Mellon Foundation, $181.9M to 328 grants
- Annenberg Foundation, $96M to 231 grants
- Lilly Endowment, $89M to 92 grants
- Arison Arts Foundation, $87M to 13 grants
- Ann and Gordon Getty Foundation, $73M to 3,460 grants
- William and Flora Hewlett Foundation, $57.9M to 309 grants
- Minneapolis Foundation, $48.7M to 1,251 grants
- The William Penn Foundation, $45.5M to 111 grants
- Greater Kansas City Community Foundation, $44.3M to 1,829 grants
- John S. and James L. Knight Foundation, $43.1M to 198 grants

successor to the Rockefeller's Recorded Anthology of American Music (RAAM). The Los Angeles–based Annenberg Foundation was the second-largest funder in music, as well as the top donor of the Philadelphia Orchestra, giving it two big $15 million gifts in 2006 and 2007. Annenberg also made several substantial donations to the Metropolitan Opera Association, totaling $25 million between 2006 and 2010, as well as two gifts of $5 million to the Academy of Music in Philadelphia ("the oldest opera house in the United States still hosting performances") in 2006, and the Los Angeles Philharmonic in 2015.

After a while, tens of millions and hundreds of millions of dollars begin to blur together in a sea of zeros, but one final foundation is worth highlighting. The Arison Arts Foundation's thirteen grants to music totaling $87 million went almost entirely to New World Symphony. The second largest recipient of foundation money, the symphony is a Miami-based training and fellowship program established by Michael Tilson Thomas and Lin and Ted Arison for conservatory graduates to take on leadership roles in professional orchestras. Of the five largest grants to music, the Arison Arts Foundation made two of them to New World Symphony (the highest was $45 million in 2009, preceded by one for $28.6 million the year prior).

Compared to its extensive philanthropic support in the 1950s, 1960s, and 1970s, the Rockefeller Foundation gives a fraction of what it used to in the arts and humanities. Between 2006 and 2015, it gave only seventeen grants to music, totaling $5.3 million, averaging just over half a million dollars a year. Most of the money went to Jazz at Lincoln Center. The Ford Foundation has been making a few more headlines, especially with Darren Walker's new initiatives on art funding and social justice. In the decade leading up to Walker's presidency, though, the foundation averaged a little less than $2 million a year in music (total $18.1 million for ninety-three grants), a much smaller fraction (which is even lower after factoring in inflation) compared to its tens of millions a year in the 1960s and 1970s.

The music organizations that received the most foundation funds were all Western art institutions, as seen in Box E.2, including three major opera companies and five major symphony orchestras. The largest recipient during these years was the Metropolitan Opera. When one combines the Metropolitan Opera Association with the Metropolitan Opera (the Met, which the association officially operates), their grants total over a quarter billion dollars, or more than twice the fundraising of the second-highest recipient. Just missing the top ten list was Jazz at Lincoln Center, which came in eleventh place, at $57.6 million from 792 grants. While not within the traditional Western art music canon, Jazz at Lincoln Center is affiliated with, as its name indicates, the prestigious New York City landmark that is home to two others on the list, the Met and the New York Philharmonic, in addition to the Juilliard School.[33]

BOX E.2

THE TOP TEN FOUNDATION RECIPIENTS IN MUSIC, 2006–15

- The Metropolitan Opera, $176.3M from 2,059 grants
- New World Symphony Inc., $107.6M from 217 grants
- Metropolitan Opera Association, $88.4M from 1,327 grants
- The Philadelphia Orchestra, $86.1M from 722 grants
- San Francisco Symphony, $76.5M from 1,430 grants
- Detroit Symphony Orchestra, $67.8M from 679 grants
- New York Philharmonic, $67.6M from 1,380 grants
- Lyric Opera of Chicago, $66.3M from 1,365 grants
- Los Angeles Opera Company, $64.6M from 607 grants
- Minnesota Orchestral Association, $64M from 990 grants

One cannot emphasize enough the magnitudes of disparity. The Metropolitan Opera alone received more than six times what all folk and indigenous music groups got *combined*. The top ten recipients in music obtained more than twenty-two times all 221 folk and indigenous organizations' gifts together. As Pam Breaux argues, grants of more than half a million dollars account for 58% of foundation arts grantmaking.[34] Smaller arts organizations—those in primarily underserved communities—are left out of the picture. To point out the difference between large foundation giving and governmental giving, the average size of an NEA grant is $25,000, and a state arts agency grant, $4,390. Public funding achieves unquestionably more accessible and democratic grantmaking.

How society regulates private giving is especially crucial given the exponential increase in the number of wealthy individuals choosing to direct their philanthropy through foundations. In 1930, there were two hundred private foundations. In 1959, there were two thousand. In 1985, there were thirty thousand. In 2017, there were ninety thousand.[35] The wealthiest Americans are channeling money away from the government and toward their personal preferences. At the same time, the 0.1% of American society continues to get richer.

New Ways of Giving, Old Ways of Taxing

While the Tax Reform Act of 1969 was the last time Congress carefully looked at the tax-exempt status of philanthropic foundations, the tax deduction for *individuals* and their federal income tax have gone even longer without revision. Over a century has passed since the War Revenue Act of 1917, originally conceived to raise money during the Great War. The tax deduction allows for individuals to make gifts to "corporations or associations organized and operated exclusively for religious, charitable, scientific, or educational purposes, or to societies for the prevention of cruelty to children or animals." For the most part, the provision has not changed despite an ever increasingly complex tax code, an expansion of government services (and debt), and mounting economic and political inequality. The federal income tax deduction provides an incentive for citizens—especially wealthy ones who have greater sources of disposable income—to channel money away from government coffers to private interests, even if in nonprofit sectors of society.

Philanthropic giving in the United States amounted to $390 billion in 2016.[36] In rank order, it went to religion (32%), education (15%), human services (12%), health (8%), and public-society benefit (8%). "Arts, culture, and humanities" came eighth on the list, at 5% and $18.21 billion. Of total giving to eligible nonprofit organizations, foundations made up 15% and individuals made up over 70% percent, with the remainder from bequests and corporations. Data from the Foundation Center show that private foundations tend to give at a higher proportion to "arts and culture," at roughly 10%. Yet even greater than foundation giving to arts and culture is the percentage donated by individuals from households with incomes greater than $1 million.

The Russell Sage Foundation has reported that wealthy people largely express different preferences and beliefs compared to the general public. Higher-income individuals are more likely to be fiscally conservative, favor deficit reduction, and approve free trade measures than the general public; they are much less likely to support a higher minimum wage, expanded tax credits for low-income workers, and government-initiated job creation.[37] And as it turns out, they give to arts and culture organizations at much higher levels as well. While individuals overall give roughly 2% of their contributions to arts and culture, households with incomes over $1 million donate 15% of their contributions. Wealthy Americans care more, as political scientist Rob Reich argues, and thus give more, to arts, culture, education, and health, even at greater levels than the provision of societal basic needs.[38]

In theory, and in line with the First Amendment, there is no moral objection to individuals, rich or poor, who give away money to causes in which they believe. In practice, however, these individuals are not donating just their own money. The federal government subsidizes their philanthropy by forgoing tax income it would otherwise spend (called "tax expenditures"). In 2011, tax deductions for charitable giving cost the U.S. Treasury $53 billion.[39] Furthermore, Reich points out how much the wealthy skew the U.S. tax system toward their interests, and that there are both theoretical problems with subsidizing preferences and practical obstacles that prevent all Americans from claiming tax deductions. Ninety percent of U.S. households make charitable contributions every year, but only those who itemize their deductions (i.e. predominantly high-income earners) can claim these refunds.[40]

Reich argues that tax brackets produce an "upside-down effect" where the tax deduction becomes an even greater subsidy the higher one's income is. Those in the highest tax bracket—in 2017, 39.6%—receive the greatest tax deduction, compared to those in the lowest tax bracket, 10% in 2017. In fact, those making $200,000 and above claimed 70% of total tax deductions for charitable contributions.[41] Those in the lowest tax bracket were unlikely to itemize their deductions in the first place, even though they tended to give away more money as a percentage of their income.[42] As Reich criticizes, in addition to the tax deduction incentive applying "unequally to donors of different tax-filing statuses and income levels," it also means that "public funds forgone in the tax deduction are flowing disproportionately to the favored charitable organizations of the rich."[43] At least two solutions could address this inequality in the tax policy: allowing nonitemizers to deduct their charitable contributions and establishing a capped tax credit, which would limit the incentivized benefit to a fixed ceiling amount.

Amid these already outdated tax structures, some are trying to find even newer forms of philanthropy, while also encouraging their peers to do more. Bill and Melinda Gates and Warren Buffet started the Giving Pledge in 2010, an open invitation to billionaires ("or those who would be if not for their giving") to commit more than half of their wealth to philanthropy or charity.[44] Its aim is to "help shift the social norms of philanthropy toward giving more, giving sooner, and giving smarter." The amount held by U.S. billionaires alone who have committed to the pledge (there are global pledgers as well) is almost as much money as the combined assets of all ninety thousand U.S. foundations currently in existence.[45]

Five years later, in 2015, coinciding with the announcement of their daughter Max's birth, Mark Zuckerberg and Priscilla Chan pledged to give away 99% of their Facebook shares, at the time worth $45 billion. Their giving, however, was through a limited liability company, or LLC, rather than a traditional private foundation. By forgoing the tax deduction to set up an otherwise nonprofit entity, Chan and Zuckerberg gained other privileges, including zero reporting requirements on their activities, zero annual payout minimums, and the ability to make political contributions to campaigns and parties, should they choose. LLCs do not pay taxes themselves—owners cover profits and losses through their personal tax returns—and unlike a formal company, LLCs do not need a board of directors, thereby allowing owners to retain even greater control of their finances and activities.

Finally, one further philanthropic evolution is the donor-advised fund, the fastest-growing "charitable intermediary." As legal scholar Ray D. Madoff explains, these funds are entities where contributors can park their charitable dollars before they want to use them.[46] The donor can claim the full tax benefit of the gift, "without any temporal requirement imposed on money to *leave*," that is, to go to a charitable organization.[47] The funds grow tax free, and unlike with foundations, there is no government payout rule, which is otherwise 5%. In essence, they allow wealthy donors to set aside tax-deductible money without needing to set up their own foundation. The fund—one of the biggest includes Fidelity Charitable, created in 1991—distributes the grant money and charges a small percentage as a fee. Most significantly, donors can remain anonymous. The fund has to report where the money goes, but not who the donors are. In 2015, donor-advised funds gave more than $13 billion in grants.[48] Donor-advised funds are thus a growing and severely underregulated form of philanthropy. They have the potential of stockpiling investments with no payout requirement, all while their donors can remain anonymous.

What worries many critics of recent large-scale philanthropy is how "profoundly undemocratic" the new giving can be.[49] As David Callahan writes, "philanthropy is becoming a much stronger power center and, in some areas, is set to surpass government in its ability to shape society's agenda."[50] Mark Zuckerberg can give away hundreds of millions of dollars to the Newark Public School System, or to Planned Parenthood, but such massive and unprecedented giving can introduce problems of political illegitimacy and money-powered super-individuals. Already, philanthropic funds have had significant impacts in charter school education, same-sex marriage policies, and medical research. And as it is, donations to the Heritage Foundation, the Cato Institute, or the Progressive Policy Institute are tax deductible because those essentially political organizations are 501(c)(3)s.

The newer generation of wealthy philanthropists are approaching the work differently than their older counterparts. Younger ones are, for example, donating earlier rather than waiting until their retirement, and are including sunset clauses, which maintain that the funds have to be spent within a certain time after their death. Those who've made their wealth in tech, big data, or finance have also called on their training and work experience to prioritize quantifying impact and needs through metrics, analytics, machine learning, and algorithms. Some scholars have questioned the overreliance on quantifying metrics and the fetishizing of numbers over lived human experiences.[51] Callahan has additionally observed, "when the wealthy get into giving they tend to turn to friends for guidance, who are often peers in their industry. They may kick in for the same causes, use the same philanthropic advisors, and embrace the same approaches as others around them."[52] This tight and interlocking social capital means that vast sums of money and influence are pooled in the hands of a "billionaires club." As discussed in *Ask the Experts*, tight social networks also led to an exclusionary and inegalitarian system of arts funding. And as Callahan writes, "just because you're good at making money doesn't mean you'll be any good at giving it away."[53]

A more serious look at tax-deductible giving, the regulation of foundations, the development of LLCs and donor-advised funds, and the monitoring of non-profit organizations, is a complex, but necessary, task. At the moment, there is very little Internal Revenue Service (IRS) verification, monitoring, or enforcement of nonprofit status. Furthermore, funders are not required to reveal who they make grants to, and by the same token, nonprofits do not have to reveal their donors. Callahan recommends the establishment of a new government agency to over-see all philanthropic and nonprofit organizations: a U.S. federal office of charita-ble affairs. It would parallel the work of the Congressional Budget Office or the Government Accountability Office. The federal government could pay for the new agency through the 2% excise tax foundations already pay on their annual invest-ment income. While the arts might be higher hanging fruit in this endeavor, they are not free from criticism.

Western Art Music in the Twenty-First Century

The broad category of "arts and culture" makes up a small fraction of charitable giv-ing (5% of overall giving; 10% of foundation giving), but it still represents over $15 billion annually in private donations and it is greatly imbalanced. As the most recent data indicate, three out of every five foundation dollars goes to orchestral or operatic music. By comparison, eighty-two cents of every one hundred foundation dollars goes to folk and indigenous music. The scales are astonishing. Interlocking matching requirements set—and met—by funding organizations and wealthy individuals, as well as the publicity and recognition large gifts bestow upon grant recipients, mag-nify the discrepancies even further. When tax dollars are lost, the U.S. federal gov-ernment subsidizes the preferences and tastes of wealthy individuals. These dollars could otherwise be spent on the artistic and cultural practices of those most often left out of institutionalized funding structures. This argument is not a critique of Western art music over others, per se, but a recognition that arts funding inequality mirrors class and racial inequalities in American society.

A similar argument could be made about the disconcerting fine arts market, where individuals and institutions are increasingly buying paintings valued at over hun-dreds of millions of dollars as "investments." Publicly funded museums play a role in subsidizing, insuring, and sustaining this system. Over the past decade, ten paint-ings worldwide have sold for over $165 million *each*. In 2017, Leonardo da Vinci's *Salvator Mundi* sold for $453 million. In 2015, Willem de Kooning's *Interchange* went for $312 million. The market has ascribed an absurd premium on authenticity and scarcity, yet perhaps laughably, few can tell the difference between a "real" painting and a forgery, or what special aura an "original" has over a print.[54] The NEA's indemnity program admirably saves museums hundreds of millions of dollars in insurance costs—it guarantees by the "full faith and credit of the United States" to pay for claims "in the event of loss or damage to an indemnified object"—but it also buoys a market whereby publicly funded museums participate in, and promote, the capitalistic fetishizing of Western artwork.[55]

One response is to take advantage of this bloated fine arts market and advance social justice. In June 2017, arts patron and philanthropist Agnes Gund established with a $100 million gift the Art for Justice Fund, which supports organizations addressing mass incarceration in the United States. Gund initiated it through the sale of her most prized Roy Lichtenstein painting, *Masterpiece*, as well as other artwork from her personal collection. She and the fund work in partnership with the Ford Foundation (which pays for program design and operating costs) and Rockefeller Philanthropy Advisors.[56]

Returning to the market of Western art music, a question to ask is: despite its beauty, do we hear classical music differently in a society of vast inequality? Or, put another way, at what extraordinary societal and economic costs are subsidized access to classical music, opera, or museums made? These questions are not to challenge public or private support of music and the arts, but the relative differences paid to various forms. To exaggerate the thought experiment even further, if there is an aesthetic experience to drinking champagne, as substantiated by point scores, tasting notes, and competitions, should there not also be concerted efforts to "increase access," through "reduced prices" or "student passes," for those who cannot afford to purchase champagne?[57] (The United Nations Educational, Scientific and Cultural Organization, UNESCO, granted the champagne industry world heritage status, citing it as "an outstanding example of grape cultivation and wine production developed since the high middle ages."[58] It joins other UNESCO world heritage sites like the Taj Mahal, the Great Wall of China, and Machu Picchu.) Some might criticize the analogy by pointing out that the wine industry is alive and kicking, surviving on its profits, and thus government subsidy is unnecessary (although there are subsidies for wine producers in the European Union). But there does also exist for-profit "classical" music, as evidenced by sold-out concerts to 2Cellos, the Piano Guys, the Three Tenors, and Bond.

In a world where artistic excellence exists in so many types, varieties, and cultures, then perhaps "quality" should not be monopolized by a single kind. It need not trickle down from the top, requiring large pools of financial and cultural resources, because it permeates the entire environment. Many cultural practices of music in the

United States are the result of inspiring creativity and intricate care, and evidence of years of apprenticeship, training, and formalized and informalized education.

Some orchestras and opera companies are indeed making greater efforts to open up to more diverse audiences, like the San Diego Symphony's Harry Potter, Star Wars, and Broadway show tunes concerts, as well as its collaboration with artists like Common and Chaka Khan. The Du Bois Orchestra, formed by Harvard students in 2015, is another instance of making music "a means of overcoming social exclusion," through the performance of "underrepresented composers" to "large, diverse audiences."[59] There still persist, however, other examples of retrenchment. Local musicians and educators, for example, criticized in 2017 the Boston Symphony Orchestra for programming seventy-two white male composers out of its total of seventy-three in the season.[60] The overall picture of aging and dwindling classical music audiences paints a grim picture in the absence of revolutionary change.

Would the "arts" disappear if the U.S. government eliminated or reduced the current tax deduction to charities? Such a scenario is impossible to predict, but cultural practices of music have always evolved, given changing social, political, and economic situations. The U.S. music industry alone generated close to $20 billion in 2018, and globally, the figure was over $50 billion.[61] This fact is evidence that Americans spend money on music and other arts, and *even pay a sales tax*, the opposite of a subsidy. Musicologist William Robin shows the ways contemporary music ensembles have had to come to terms with a neoliberal market economy, even forming LLCs of their own. They demonstrate that groups can adapt.[62] Some might ardently object that noncommercial arts—or even true "Art"—will disappear because it cannot survive in the marketplace without private donations. It is important to remember, though, that individuals can still make gifts to whichever art they value. No one would stop them from exercising their freedom of speech; they would just do so without tax deduction.

If in the end American society believes that charity to nonprofit arts institutions provides an overall public benefit (e.g., increased diversity and cultural pluralism), then a compromise is a capped tax credit (e.g., 50% on the first $1,000), rather than a full, unlimited deduction. As with the critiques mentioned by Reich, a tax credit would actually democratize charitable giving to more people, instead of just the wealthy few who itemize their deductions. In terms of free speech, a capped credit is also more equitable because a greater number of voices are heard and the volume of one's voice is less tied to the amount of money given away. A capped tax credit is not a permanent fix; it is a possible solution for the present, given the current system of social and economic inequality. When new inequalities develop, society can re-evaluate and change the system again. Last but not least, this revision of the tax code would hopefully be accompanied by a substantial increase in local, state, and federal arts funding, along the values of wide distribution to diverse cultural practices.

Expertise, Influence, and Ethics

In today's society, the concept of the "expert" has progressively morphed into different actors: the "influencers," "thought leaders," "public intellectuals," and "curators."[63] Perhaps not all of these people have developed their knowledge through extensive training and study, or the acquisition of significant experience in a particular field, but they are all playing a role in how society sees and interprets the world, what it consumes, the pleasure it derives from consuming, and how it determines value. Given the rise of many of these actors, has society truly democratized who can be an expert, or has it filled the room with allegedly vested interests? Has expertise become too instrumental in advancing certain political and social goals, for both good and bad?

Whom society deems to be experts and how seriously it takes experts' opinions mirrors economic and political inequalities. Exclusivity remains a central issue. To become a true expert—and not just a snake-oil salesman—requires large amounts of time and resources, which are not available to all members of society. The ascent of civic inequality is no surprise in light of concentrated decision making in the hands of the few, combined with higher levels of wealth disparity. During a time when some people question even basic science and others blithely and self-assuredly declare a fact they disagree with as "fake news," an ethics of expertise and influence is even more critical.[64] Such ethics can begin with, perhaps, the most "subjective" and preference bound of fields: art.

Of critical importance, I have not argued in this book that arts grantmakers and arts experts in the midcentury were not actually experts, that they had multifarious intentions, or that their work was prejudicial. A critique of subjectivity is almost too easy—of course, everyone has their own preferences. To boot, unabashed criticism would be extraordinarily difficult because many of these officials, consultants, and practicing artists sacrificed, donated, and worked tirelessly to sustain a creative practice that they were passionate about and loved. They had the best of intentions and they were clearly successful in expanding the tradition of Western art music after World War II. The point is not to question their motives or whether or not they were experts, but to understand what consequences arose because they were regarded, treated, and *asked* as experts—or, how seemingly nonsubjective formal structures based on expertise led to unequal outcomes. Not just experts in classical music worked and sacrificed during this period, but also many others.

Similarly, I have *not* argued that connections or social capital is inherently bad. Without connections, we would be isolated individuals; society would not exist. Social capital is a resource just like economic capital—a resource that can generate greater good. A college student can call on her friends to help her with her writing assignment; she can reach out to her professor, a mentor, or a tutor. Program directors at the NEA used social networks to increase the diversity of their panelists in Expansion Arts. At the same time, capital can be exclusive—just as a rich person can hoard his or her wealth, the powerful can be exclusionary. The goal should be figuring out how society can utilize expertise and social capital to generate positive societal benefits in inclusive ways. At the least, society should be more conscious of the way it employs social connections in grantmaking, recognizing that there are fewer means of redistributing social capital.

Perhaps, then, a central takeaway from this study is to remember again the simple idea that individuals should trust experts to the extent that they understand that informed expert opinions are, nevertheless, still opinions. Likewise, experts should feel obligated to act and advise transparently, indicating whenever there exist conflicts of interest, undue influence, or other rewards to be gained. Additionally, and importantly, there may be many unrecognized forms of expertise right beneath society's nose. Rather than an aristocratic model of expertise, society should seek historically underrepresented experts for their perspectives and insights. This democratization of expertise requires an attendant effort to democratize social capital, the form of capital most significant in the spread and legitimacy of the arts.

Alternative models of grantmaking in the arts might also lead to a fairer, more egalitarian distribution of resources. One way to prevent cronyism, for instance, is the anonymization of grant applicants, where reviewers do not know who the applicant is. Evaluators are left with the art work alone, with fewer pressures to select their friends—or unselect their foes. Anonymization has its downsides, however, because it assumes that the playing field is level, and at times, affirmative intervention would be beneficial, as in the cultivation of minority art forms. Or, an even more radical solution is a grants lottery, that is, a completely randomized selection of winners and losers. Anyone can enter; anyone has the possibility of being chosen. If this option is too alarming, then the grantmaker can establish criteria regarding who can enter (e.g., qualifications, a statement or commitment of interest and sincerity, etc.).

An unfortunate answer might be to abolish human experts in the selection process altogether, or throwing the baby out with the bath water. Technology complicates social interactions in positive and negative ways, but a "machine-driven curation, based on sophisticated algorithms and data mining," should not serve as a complete replacement of human decision making.[65] There is an allure to the notion of complete and fair objectivity, in selecting without discrimination, in a consistent and rational way. But the appeal is nevertheless a mirage, masked by the fact that humans still write the code that computers run, a code that is nonetheless evidence of the coders' preferences and biases. Ultimately, as Michael Bhaskar states, "curation is, in part, about what machines cannot do."[66]

In a world where basic needs are not being met, of a lack for food and housing, and healthcare, perhaps it is more difficult to justify elite preferences for expensive art. Yet, in art's strong defense, it has important positive social and human developmental capacities, and its support should persist.[67] The strongest contribution that arts experts provide is their wealth of knowledge and experience, and at their best, arts panelists and evaluators know what has and has not been successful, based on years of practice in their field. But different experiences and backgrounds should also be prioritized. Membership in elite institutions or prestigious organizations is not inherently a greater source of expertise than work in a local community context or rural setting. Foundation and government program directors should be committed to, and cognizant of, issues of injustice and inequality. Otherwise, ignorance of nondominant cultural forms amounts to their exclusion.

As things stand, minority applicants are often less equipped to directly seek grants offered by philanthropic institutions and government agencies. In general, their social networks are more limited than those of artists and organizations that have received public and private funding for decades. Even for minority applicants who know about the availability of grants, they may nevertheless lack the technical experience to apply. They frequently lack development offices or grant writers that larger, more mainstream arts organizations normally employ. To truly lay the groundwork for a more egalitarian and multicultural system of arts funding, reaching out to those who have been routinely left out of the system is necessary. Plant seeds through initial grants; provide awards; and afford recognition. Do not just publish guidelines, but actively visit, recruit, and promote. Equip artists and organizations not only with financial resources but also know-how to empower them to manage their budgets, reach out to other funders, and network with their peers. Do not expect arts organizations to become self-sufficient within a limited number of years, and remember that systemic inequality and prejudice have disadvantaged poor and working-class people, individuals with disabilities, women, and people of color over multiple generations.

As a final suggestion: do not listen only to the same voices. Do not go to the same people for consultation and expertise over and over again. Money speaks loudly on its own, and privilege affords the means to speak and be heard. Instead, listen to those who have been ignored in the past, and to those who speak in different languages and from different perspectives. Reach out to those who have been marginalized or feel that they do not have a stake or a right in the system. Those are the expert voices I would want to hear.

Appendix

Ford Foundation Budgets, 1953–77

Fiscal Year	Income	Total Grants	Music Specific	Music as %
1953	$48,248,006	$58,905,570	$0	0%
1954*	$19,958,899	$49,438,558	$30,000	0%
1955	$133,576,771	$64,957,658	$0	0%
1956	$165,888,263	$557,778,481	$0	0%
1957	$102,908,434	$153,393,616	$2,980,000	2%
1958	$92,570,289	$79,033,884	$385,000	0%
1959	$84,625,525	$109,353,966	$203,500	0%
1960	$127,353,638	$160,752,733	$304,200	0%
1961	$130,503,706	$144,550,898	$596,000	0%
1962	$136,578,174	$223,258,476	$867,724	0%
1963	$140,311,913	$212,285,581	$16,558,598	8%
1964	$146,943,393	$225,136,327	$1,664,400	1%
1965	$145,406,691	$281,588,729	$5,832,189	2%
1966	$157,440,736	$341,627,172	$81,357,500	24%
1967	$158,089,844	$234,083,307	$874,000	0%
1968	$154,536,363	$175,730,176	$2,276,905	1%
1969	$149,199,705	$198,968,415	$495,502	0%
1970	$142,250,556	$192,307,414	$1,265,037	1%
1971[†]	$183,224,531	$176,178,236	$15,359,809	9%

Fiscal Year	Income	Total Grants	Music Specific	Music as %
1972	$110,393,962	$176,052,095	$3,643,439	2%
1973	$103,979,000	$210,215,881	$3,477,571	2%
1974	$101,196,000	$220,228,940	$3,418,378	2%
1975	$85,213,000	$172,441,924	$600,162	0%
1976	$86,448,000	$137,065,998	$369,278	0%
1977	$87,978,000	$98,445,371	$499,885	1%

* Nine-month period, change in calendar year.

† Ford changed its accounting method for investment income.

Rockefeller Foundation Budgets, 1953–77

Fiscal Year	Income	Total Grants	Music Specific	Music as %
1953	$18,595,820	$16,771,582	$604,840	4%
1954	$18,990,490	$19,107,665	$197,550	1%
1955	$20,915,631	$19,152,353	$438,587	2%
1956	$27,110,400	$30,075,305	$190,200	1%
1957	$44,502,540	$42,798,916	$7,808,798	18%
1958	$30,919,413	$31,592,157	$559,625	2%
1959	$30,812,404	$34,189,340	$249,380	1%
1960	$29,703,566	$32,833,971	$200,095	1%
1961	$36,513,418	$36,513,418	$94,475	0%
1962	$24,266,248	$30,047,036	$312,585	1%
1963	$26,066,960	$37,146,072	$5,315,690	14%
1964	$27,276,570	$40,402,429	$1,003,200	2%
1965	$29,137,115	$35,938,896	$1,221,674	3%
1966	$30,784,237	$41,843,499	$1,013,162	2%
1967	$32,188,393	$39,142,415	$1,525,170	4%
1968	$32,838,247	$42,559,795	$487,562	1%
1969	$31,977,066	$47,275,315	$692,097	1%
1970	$29,139,492	$53,932,035	$1,712,017	3%
1971	$27,994,801	$41,934,380	$606,950	1%
1972	$25,202,354	$43,743,006	$928,929	2%
1973	$27,563,857	$40,271,699	$1,093,690	3%

Fiscal Year	Income	Total Grants	Music Specific	Music as %
1974	$35,388,757	$42,103,720	$192,313	0%
1975	$33,006,513	$40,746,314	$470,200	1%
1976	$37,361,444	$42,861,974	$1,617,750	4%
1977	$38,926,714	$39,415,573	$1,407,800	4%

National Endowment for the Arts (NEA) Budgets, 1965–77

Fiscal Year	Appropriations	Gifts to NEA	Total Grants	Music Specific	Music as %
1965	$50,000.00		$50,000.00		0%
1966	$2,500,000.00	$34,308.23	$2,534,308.23	$183,575.00	7%
1967	$7,965,692.00	$1,983,075.00	$9,948,767.00	$653,858.00	9%
1968	$7,170,791.00	$674,291.00	$11,092,451.00	$1,154,969.00	11%
1969	$7,756,875.00	$2,356,875.00	$10,751,917.00	$861,620.00	14%
1970	$8,250,000.00	$2,000,000.00	$15,718,477.00	$2,252,195.00	17%
1971	$15,090,000.00	$2,500,000.00	$20,482,542.00	$5,188,383.00	29%
1972	$29,750,000.00	$3,500,000.00	$36,321,887.00	$9,745,797.00	29%
1973	$38,200,000.00	$3,631,898.00	$45,286,183.00	$10,382,210.00	25%
1974	$60,775,000.61	$7,280,867.61	$71,817,983.78	$16,116,310.73	24%
1975	$74,750,000.00	$7,710,271.00	$86,946,671.00	$14,894,833.00	18%
1976	$82,000,000.00	$7,520,000.00	$95,617,421.00	$17,249,296.00	19%
Transition Quarter	$33,937,000.00	$510,000.00	$37,644,209.00	$9,724,680.00	27%
1977	$94,000,000.00	$16,600,824.00	$114,451,507.00	$25,131,074.00	22%

Notes

INTRODUCTION

1. These figures are based on analysis of the annual reports of each institution. For calculations of present-day value, reference http://www.measuringworth.com.

2. The Ford Foundation, "The Ford Foundation: Millions for Music—Music for Millions," *Music Educators Journal* 53, no. 1 (1966): 83–86.

3. Ralph Smith, "The New Policy-Making Complex in Aesthetic Education," *Curriculum Theory* 4, no. 2 (1974): 159–68.

4. Howard S. Becker, *Art Worlds* (Berkeley: University of California Press, 1982).

5. For example, see John Harris, *Government Patronage of the Arts in Great Britain* (Chicago: University of Chicago Press, 1970); Andrew Sinclair, *Arts and Cultures: The History of the 50 Years of the Arts Council of Great Britain* (London: Sinclair-Stevenson, 1995).

6. Robert Evans, "The Sociology of Expertise: The Distribution of Social Fluency," *Sociology Compass* 2, no. 1 (2008): 281–98.

7. Charles Wright Mills, *The Power Elite*, New ed. (Oxford: Oxford University Press, 2000).

8. By comparison, the National Science Foundation was founded in 1950, also as a postwar grantmaking institution.

9. Pierre Bourdieu, "The Forms of Capital," in *Handbook of Theory and Research for the Sociology of Education*, ed. John Richardson (New York: Greenwood, 1986), 241–58; Pierre Bourdieu, *Distinction: A Social Critique of the Judgement of Taste* (London: Routledge & Kegan Paul, 1986).

10. Alexis de Tocqueville, *Democracy in America*, 2nd ed. (New York: Vintage Books, 1990); Thorstein Veblen, *The Theory of the Leisure Class: An Economic Study in the Evaluation of Institutions* (New York: MacMillan, 1899).

11. See Ralph P. Locke and Cyrilla Barr, eds., *Cultivating Music in America: Women Patrons and Activists Since 1860* (Berkeley: University of California Press, 1997); Carol Oja, *Making Music Modern: New York in the 1920s* (Oxford: Oxford University Press, 2000).

12. http://www.rockefellerfoundation.org/about-us (Accessed 12 11 2013).

13. Steve Hargreaves, "The Richest Americans in History," CNN Money, June 2, 2014, http://money.cnn.com/gallery/luxury/2014/06/01/richest-americans-in-history (Accessed 24 04 2017).

14. Finances of the Ford Foundation, 14 09 1962, Folder: Staff Memos—Miscellaneous 1962–1964, Box 6, Series IV, FA582, Ford Foundation (FF), Rockefeller Archive Center, Tarrytown, New York (RAC).

15. Richard Magat, *The Ford Foundation at Work: Philanthropic Choices, Methods, and Styles* (New York: Plenum Press, 1979), 18.

16. Ford Foundation, "Annual Report 1966."

17. These numbers are based on my calculations of each foundation's annual report budgets, with assistance from John Griffin. For individual histories of each music program, see Chapter 1 in Michael Sy Uy, "The Big Bang of Music Patronage in the United States: The National Endowment for the Arts, the Rockefeller Foundation, and the Ford Foundation" (Harvard University, 2017).

18. Nick Taylor, *American-Made: The Enduring Legacy of the WPA: When FDR Put the Nation to Work* (New York: Bantam Books, 2008).

19. Gary Larson, *The Reluctant Patron: The United States Government and the Arts, 1943–1965* (Philadelphia: University of Pennsylvania Press, 1983).

20. http://arts.gov/open-government/nea-budget-planning-information/national-endowment-arts-appropriations-history (Accessed 22 01 2014).

21. These numbers are based on my calculations of the NEA's annual report budgets, with assistance from John Griffin.

22. See, for example, Frances Stonor Saunders, *Who Paid the Piper? The C.I.A. and the Cultural Cold War* (London: Granta, 1999); as well as Mark Carroll, *Music and Ideology in Cold War Europe* (Cambridge: Cambridge University Press, 2003). Also see Andrea Bohlman, *Musical Solidarities: Political Action and Music in Late Twentieth-Century Poland* (Oxford: Oxford University Press, 2019); and Lisa Jakelski, *Making New Music in Cold War Poland: The Warsaw Autumn Festival, 1956–1968* (Berkeley: University of California Press, 2016), among others.

23. Donna Binkiewicz, *Federalizing the Muse: United States Art Policy and the National Endowment for the Arts, 1965–1980* (Chapel Hill: University of North Carolina Press, 2004), 4.

24. Frank Thompson Jr., "Are the Communists Right in Calling Us Cultural Barbarians?," *Music Journal* 13, no. 6 (1955), 5.

25. For instance, in Commissioner General Cullman's petition for funds for the 1958 Brussels Universal and International Exhibition, he argued, "we can do a *Sputnik* culturally, intellectually, and spiritually." In Walter Hixson, *Parting the Curtain: Propaganda, Culture, and the Cold War, 1945–1961* (Basingstoke: MacMillan, 1997), 142.

26. See Emily Abrams Ansari's work on musical Americanism and Danielle Fosler-Lussier's examination of the State Department's Cultural Presentations Program. Emily Abrams Ansari, *The Sound of a Superpower: Musical Americanism and the Cold War* (Oxford: Oxford University Press, 2018); Ansari, "Shaping the Politics of Cold War Musical Diplomacy: An Epistemic Community of American Composers," *Diplomatic History* 36, no. 1 (2012): 41–52; Danielle Fosler-Lussier, *Music in America's Cold War Diplomacy* (Berkeley: University of California Press,

2015). Also see Penny von Eschen, *Satchmo Blows Up the World: Jazz Ambassadors Play the Cold War* (Cambridge, MA: Harvard University Press, 2004).

27. Joan Roelofs, *Foundations and Public Policy: The Mask of Pluralism* (Albany: State University of New York Press, 2003), 13.

28. Ibid.

29. Ibid., 13–14.

30. Folder: Bennington College—Composers Conferences 1954–1958, 1961, Box 297, Series 200R, Subgroup 2, Record Group 1 (RG1), Rockefeller Foundation (RF), RAC.

31. I came across no archival instances, however, of when the foundation clearly rejected a recipient due to his or her political membership or affiliation.

32. Magat, *The Ford Foundation at Work: Philanthropic Choices, Methods, and Styles*, 33.

33. Ford Foundation Oral History Project, 27 09 1973, Folder: Ylvisaker, Paul, Box 3, Series IV, FA618, FF, RAC.

34. For example, "Lincoln Center Aide Sees Boom in Culture Taking Place in U.S.," *New York Times*, April 2, 1960; "Cultural Centers Are Springing Up in Cities Big and Small: Culture Booms in Many Cities," *New York Times*, July 29, 1962.

35. Rockefeller Brothers Fund, *The Performing Arts: Problems and Prospects: Rockefeller Panel Report on the Future of Theatre, Dance, Music in America* (New York: McGraw-Hill Book Company, 1965); William J. Baumol and William G. Bowen, "On the Performing Arts: The Anatomy of Their Economic Problems," *American Economic Review* 55, no. 1/2 (1965): 495–502; William J. Baumol, *Performing Arts: The Economic Dilemma: A Study of Problems Common to Theater, Opera, Music, and Dance* (New York: Twentieth Century Fund, 1966).

36. Rockefeller Brothers Fund, *The Performing Arts: Problems and Prospects*, v.

37. Fannie Taylor and Anthony Barresi, *The Arts at a New Frontier: The National Endowment for the Arts* (New York: Plenum Press, 1984), 17, 23.

38. Both went on to have eminent careers in academia and public affairs. Bowen later became president of Princeton from 1972 to 1988 and president of the Mellon Foundation from 1988 to 2006. Baumol wrote over eighty books and hundreds of journal articles, as well as taught at Princeton and New York University, where he was director of the Berkley Center for Entrepreneurship and Innovation.

39. Baumol and Bowen, "On the Performing Arts: The Anatomy of Their Economic Problems," 499.

40. Ibid., 500.

41. Baumol and Bowen, *Performing Arts: The Economic Dilemma*. The report was published in 1966 by the Twentieth Century Fund, where August Heckscher was director.

42. The problem was one shared across the performing arts, in addition to other "stagnant" sectors of the economy (e.g., education).

43. Robert H. Bremner, *American Philanthropy*, 2nd ed. (Chicago: University of Chicago Press, 1988), 191.

44. Robert Margo, "Chapter 7: Foundations," in *Who Benefits from the Nonprofit Sector?*, ed. Charles T. Clotfelter (Chicago: University of Chicago Press, 1992), 216.

45. Pierre Bourdieu and Randal Johnson, *The Field of Cultural Production: Essays on Art and Literature* (New York: Columbia University Press, 1993).

46. See especially Georgina Born, *Rationalizing Culture: IRCAM, Boulez, and the Institutionalization of the Musical Avant-Garde* (Berkeley: University of California Press,

1995); Henry Kingsbury, *Music, Talent, and Performance: A Conservatory Cultural System* (Philadelphia: Temple University Press, 1988); Richard Kurin, *Reflections of a Culture Broker: A View from the Smithsonian* (Washington, DC: Smithsonian Institution Press, 1997).

47. Paul DiMaggio, "Decentralization of Arts Funding from the Federal Government to the States," in *Public Money and the Muse: Essays on Government Funding for the Arts*, ed. Stephen Benedict (New York: W. W. Norton, 1991), 249.

48. Eduardo Herrera, "The Rockefeller Foundation and Latin American Music in the 1960s: The Creation of Indiana University's LAMC and Di Tella Institute's CLAEM," *American Music* 35, no. 1 (2017): 51–74.

49. Scholars and some former officers have begun to document Ford's, Rockefeller's, and the NEA's histories and analyze their work. In addition to Taylor, Barresi, and Binkiewicz, others have also begun to address different areas of government funding including arts education, dance, and state arts agencies: Constance Marie Bumgarner, "Artists in the Classroom: An Analysis of the Arts in Education Program of the National Endowment for the Arts" (Pennsylvania State University, 1993); Angela Helen Graham, "The National Endowment for the Arts Dance Program, 1965 to 1971: A Social and Cultural History" (Temple University, 1996); Keith D. Lee, "Supporting the Need: A Comparative Investigation of Public and Private Arts Endowments Supporting State Arts Agencies" (Ohio State University, 2007). Historians and other scholars working on the Ford and Rockefeller Foundations have primarily focused on the institutions' work in international affairs, domestic policy, and medical research. Richard Magat has written a comprehensive history of the institution but touched upon the music and arts programs only in pieces. Magat, *The Ford Foundation at Work: Philanthropic Choices, Methods, and Styles*. Two recent works, however, have considered some of the Ford Foundation's music programs, including support of the Music Educators National Conference and the New York City Opera commissions. Paul Michael Covey, "The Ford Foundation—MENC Contemporary Music Project (1959–1973): A View of Contemporary Music in America" (University of Maryland, College Park, 2013); Tedrin Blair Lindsay, "The Coming of Age of American Opera: New York City Opera and the Ford Foundation, 1958–1960" (University of Kentucky, 2009). The Rockefeller Foundation's arts and humanities work is similarly under-explored, although some scholarship has focused on specific music programs. For example, Jeanne Marie Belfy, *The Commissioning Project of the Louisville Orchestra, 1948–1958: A Study of the History and Music* (Louisville: UMI Publishers, 1986). Eduardo Herrera's work on the Rockefeller-funded Torcuato di Tella Institute is a necessary contribution to understanding the foundation's funding, foreign policy networks, and identity formation of avant-garde composers. Eduardo Herrera, *Elite Art Worlds: Philanthropy, Latin Americanism, and Avant-Garde Music* (Oxford: Oxford University Press, forthcoming).

50. By contrast, in historical musicological terms, "classical music" refers more specifically to the Gallant style from the eighteenth century.

51. For a history of Western art music, see Richard Taruskin, *Oxford History of Western Music* (Oxford: Oxford University Press, 2009).

52. H. Wiley Hitchcock, *Music in the United States: A Historical Introduction* (Englewood Cliffs, NJ: Prentice-Hall, 1969).

53. Research Division National Endowment for the Arts, "Minorities and Women in the Arts: 1970," 1978, https://www.arts.gov/sites/default/files/NEA-Research-Report-7.pdf (Accessed 13 12 2019).

54. From Kenneth W. Thompson to Lukas Foss, 30 10 1963, Folder: University of Buffalo—Creative Music Associates—(Lukas Foss, Allen D. Sapp) 1963–1969, Box 432, Series 200R, Subgroup 2, RG1, RF, RAC.

55. Pam Breaux, "Better Together: Public and Private Funding for the Arts," June 2017, https://mellon.org/resources/shared-experiences-blog/better-together-public-and-private-funding-arts/ (Accessed 02 07 2019).

56. Shamus R. Khan, *Privilege: The Making of an Adolescent Elite at St. Paul's School* (Princeton, NJ: Princeton University Press, 2011), and Stephen J. McNamee and Robert K. Miller Jr., *The Meritocracy Myth*, 2nd ed. (Lanham, MD: Rowman & Littlefield Publishers, 2009).

57. William Cheng, "Staging Overcoming: Narratives of Disability and Meritocracy in Reality Singing Competitions," *Journal of the Society for American Music* 11, no. 2 (2017): 184–214.

CHAPTER 1

1. Harry Collins and Robert Evans, *Rethinking Expertise* (Chicago: University of Chicago Press, 2007).

2. Tom Nichols, *The Death of Expertise: The Campaign Against Established Knowledge and Why It Matters* (Oxford: Oxford University Press, 2017), xi, emphasis in original.

3. Ibid., 20.

4. For the most comprehensive review of the concept of expertise, see K. Anders Ericsson et al., eds., *The Cambridge Handbook of Expertise and Expert Performance* (Cambridge: Cambridge University Press, 2006).

5. K. Anders Ericsson, "Chapter 1: An Introduction," in *The Cambridge Handbook of Expertise and Expert Performance* (Cambridge: Cambridge University Press, 2006), 10.

6. Dean K. Simonton, "Creative Productivity, Age, and Stress: A Biographical Time-Series Analysis of 10 Classical Composers," *Journal of Personality and Social Psychology* 35 (1977): 791–804.

7. Pierre Bourdieu, "The Forms of Capital," in *Handbook of Theory and Research for the Sociology of Education*, ed. John Richardson (New York: Greenwood, 1986), 241–58; Pierre Bourdieu, *Distinction: A Social Critique of the Judgement of Taste* (London: Routledge & Kegan Paul, 1986). Max Weber argued that rational legitimacy is accomplished through the application of impersonal and consistent rules, despite the persistence of idiosyncratic tastes. This rationalization helps sustain a collective belief of fairness in the process. Instead, preferences and tastes themselves are folded into formal criteria of evaluation, for example, defining originality according to the types of originality that one's own work exhibits. In Michèle Lamont, *How Professors Think: Inside the Curious World of Academic Judgment* (Cambridge, MA: Harvard University Press, 2010), 128, 130.

8. Robert Merton, "The Matthew Effect in Science," *Science* 159, no. 3810 (1968): 56–63. Matthew 25:29, "For unto every one that hath shall be given, and he shall have abundance; but from him that hath not shall be taken even that which he hath" (King James Version).

9. Edward L. Thorndike, "A Constant Error in Psychological Ratings," *Journal of Applied Psychology* 4, no. 1 (1920): 25–29.

10. Harald Mieg, "Chapter 41: Social and Sociological Factors in the Development of Expertise," in *The Cambridge Handbook of Expertise and Expert Performance* (Cambridge: Cambridge University Press, 2006): 743–60; Julia Evetts, Harald Mieg, and Ulrike Felt, "Chapter 7:

Professionalization, Scientific Expertise, and Elitism: A Sociological Perspective," in *The Cambridge Handbook of Expertise and Expert Performance*: 105–23.

11. Pierre Bourdieu and Randal Johnson, *The Field of Cultural Production: Essays on Art and Literature* (New York: Columbia University Press, 1993).

12. Andreas C. Lehmann and Hans Gruber, "Chapter 26: Music," in *The Cambridge Handbook of Expertise and Expert Performance*, 2; Robert W. Weisberg, *Creativity: Beyond the Myth of Genius* (New York: W. H. Freeman, 1993).

13. Collins and Evans, *Rethinking Expertise*, 2.

14. Ibid., 6.

15. Michael Polanyi, *Personal Knowledge: Towards a Post-Critical Philosophy* (Chicago: University of Chicago Press, 1958).

16. Collins and Evans, *Rethinking Expertise*, 14.

17. The stages of contributory expertise are novice, advanced beginner, competence, proficiency, and expertise. These stages are similar to Robert Hoffman's proficiency scale as found in Michelene T. H. Chi, "Chapter 2: Two Approaches to the Study of Experts' Characteristics," in *The Cambridge Handbook of Expertise and Expert Performance*, 22.

18. Collins and Evans, *Rethinking Expertise*, 28.

19. Collins and Evans refer instead to interactional expertise as "parasitic," although not necessarily in a pejorative way. They write that while contributory expertise is "self-sustaining," interactional expertise is not. Ibid., 35.

20. Edge, "What Is Reputation? A Conversation with Gloria Origgi," May 11, 2015, http://edge.org/conversation/gloria_origgi-what-is-reputation (Accessed 01 10 2015).

21. John Marshall interview with Virgil Thomson, 23 12 1948, Folder: Program and Policy—Music 1948–1954, Box 5, Series 911, Subgroup 1, Record Group 3 (RG3), Rockefeller Foundation (RF), Rockefeller Archive Center, Tarrytown, New York (RAC).

22. I thank Monica Hershberger for pointing this out to me.

23. Edward F. D'Arms interview with Music Conference, 25 02 1949, Folder: Program and Policy—Music 1948–1954, Box 5, Series 911, Subgroup 1, RG3, RF, RAC. Kerr was also the executive secretary and cofounder of the American Music Center, along with Luening, Porter, Aaron Copland, and others.

24. From John Marshall to David Stevens, Charles Fahs, Edward F. D'Arms, Chadbourne Gilpatric, Inter-office correspondence, 14 03 1949, Subject: Composers Conference on February 25, ibid.

25. From John Marshall to Virgil Thomson, Otto Luening, Quincy Porter, 13 04 1949, ibid.

26. Harrar was previously director of agriculture and vice president of the foundation.

27. Jacob G. Harrar, "Proposals for the Future Program of the Rockefeller Foundation 12/1/62," Folder: Program and Policy Reports Pro-46–Pro-49 1953–1963, Box 29, Series 900, Subgroup 2, RG3, RF, RAC.

28. Anthony Giddens, *The Consequences of Modernity* (Palo Alto, CA: Stanford University Press, 1990).

29. Harald Mieg, *The Social Psychology of Expertise* (Mahwah, NJ: Erlbaum, 2001).

30. From Kenneth W. Thompson to Lukas Foss, 30 10 1963, Folder: University of Buffalo—Creative Music Associates—(Lukas Foss, Allen D. Sapp) 1963–1969, Box 432, Series 200R, Subgroup 2, RG1, RF, RAC.

31. Folder: Program and Policy 1962–1963, Box 1, Series 925, Subgroup 2, RG1, RF, RAC.

32. The University of Buffalo received the grant of $200,000 ($1.6 million in 2017) toward the establishment of its center of performing and creative arts under the joint direction of Lukas Foss and Allen Sapp. Foss had submitted the application before he was invited to serve on the committee and specified that he would only participate if his application received fair judgment. He was, however, on the committee when that recommendation was made. Also see Renee Levine Packer, *This Life of Sounds: Evenings for New Music in Buffalo* (Oxford: Oxford University Press, 2010).

33. Folder: Symphony Orchestras—Composers-in-Residence 1965–1970, Box 425, Series 200R, Subgroup 2, RG1, RF, RAC.

34. Other individual awards included those to creative writers, theater directors, visual artists, and choreographers. Folder: Concert Artists Program 1971, Box 10, Series VI, FA640, Ford Foundation (FF), RAC. These competitions were designated Foundation Administered Projects (FAPs). FAPs were approved "when the Foundation believe[d] it [could] advantageously supervise an activity itself and thus [did] not need or desire an outside organization as grantee." Willard Hertz, "Questions and Answers Regarding Philanthropic and Financial Practices and Policies," 18 06 1963, Report 10457, Catalogued Reports, FF, RAC. These types of projects, a form of self-granting, were unique to the Ford Foundation, at least in the arts category, and did not exist within the grantmaking of the Rockefeller Foundation. Both foundations greatly preferred to serve the role of grantmaker, providing grants to other organizations, rather than operating the programs themselves. Given this stance, Ford FAPs were especially rare. In 1962, for example, only $3.6 million ($29.2 million in 2017) was spent on FAPs, compared to its overall grants outlay of $223.3 million ($1.81 billion).

35. From W. McNeil Lowry, 05 01 1975, Folder: Concert Artists Program 1971, Box 10, Series VI, FA640, FF, RAC.

36. Request for Grant Action, ibid.

37. "Transcript: H/A Conference January 3 & 4, 1958," Folder: Meeting of January 3–4, 1958—Economic & Social Positions of the Arts & the Artist, Box 36, Series XI, FA640, FF, RAC.

38. "The Arts and the Ford Foundation," 12 1968, Folder: The Arts and the Ford Foundation, December 1968, Box 7, Series IV, FA582, FF, RAC.

39. "Arts Program Evaluation (1957–1961) and Statement of Current Objectives and Policies," 12 1961, Report 07516, Catalogued Reports, FF, RAC.

40. In her statement at the Senate hearings before the Subcommittee on Foundations in 1974, Hanks claimed that the use of "professional advisers in developing policies and recommending on specific applications" were developed by foundations in their fellowships to individual artists and then similarly adopted by the Arts Endowment. Folder: Statement: SubComm on Foundations (Senate) Nov. 25, 1974, Box 4, A1 Entry 5, Record Group 288 (RG288), the National Archives at College Park, Maryland (Archives II). The Rockefeller Brothers Fund was distinct from the Rockefeller Foundation and was considered more a project of John D. Rockefeller Jr.'s sons, John D. Rockefeller III, Nelson, Laurance, Winthrop, and David, but its ties with the Rockefeller Foundation were still strong.

41. "Proposed Panel Resolution," Folder: NCA Third Meeting (Nov. 12–14, 1965), Box 1, A1 Entry 18, RG288, Archives II.

42. Ibid.

43. From Roger Stevens to Aaron Copland, 04 07 1967, Folder: C, Box 6, A1 Entry 20, RG288, Archives II.

44. "Proceedings, November 3, 1967," Folder: Tenth Meeting (Nov. 3, 1967), Box 3, A1 Entry 18, RG288, Archives II.

45. From Roger Stevens to Harold Weston, 29 05 1967, Folder: V, Box 11, A1 Entry 20, RG288, Archives II.

46. From Roger Stevens to Congressman Joelson, 09 06 1967, Folder: J, Box 8, A1 Entry 20, RG288, Archives II.

47. From Michael Straight to Nancy Hanks, 20 11 1971, Folder: Duty Statement, Box 9, A1 Entry 26, RG288, Archives II.

48. "Panels: Definition, Endowment Program Use, Responsibilities, Membership, Criteria for Selection, Solicitations for Membership, Selection Procedures," 05 1975, Folder: Guide Forms for Program Use, Box 9, A1 Entry 26, RG288, Archives II.

49. "Draft of Letter to Music Panel Members," 21 11 1969, Folder: A, Box 1, A1 Entry 3, RG288, Archives II.

50. "Michael Straight's Response to Insert 1533: How Panelists Are Selected," 12 02 1976, Folder: Panel Procedures, Box 9, A1 Entry 26, RG288, Archives II.

51. From Walter Anderson to Nancy Hanks, Subject: Suggested Changes in Panel Structure, 11 11 1971, Folder: Harlow Heneman—Chairman of Task Force, Box 5, A1 Entry 1, RG288, Archives II.

52. Howard Pollack, *Aaron Copland: The Life and Work of an Uncommon Man* (New York: Henry Holt and Company, 1999). For example, Pollack cites composer William Schuman, who said that "Aaron was always tactful," as well as theater director Harold Clurman, who noted that Copland was "the most tactful, knowing exactly what to say to each person. . . . He always knows exactly the right thing to say in the right circumstances," 5.

53. From Tom Freeman to Nancy Hanks and Michael Straight, Re: Survey of Panel Operations, 08 10 1974, Folder: M. Straight—Policy Papers, Box 9, A1 Entry 26, RG288, Archives II. By contrast, currently an electronic, web-based voting software is used today.

54. The dance program, on the other hand, had experimented with, and adopted, a ballot method of voting. All applications were discussed first, and then voting took place at the end of the meeting. There were perceived advantages to this system: it enabled panelists to gain a better perspective and overview of all the grants; it helped avoid prolonged discussion or last-minute emotional comments that might negatively influence voting; and it allowed panelists to vote independently and secretly. A central disadvantage was that without transparency, panelists could not be held accountable for the way they voted.

55. From Gunther Schuller to Nancy Hanks, 05 10 1976, Folder: Guide Forms for Program Use, Box 9, A1 Entry 26, RG288, Archives II.

56. From Walter Anderson to Gunther Schuller, 16 11 1976, ibid.

57. I would like to thank Carol Oja for allowing me to borrow Mark Tucker's collection of RAAM.

58. "Report on the Recorded Anthology of American Music," Folder 35, Box 6, Series 925, Subgroup 2, RG3, RAC.

59. Ibid.

60. Mario di Bonaventura, "Preliminary Conclusions," 20 12 1972, Folder: Recording April 1973, Box 7, Series 925, Subgroup 2, RG3, RF, RAC.

61. From Charles Hamm to Howard Klein, Subject: The Proposed American Music Recording Project by the Rockefeller Foundation, ibid.

62. For a more in-depth study, see Michael Sy Uy, "The Recorded Anthology of American Music and the Rockefeller Foundation: Expertise, Deliberation, and Commemoration in the Bicentennial Celebrations," *American Music* 35, no. 1 (2017): 75–93.

63. Herman Krawitz, "Final Report," 10 09 1979, Folder 48L, Box 8B, Series 925, Subgroup 2, RG3, RF, RAC.

64. Folder: Recording Minutes 1973–1984, Box 9, Series 925, Subgroup 2, RG3, RF, RAC (my emphasis).

65. "Reports Resulting from Meeting, April 18, 1973," Folder 39, Box 7, Series 925, Subgroup 2, RG3, RF, RAC (my emphasis).

66. Carol Oja, "'Picked Young Men,' Facilitating Women, and Emerging Composers: Establishing an American Prix de Rome," in *Music and Musical Composition at the American Academy in Rome*, ed. Martin Brody (Rochester, NY: University of Rochester Press, 2014), 160.

67. Jann Pasler, "Chapter 11: The Political Economy of Composition in the American University, 1965–1985," in *Writing Through Music: Essays on Music, Culture, and Politics* (Oxford: Oxford University Press, 2008): 318–62.

68. Pasler noted that before 1975, no women served on the NEA's music advisory panel.

69. Emily Abrams Ansari, "'Masters of the President's Music': Cold War Composers and the United States Government" (Harvard University, 2009), 8; and Emily Abrams Ansari, *The Sound of a Superpower: Musical Americanism and the Cold War* (New York: Oxford University Press, 2018). Examining the American National Theater and Academy and the U.S. Information Agency, Ansari points out that many of the composers represented "the compositional mainstream," were trained at institutions mostly on the East Coast, and wrote music for "traditional ensembles in mostly tonal and chromatic harmonic language," 5.

70. From Nancy Hanks to Senator Lee Metcalf, 22 04 1975, Folder: Panel Procedures, Box 9, A1 Entry 26, RG288, Archives II.

71. Collins and Evans, *Rethinking Expertise*, 64. Collins and Evans point out that the term "referred" is taken from the idea of "referred pain"—for example, when a back injury results in pain in the leg.

72. It should be noted that the NEA's criteria of evaluation—as has the composition of its panels—have continuously evolved and changed over the years. Currently, the Art Works program reviews applications according to "artistic excellence," or the quality of the artists, the organizations, and the significance of the project, and "artistic merit," or the project's creativity and innovation, engagement with the public, and overall meeting the "highest standards of excellence." http://arts.gov/grants-organizations/art-works/application-review (Accessed 03 10 2015).

73. At the Eleventh Meeting of the NCA in April 1968, the majority of applications were rejected because there was "no program at this time [that] cover[ed] this type of activity." Among other reasons were that the organization could receive other sources of funding, that the Arts Endowment did not support deficit funding, or that new projects essentially duplicating existing ones were not funded. Folder: Eleventh Meeting (Apr. 19–21, 1968), Box 3, A1 Entry 18, RG288, Archives II.

74. Ibid.

75. Interview with Joshua Rifkin, 10 09 2015.

76. Interview with Herman Krawitz, 02 02 2016.

77. Pollack, *Aaron Copland*, 193.

78. Nigel Simeone, ed., *The Leonard Bernstein Letters* (New Haven, CT: Yale University Press, 2013).

79. Numerous correspondences could be found between Foss and Bernstein in the edited letters.

80. Pollack, *Aaron Copland*, 200.

81. From Roger Stevens to Aaron Copland, 08 07 1967, Folder: C, Box 6, A1 Entry 20, RG288, Archives II. Stevens had left the choice of a third member completely up to Copland.

82. Paul Michael Covey, "'No Restrictions in Any Way on Style': The Ford Foundation's Composers in Public Schools Program, 1959–1969," *American Music* 33, no. 1 (2015): 89–130.

83. Raymond Murphy, *Social Closure: The Theory of Monopolization and Exclusion* (Oxford: Clarendon Press, 1988).

84. From Gunther Schuller to Norman Lloyd, 06 12 1965, Subject: Regarding the Evaluation of the Modern and Contemporary Music Program at Iowa, Folder: University of Iowa—Music 1965 (contemporary works), Box 449, Series 200R, Subgroup 1, RG1, RF, RAC.

85. Edge, "What Is Reputation?"

CHAPTER 2

1. Dwight Macdonald, "The Philanthropoids," *New Yorker*, December 10, 1955, 98. Also published in Dwight Macdonald, *The Ford Foundation: The Men and the Millions* (New York: Reynal, 1956), 57.

2. Ibid., 68.

3. My use is also in contrast to foundation-specific use of the term "officer" to refer only to those positions with chief executive responsibilities, e.g., the president, vice presidents, the treasurer, etc.

4. The Ford Foundation was the exception because it paid a salary to its board of trustees members.

5. Independent Commission, "A Report to Congress on the National Endowment for the Arts," 09 1990. I thank NEA music specialist Court Burns for this reference.

6. Ibid., Congressional Record, 15 09 1965.

7. Interview with Ana Steele, 23 02 2015.

8. Straight, *Nancy Hanks, An Intimate Portrait*, 185.

9. From Howard Klein to John H. Knowles, Inter-office correspondence, 18 09 1974, Folder: Program and Policy July–December 1974, Box 2, Series 925, Subgroup 2, Record Group 3 (RG3), Rockefeller Foundation (RF), Rockefeller Archive Center, Tarrytown, New York (RAC).

10. "Guidelines for Foundation Staff: Grants to Organizations," 24 08 1972, Report 9547, Catalogued Reports, Ford Foundation (FF), RAC.

11. From Nancy Hanks to Robert P. Mayo, Director, Bureau of the Budget, 02 03 1970, Folder: Office of Management & Budget, Box 20, A1 Entry 2, RG288, Archives II.

12. Folder: Grant Requests 1972 2/3, Box 7, Series IV, FA582, FF, RAC.

13. Howard Klein, "'The Arts: Beyond the Cultural Boom': A Report on the Program in Cultural Development, The Rockefeller Foundation 1968–1972," 1972, Folder: Program and Policy Reports Pro-1–Pro-2 1966, Box 3, Series 925, Subgroup 2, RG3, RF, RAC.

14. From Chadbourne Gilpatric to John S. Edwards, 16 04 1963, Folder: American Symphony Orchestra League (general support) 1963–1968, Box 283, Series 200R, Subgroup 2, RG1, RF, RAC.

15. Formally, one's habitus is the set of "durable" and "transposable" dispositions (i.e., worldview and experiences) that simultaneously reflect a "structured structure" (i.e., a system that is set) and a "structuring structure" (i.e., a system that is set but also changing over time). Pierre Bourdieu, *Distinction: A Social Critique of the Judgement of Taste* (London: Routledge & Kegan Paul, 1986), 53.

16. By "durable," Bourdieu means that these dispositions are long lasting and steadily affect life trajectories.

17. Kwame Anthony Appiah, *The Lies That Bind: Rethinking Identity* (New York: Liveright Publishing Corporation, 2018), 11.

18. Mahzarin R. Banaji and Anthony G. Greenwald, *Blindspot: Hidden Biases of Good People* (New York: Delacorte Press, 2013).

19. http://spottheblindspot.com/the-iat/ (Accessed 19 11 2015).

20. Also see David Brackett, *Categorizing Sound: Genre and Twentieth-Century Popular Music* (Oakland: University of California Press, 2016) on genres and the mapping of musical style and categories of group identification.

21. Banaji and Greenwald, *Blindspot: Hidden Biases of Good People*, 4.

22. Mary Brucker and Merrimon Cuninggim, "The Foundation's People and Their Work," 18 02 1975, Report 11002, Catalogued Reports, FF, RAC.

23. There was some overlap between teaching and academic administration experience. Brucker and Cuninggim had data on 254 total professional staff.

24. Macdonald, "The Philanthropoids," 57.

25. Mary Brucker and Merrimon Cuninggim, "The Foundation's People and Their Work," 18 02 1975, Report 11002, Catalogued Reports, FF, RAC.

26. Joel Colton and Malcolm Richardson, "The Humanities and 'The Well-Being of Mankind,'" 1982, Folder: Program and Policy History Supplementary Material ". . . A Half-Century of the Humanities at the R.F.," Box 8, Series 911, Subgroup 2, RG3, RF, RAC.

27. From J. G. Harrar to Barry Bingham, 15 10 1963, marked personal, Folder: Program and Policy 1960–1971, Box 2, Series 911, Subgroup 2, RG3, RF, RAC. The restructuring of the divisions in 1962, however, involved some shuffling and frustration, and Fahs left the foundation to become the cultural attaché to the American embassy in Japan. Boyd Compton, Robert Crawford, and Gerald Freund, who became a nucleus for an emerging arts program, also divided their time with the humanities and social sciences.

28. "Five Years of the Rockefeller Foundation 1952–1957: A Review and Appraisal by a Committee of the Foundation's Board of Trustees," 04 11 1958, marked confidential, Folder: Program and Policy 1958–1960, Box 27, Series 911, Subgroup 2, RG3, RF, RAC.

29. The Rockefeller Foundation Grant Evaluation Form, Folder: Recording 1963–1966, Box 6, Series 925, Subgroup 2, RG3, RF, RAC.

30. From Edward F. D'Arms to Charles B. Fahs, John Marshall, and Chadbourne Gilpatric, Inter-office correspondence, 19 01 1954, Subject: DH Program - II, Folder: Program and Policy 1951–1954, Box 1, Series 911, Subgroup 1, RG3, RF, RAC.

31. Michèle Lamont, *How Professors Think: Inside the Curious World of Academic Judgment* (Cambridge, MA: Harvard University Press, 2010), 8.

32. Ibid., 46.

33. Ibid., 113. This expectation was in addition to showing up fully prepared for discussion, a strong sense of responsibility and work ethic, demonstrated intellectual breadth, openness to interdisciplinary endeavors, and respecting others' expertise.

34. From Nancy Hanks, Memorandum for Program Directors, 12 01 1970, Subject: Panel or Advisory Meetings, Folder: Panel Procedures, Box 9, A1 Entry 26, RG288, Archives II.

35. From Robert Goheen to George Harrar, "Request for a Grant for Musical Research to Be Done with the Aid of Computers," 10 08 1964, Folder: Princeton—Musical Research 1964–1967, Box 408, Series 200R, Subgroup 2, RG1, RF, RAC.

36. From Martin Bookspan to Gerald Freund, 29 06 1964, ibid.

37. By comparison, a grant to the Columbia-Princeton Electronic Music Center was decided in the same year, and Bookspan's recommended evaluators to Freund were Harold Schonberg, Jay Harrison, Everett Helm, Eugene Ormandy, Leopold Stokowski, George Szell, Alfred Frankenstein, and Gunther Schuller. From Martin Bookspan to Gerald Freund, 10 04 1964, Folder: Columbia University—Electronic Music (Luening, Otto) (Ussachevsky, Vladimir) 1964–1966, 1981, Box 315, Series 200R, Subgroup 2, RG1, RF, RAC.

38. I state at least one because Jacques Barzun (Columbia University) reported in a speech entitled "Man and the Machine" at a conference at Yale that "two of the five judges said that this was good, and three said that this was bad." Based on the correspondence kept in the archival file, this was not the case.

39. From Richard Franko Goldman to Gerald Freund, 15 07 1964, Folder: Princeton—Musical Research 1964–1967, Box 408, Series 200R, Subgroup 2, RG1, RF, RAC.

40. From Gerald Freund to Martin Bookspan, 17 07 1964, ibid.

41. From Martin Bookspan to Gerald Freund, 24 07 1964, ibid.

42. From Stefan Bauer-Mengelberg to Gerald Freund, 10 08 1964, ibid.

43. William H. Whyte Jr., "What Are the Foundations Up To?," *Fortune*, October 1955.

44. Inderjeet Parmar, *Foundations of the American Century: The Ford, Carnegie, and Rockefeller Foundations in the Rise of American Power* (New York: Columbia University Press, 2012), 31.

45. Interview with Ana Steele, 23 02 2015.

46. Other major contributors to the establishment of the BCA included David Rockefeller ($50,000; $360,000 in 2017), John D. Rockefeller III ($50,000), the Old Dominion Foundation ($75,000; $550,000 in 2017), the Rockefeller Brothers Fund ($225,000; $1.7 million in 2017), and the Ford Foundation ($225,000). From G. A. McLellan to Norman Lloyd, 14 08 1968, Folder: Business Committee for the Arts, Inc. (general support) 1967–1969, Box 304, Series 200R, Subgroup 2, RG1, RF, RAC.

47. From Gerald Freund to Norman Lloyd, Inter-office correspondence, 07 05 1968, Subject: RF Grant for Business Committee for the Arts, Inc., Folder: Business Committee for the Arts, Inc. (general support) 1967–1969, Box 304, Series 200R, Subgroup 2, RG1, RF, RAC.

48. Mary Anna Culleton Colwell, "The Foundation Connection: Links Among Foundations and Recipient Organizations," in *Philanthropy and Cultural Imperialism: The Foundations at Home and Abroad*, ed. Robert F. Arnove (Boston: G. K. Hall & Co., 1980), 413–52.

49. Colwell, "The Foundation Connection," 416.

50. These actions included not submitting applications under their names, voting on certain proposals, being present at certain discussions, and avoiding certain activities for up to a year after leaving the NEA. From Robert Wade to NEA Panel and Council Members,

06 1972, Subject: Conflict of Interest, Folder: General Counsel, Box 5, A1 Entry 1, RG288, Archives II.

51. Pierre Bourdieu, *Distinction*, 66.

52. Harry Collins and Robert Evans, *Rethinking Expertise* (Chicago: University of Chicago Press, 2007), 119.

53. Ibid., 8.

54. Parmar, *Foundations of the American Century*, 15.

55. Ibid.

56. Frank Fischer, *Democracy and Expertise* (Oxford: Oxford University Press, 2009), 5.

57. Ibid.

58. The Danish consensus conference is a standard model.

59. Robert F. Arnove, ed., "Introduction," in *Philanthropy and Cultural Imperialism: The Foundations at Home and Abroad* (Boston: G. K. Hall & Co., 1980), 18.

CHAPTER 3

1. National Endowment for the Arts, "Annual Report 1975," 2.

2. Joan Roelofs, *Foundations and Public Policy: The Mask of Pluralism* (Albany: State University of New York Press, 2003). The civic sector goes by other names as well, including the third sector, the nonprofit sector, the voluntary sector, the independent sector, or civil society, more generally.

3. Joel L. Fleishman, *The Foundation: A Great American Secret: How Private Wealth Is Changing the World* (New York: Public Affairs, 2007), 3.

4. Pierre Bourdieu and Randal Johnson, *The Field of Cultural Production: Essays on Art and Literature*, European Perspectives (New York: Columbia University Press, 1993). The concept of the field has played a key role in much of Bourdieu's writings on the sociology of art, such as *Distinction* (1984), *The Field of Cultural Production* (1993), and *The Rules of Art* (1996).

5. Antonia Pantoja, Wilhemina Perry, and Barbara Blourock, "Towards the Development of Theory: Cultural Pluralism Redefined," *Journal of Sociology and Social Welfare* 4, no. 1 (1976): 126.

6. The question of government crowding out was one of the primary objections against the founding of the Arts Endowment—in fact, Helen Thompson, director of the American Symphony Orchestra League, had initially testified that 91% of orchestras were against government funding, for fear that it would reduce private contributions. Fannie Taylor and Anthony Barresi, *The Arts at a New Frontier: The National Endowment for the Arts* (New York: Plenum Press, 1984), 44. Representative Thomas B. Curtis (R-MO) facetiously named his theory that government intervention drove out private incentives or obligations to give the "Curtis law," after himself.

7. Margaret Wyszomirski, "Congress, Presidents, and the Arts: Collaboration and Struggle," *Annals of the American Academy of Political and Social Science* 499 (1988): 130.

8. Pierre Bourdieu, *Distinction: A Social Critique of the Judgment of Taste*, trans. Richard Nice (Cambridge, MA: Harvard University Press, 1984), 231.

9. A Bourdieusian analysis of the field includes examining the position of the field vis-à-vis the field of power, mapping out the objective structure of relations between the positions occupied by agents who compete for legitimate forms of authority in the field, and analyzing the habitus of agents—the systems of dispositions they have acquired. Pierre Bourdieu and Loïc J. D. Wacquant, *An Invitation to Reflexive Sociology* (Chicago: University of Chicago Press, 1992), 104–7.

10. Howard S. Becker, *Art Worlds* (Berkeley: University of California Press, 1982), x. Yet the advantage of examining "fields" over "art worlds" is how the concept of the field is mutually bound with Bourdieu's other ideas on "capital" and "habitus."

11. Education scholar Patricia Thomson further clarifies, "agents who occupy particular positions understand how to behave in the field, and this understanding not only feels 'natural' but can be explained using the truths, or *doxa*, that are common parlance within the field." Patricia Thomson, "Field," in *Pierre Bourdieu Key Concepts*, ed. Michael Grenfell, 2nd ed. (Durham, NC: Acumen, 2012), 68. Doxa, or "the rules of the game," are so taken for granted that they are nondiscursive and accepted as "the way things are." They are naturalized in a way, however, that is misrecognized so that individuals in society fail to see that these unwritten rules are arbitrarily determined, are perpetuated under systems of hierarchy, and are reinforced by actors within society.

12. Pierre Bourdieu, "The Forms of Capital," in *Handbook of Theory and Research for the Sociology of Education*, ed. John Richardson (New York: Greenwood, 1986), 241–58.

13. Regarding musical scores as a form of cultural capital, see especially Louis K. Epstein, "Toward a Theory of Patronage: Funding for Music Composition in France, 1918–1939" (Harvard University, 2013).

14. As Bourdieu notes, changes in habitus occur slowly because of the "durability" of one's habitus. He also refers to the gap in time between changes in the field and changes in habitus as "hysteresis."

15. Kathleen McCarthy, "From Cold War to Cultural Development: The International Cultural Activities of the Ford Foundation, 1950–1980," *Daedalus* 116, no. 1 Philanthropy, Patronage, Politics (1987): 93.

16. Rockefeller Foundation, "Annual Report 1953," 7–8.

17. Ibid.

18. Rockefeller Foundation, "Annual Report 1957," 16–17.

19. "An Enlarged Program in the Arts: Humanities and the Arts Program Policy Discussion Paper," 17-18 03 1960, Report 02782, Catalogued Reports, Ford Foundation (FF), Rockefeller Archive Center, Tarrytown, New York (RAC).

20. "The Arts and the Ford Foundation: 1969," Folder: The Arts and the Ford Foundation December 1968, Box 7, Series IV, FA582, FF, RAC.

21. Folder: An Enlarged Program in the Arts March 1960, Box 6, Series IV, FA582, FF, RAC.

22. The passing of the National Foundation on the Arts and Humanities Act of 1965 was not a surprise. The year before, the NCA was established through the National Arts and Cultural Development Act of 1964.

23. Rockefeller Foundation, "Annual Report 1965," 6.

24. From Henry T. Heald to Officers and Directors, Subject: Relations with Government Programs, 04 05 1965, Folder: Henry T Heald/W McNeil Lowry Memoranda 1/1/61-5/4/65, Box 16, Series IV, FA582, FF, RAC.

25. "The Ford Foundation Programs and Developing Federal Activities," ibid.

26. From E. S. Staples to Policy Planning Files, Subject: Conversation with James Armsey on Policy and Planning Questions, 11 06 1965, Folder: Policy and Planning Questions—Meetings with Domestic Programs 3/30/65–6/11/65, Box 21, Series IV, FA582, FF, RAC.

27. Gerald Freund, "Concerning a Philosophy of the Arts Program," Folder: Program and Policy 1964–1968, Box 1, Series 925, Subgroup 2, Record Group (RG) 3, Rockefeller Foundation (RF), RAC.

28. From Frederick Gash to Norman Lloyd, 31 03 1967, Folder L, Box 8, A1 Entry 20, Record Group 288 (RG288), The National Archives at College Park, Maryland, (Archives II). "Obituary: Frederick Gash, 82, A Patron of the Arts," *New York Times*, October 6, 1993.

29. "Proceedings, Saturday Morning Session, November 13, 1965," Folder: NCA Third Meeting (Nov. 12–14, 1965), Box 1, A1 Entry 18, RG288, Archives II.

30. Ibid.

31. Merrimon Cuninggim, *Private Money and Public Service: The Role of Foundations in American Society* (New York: McGraw-Hill Book Company, 1972), 12.

32. Ibid., 13

33. "Proceedings, Saturday Morning Session, November 13, 1965," Folder: NCA Third Meeting (Nov. 12–14, 1965), Box 1, A1 Entry 18, RG288, Archives II.

34. From Donald Engle to Roger Stevens, 29 11 1967, Folder E, Box 6, A1 Entry 20, RG288, Archives II.

35. National Endowment for the Arts, "Annual Report 1970," 56.

36. Rockefeller Foundation, "Annual Report 1972," 8.

37. Robert H. Bremner, *American Philanthropy*, 2nd ed. (Chicago: University of Chicago Press, 1988).

38. From Nancy Hanks, "Memorandum for Program Directors," 12 06 1974, Folder: Memorandums 1973–1974, Box 7, A1 Entry 1, RG288, Archives II. Emphasis in original.

39. Rockefeller Brothers Fund, *The Performing Arts: Problems and Prospects: Rockefeller Panel Report on the Future of Theatre, Dance, Music in America* (New York: McGraw-Hill Book Company, 1965), 147.

40. Folder: Office of Management & Budget, Box 20, A1 Entry 2, RG288, Archives II. The two other operating principles were "selectivity and professional quality" and "cooperating with the artistic and arts education communities."

41. Ibid.

42. Frederick de W. Bolman, "Caution Needed in Matching Grants," *Foundation News*, Folder: B, Box 5, A1 Entry 20, RG288, Archives II.

43. Ibid.

44. "Gifts and Matching Fund Opportunities Through the National Endowment for the Arts Treasury Fund," 11 04 1970, Folder: Memorandums to Staff, Box 6, A1 Entry 1, RG288, Archives II. Emphasis in original.

45. National Endowment for the Arts, "Annual Report 1966."

46. National Endowment for the Arts, "Annual Report 1969."

47. To Robert P. Mayo, Director, Bureau of Budget, "National Foundation on the Arts and the Humanities, Justification for Request for Supplemental Appropriation of $4 Million in Federal Matching Funds for Fiscal Year 1970," 21 10 1969, Folder: Budget Bureau, 1966-69, Box 3, A1 Entry 21, RG288, Archives II.

48. Ibid.

49. National Endowment for the Arts, "Annual Report 1970," "Annual Report 1971," "Annual Report 1972," "Annual Report 1973," "Annual Report 1974," "Annual Report 1975," "Annual Report 1976."

50. The NEA funded the tours of the American Ballet Company, American Ballet Theatre, City Center Joffrey Ballet, and Martha Graham Center of Contemporary Dance in this way.

51. The program included grants to the Dallas Civic Opera Company ($751,110), the Lyric Opera of Chicago ($1 million), the New York City Opera ($1 million), the San Francisco Opera Association ($1 million), and the Kentucky Opera Association ($61,593), *inter alia*.

52. Fleishman, *The Foundation*, 53.

53. Roelofs, *Foundations and Public Policy*. In 1978, Congress reduced the excise tax from 4% to 2%, when it determined that the IRS was collecting three times the actual cost of monitoring foundation operations. Bremner, *American Philanthropy*, 190.

54. Rockefeller Foundation, "Annual Report 1969," section on "The Congress and Foundations," 3.

55. From Richard Magat to McGeorge Bundy, 06 10 1966, Folder: Bundy, 1966, Box 6, Series I, FA728, FF, RAC.

56. From Harlow Heneman to Nancy Hanks, 01 10 1973, Folder: Harlow Heneman— Chairman of Task Force, Box 5, A1 Entry 1, RG288, Archives II.

57. "Report of the Task Force on Policies and Operations of the National Endowment for the Arts," 10 1973, ibid.

58. Folder: Program and Policy March–June 1974, Box 2, Series 925, Subgroup 2, RG3, RF, RAC.

59. Folder: Rockefeller Foundation, Box 16, A1 Entry 2, RG288, Archives II.

60. "How Can Foundations Help the Arts?," Folder: Program and Policy Reports Pro-6a– Pro-6b 1974, Box 3, Series 925, Subgroup 2, RG3, RF, RAC. All following quotations taken from this note.

61. Ames, however, did not cite data to substantiate this claim.

62. From Nancy Hanks to John H. Knowles, 12 06 1974, Folder: K, Box 8, A1 Entry 3, RG288, Archives II.

63. Cuninggim, *Private Money and Public Service*, 79.

64. Hanks's role as "one of the boys" was reinforced by her strong background in foundation work, coming from the Rockefeller Brothers Fund, and having strong professional and personal relationships with the Rockefeller family. She thus owned a high amount of social capital that also shaped her perspectives on the role of foundation funding.

65. Roelofs, *Foundations and Public Policy*, 121.

66. Robert F. Arnove, ed., "Introduction," in *Philanthropy and Cultural Imperialism: The Foundations at Home and Abroad* (Boston: G. K. Hall & Co., 1980).

67. Michael Grenfell and Cheryl Hardy, *Art Rules: Pierre Bourdieu and the Visual Arts* (Oxford: Berg, 2007), 30–31.

CHAPTER 4

1. Winthrop Sargeant, *Listening to Music* (Westport, CT: Greenwood Press, 1958), 15.

2. To Sargeant, "the foundation style" was written by "modern composers," themselves a product of "the attempted revolution in musical technique that was initiated . . . by [Igor] Stravinsky, [Arnold] Schoenberg, and the group known in Paris as 'Les Six,'" ibid., 13–14. He equated modern composers to "formalists." Furthermore, "the music is composed, not for audiences, but for other formalist composers," 14–15. Sargeant's terminology is notably different from my own and other present-day understandings of "formalism," or even the lineage connecting Stravinsky, Schoenberg, and *Les Six*.

3. Ibid., 171.

4. Ford Foundation, *Sharps and Flats: A Report on Ford Foundation Assistance to American Music* (New York: Ford Foundation, 1980), 23.

5. For example, see Wayne Lee Gay's recent review of composer Gabriela Lena Frank, which asserts that "Frank is definitely no ivory tower composer," instead focusing on her philosophy of *"mestizaje"* and her multiracial background. Wayne Lee Gay, "Frankly Listening," *Theater Jones*, April 5, 2017, http://www.theaterjones.com/ntx/reviews/20170404064832/2017-04-05/The-Cliburn/Gabriela-Lena-Frank (Accessed 30 04 2017).

6. Nadine Hubbs, *The Queer Composition of America's Sound: Gay Modernists, American Music, and National Identity* (Berkeley: University of California Press, 2004), 162. According to Hubbs, composers associated "atonal and dissonant music" and musical serialism with "exclusivity and elitism, as well as heteronormative masculinity." See also Carol Oja, *Making Music Modern: New York in the 1920s* (Oxford: Oxford University Press, 2000).

7. Joseph N. Straus, "The Myth of Serial 'Tyranny' in the 1950s and 1960s," *Musical Quarterly* 83, no. 3 (1999): 301–43 and Joseph N. Straus, *Twelve-Tone Music in America* (Cambridge: Cambridge University Press, 2009).

8. Musicologists Anne Shreffler and Michael Broyles have pointed out in separate essays, however, certain gaps in Straus's interpretations regarding aspects of categorization and methodology. Anne Shreffler, "The Myth of Empirical Historiography: A Response to Joseph N. Straus," *Musical Quarterly* 84, no. 1 (2000): 30–39; Michael Broyles, *Mavericks and Other Traditions in American Music* (New Haven, CT: Yale University Press, 2004). Also see Peter Schmelz, "Review: Twelve-Tone Music in America," *Notes* 67, no. 2 (2010): 322; Martin Brody, "Review: Joseph Straus, Twelve-Tone Music in America," *Journal of the American Musicological Society* 65, no. 1 (2012): 291.

9. Hubbs, *The Queer Composition of America's Sound*, 164.

10. See also Anne Shreffler, "Ideologies of Serialism: Stravinsky's 'Threni' and the Congress for Cultural Freedom," in *Music and the Aesthetics of Modernity*, ed. Karol Berger and Anthony Newcomb (Cambridge, MA: Harvard University Press, 2005), 217–45.

11. Rockefeller Foundation grants went to both liberal arts colleges and research universities, but for simplicity, I refer to them both when I use the term "university."

12. "Precursors to a New Philanthropy," The Rockefeller Foundation: A Digital History, https://rockfound.rockarch.org/precursors-to-a-new-philanthropy (Accessed 18 01 2019).

13. From Norman Lloyd to Kenneth W. Thompson and John G. Harrar, Inter-office correspondence, 27 09 1968, Subject: Arts Program—Projection for Future, Folder: Program and Policy 1964–1968, Box 1, Series 925, Subgroup 2, Record Group (RG) 3, Rockefeller Foundation (RF), Rockefeller Archive Center, Tarrytown, New York (RAC).

14. Emily Abrams Ansari, *The Sound of a Superpower: Musical Americanism and the Cold War* (New York: Oxford University Press, 2018), 37.

15. Folder: Barnard College—Electronic Music 1952–1953, Box 296, Series 200R, Subgroup 2, RG1, RF, RAC. Also see Rachel Vandagriff, "The Pre-History of the Columbia Princeton Electronic Music Center" (American Musicological Society, Vancouver, Canada, 2016). I thank Vandagriff for sharing her paper with me after the conference.

16. From Vladimir Ussachevsky to Charles B. Fahs, "Memorandum on Tape Music," 12 03 1953, Folder: Barnard College—Electronic Music 1952–1953, Box 296, Series 200R, Subgroup 2, RG1, RF, RAC.

17. Ibid.

18. From Milton Babbitt to John Marshall, 14 06 1957, Folder: Columbia University—Electronic Music (Luening, Otto) (Ussachevsky, Vladimir) 1957–May 1958, Box 315, Series 200R, Subgroup 2, RG1, RF, RAC.

19. From John Marshall, Inter-office correspondence, 27 06 1957, Subject: Milton Babbitt's Proposal for Further Work in Electronic Music, ibid.

20. Interview John Marshall with Vladimir Ussachevsky, 01 05 1958, ibid.

21. From Vladimir Ussachevsky to John Marshall, 18 08 1958, Folder: Columbia University—Electronic Music (Luening, Otto) (Ussachevsky, Vladimir) June–December 1958, Box 315, Series 200R, Subgroup 2, RG1, RF, RAC.

22. Unfortunately, the memoranda do not indicate which recordings were sent.

23. From Robert S. Morison, Inter-office correspondence, 07 11 1958, Folder: Columbia University—Electronic Music (Luening, Otto) (Ussachevsky, Vladimir) June–December 1958, Box 315, Series 200R, Subgroup 2, RG1, RF, RAC. It is not known which record Ms. Morison was referring to.

24. Robert W. July interview with Vladimir Ussachevsky, 06 11 1958, ibid. The officers' fact sheet to the trustees included short biographies of the composers and recommenders involved. The fact sheets focused on academic credentials, prestigious fellowships, and important compositions, in that order.

25. From Vladimir Ussachevsky to Charles B. Fahs, 28 11 1958, Folder: Columbia University—Electronic Music (Luening, Otto) (Ussachevsky, Vladimir) June–December 1958, Box 315, Series 200R, Subgroup 2, RG1, RF, RAC.

26. From Roger Sessions to Charles B. Fahs, 18 11 1958, ibid.

27. Milton Babbitt, "Who Cares If You Listen?," *High Fidelity* 8, no. 2 (1958): 38–40, 126–27.

28. Robert W. July interview with Milton Babbitt, 10 12 1959, Folder: Columbia University—Electronic Music (Luening, Otto) (Ussachevsky, Vladimir) 1959–1963, Box 315, Series 200R, Subgroup 2, RG1, RF, RAC. Babbitt also discussed "experiments in increasing rhythmic complexity, chance selection of materials, and work based on highly organized, mathematically-inspired formulae."

29. Monica Hershberger, "Princeton Seminars 1959–1960," http://frommfoundation.fas.harvard.edu/princeton-seminars (Accessed 01 05 2016).

30. By comparison, Amy Beal shows how Babbitt avoided attending the Darmstadt Music Festival until 1964 and even after, "he disliked the participants and found the conditions unacceptable." Amy Beal, *New Music, New Allies: American Experimental Music in West Germany from the Zero Hour to Reunification* (Berkeley: University of California Press, 2006), 140. She also shows how American experimentalist composers relied more on European patronage, through festivals, radio broadcasts, and West German cultural institutions.

31. RF64017, Folder: University of Buffalo—Creative Music Associates 1963–June 1964 (Lukas Foss, Alan D. Sapp), Box 432, Series 200R, Subgroup 2, RG1, RF, RAC.

32. RF66059, ibid.

33. Ibid.

34. Nigel Simeone, ed., *The Leonard Bernstein Letters* (New Haven, CT: Yale University Press, 2013).

35. Renee Levine Packer, *This Life of Sounds: Evenings for New Music in Buffalo* (Oxford: Oxford University Press, 2010).

36. I thank William Robin for reminding me of this distinction, beginning in the 1960s, as well as sharing with me his materials on the Association of University Composers, whose membership list greatly overlapped with composers discussed throughout this chapter.

37. Packer, *This Life of Sounds*, 24.

38. Gerald Freund and Boyd R. Compton interview with Beatrice Witkin, Arthur Weisberg, and Peter Tandy, 24 03 1964, Folder: Rutgers University—Contemporary Ensemble June 1965–1966, Box 410, Series 200R, Subgroup 2, RG1, RF, RAC.

39. Boyd R. Compton interview with Contemporary Chamber Ensemble, 16 06 1965, ibid.

40. Norman Lloyd interview with Contemporary Chamber Ensemble, 05 10 1967, Folder: Rutgers University—Contemporary Chamber Ensemble 1967–1969, Box 411, Series 200R, Subgroup 2, RG1, RF, RAC.

41. Howard Klein interview with Visit to Rutgers, 09 05 1968, ibid.

42. From Alan Rich to Gerald Freund, 31 12 1963, Folder: University of Buffalo—Creative Music Associates 1963–June 1964 (Lukas Foss, Alan D. Sapp), Box 432, Series 200R, Subgroup 2, RG1, RF, RAC.

43. From Gerald Freund to Alan Rich, 06 01 1964, ibid.

44. From Gerald Freund to Martin Bookspan and Kenneth W. Thompson, emphasis in original, 06 05 1964, Folder: University of Washington—Music 1964–1966, Box 351, Series 200R, Subgroup 5, RG1, RF, RAC.

45. Gerald Freund diary with Bergsma, 04 11 1965, ibid.

46. RF67039, ibid.

47. Steve Swayne, *Orpheus in Manhattan: William Schuman and the Shaping of America's Musical Life* (New York: Oxford University Press, 2011), 273.

48. From William Schuman to Gerald Freund, 13 04 1964, Folder: University of Washington—Music 1964–1966, Box 351, Series 200R, Subgroup 5, RG1, RF, RAC.

49. Report to the Rockefeller Foundation, Final Report, 04 11 1974, Folder: University of Washington—Music 1970–1975, Box 351, Series 200R, Subgroup 5, RG1, RF, RAC.

50. Interview Norman Lloyd with Prof. Dorothy Klotzman, Department of Music, Brooklyn College, 14 06 1972, ibid.

51. Interview Gerald Freund, Orchestra Rehearsal, James Dixon, Conductor, 18 10 1965, Folder: University of Iowa—Music 1965 (contemporary works), Box 449, Series 200R, Subgroup 2, RG1, RF, RAC.

52. Interview Gerald Freund and Norman Lloyd with University of Iowa, Lunch, 18 10 1965, ibid.

53. Letters to Richard Franko Goldman, Peter Mennin, Gunther Schuller, and William Schuman from Norman Lloyd, 22 10 1965, ibid. Schuman admitted that he had not been there in a number of years but that the one visit he had was "positive" (he also confessed that he went as part of an all-William-Schuman program, with lectures and receptions). William Schuman to Norman Lloyd, 27 10 1965. Goldman was enthusiastic, also having given three lectures and conducting several concerts there over the past three years. From Richard Franko Goldman to Norman Lloyd, 28 10 1965. Mennin wrote that his memories were positive, and Schuller, writing from Berlin, acknowledged the "quite high" performance standards. From Peter Mennin to Norman Lloyd, 03 11 1965, and Gunther Schuller to Norman Lloyd, 06 12 1965.

54. RF65077, ibid.

55. From Richard B. Hervig, Professor of Composition, to Norman Lloyd, 30 07 1965, ibid.

56. Report to the Rockefeller Foundation, 10 06 1968, Folder: University of Iowa—Music 1966–1970, 1982, Box 449, Series 200R, Subgroup 2, RG1, RF, RAC.

57. Center for New Music, https://uiowa.edu/cnm/history (Accessed 04 07 2019).

58. Grant in Aid to the Cleveland Institute of Music, Folder: Cleveland Institute of Music (Erb, Donald) Contemporary Music Program, 1965–1967, 1969–1971, Box 311, Series 200R, Subgroup 2, RG1, RF, RAC.

59. Boyd R. Compton visit to Cleveland, Cleveland Institute of Music and Case Institute of Technology, 17–19 03 1966, ibid.

60. Boyd R. Compton interview with Donald Erb, 26 01 1966, Folder: North Carolina School of the Arts 1967–1969, Box 96, Series 200R, Subgroup 3, RG1, RF, RAC.

61. Interview Howard Klein with Donald Erb, Composer-in-Residence at Dallas Symphony, 18 03 1969, ibid. Erb served as composer in residence at Dallas in 1968.

62. CIM New Music Ensemble, https://www.cim.edu/academic-programs/ensembles/cim-newmusicensemble (Accessed 04 07 2019).

63. RF67077, Folder: North Carolina School of the Arts 1967–1969, Box 96, Series 200R, Subgroup 3, RG1, RF, RAC.

64. Ibid.

65. Folder: University of Michigan—Contemporary Music 1968–1969, Box 102, Series 200R, Subgroup 3, RG1, RF, RAC.

66. From Leslie Bassett to Howard Klein, 23 02 1973, Folder: University of Michigan—Contemporary Music 1970–1975, Box 102, Series 200R, Subgroup 3, RG1, RF, RAC.

67. GIA RF67082, Folder: University of Michigan—Contemporary Music 1968–1969, Box 102, Series 200R, Subgroup 3, RG1, RF, RAC.

68. Interview Norman Lloyd with Ross Lee Finney, 28 01 1969, ibid.

69. Interview Norman Lloyd with Ross Lee Finney, 02 02 1968, ibid.

70. Interview Boyd R. Compton with Morton Subotnick, 30 12 1965, Folder: Mills College—Music (Chamber Music Ensemble) 1965–1966, Box 378, Series 200R, Subgroup 2, RG1, RF, RAC.

71. Also see David Bernstein, ed., *The San Francisco Tape Music Center: 1960s Counterculture and the Avant-Garde* (Berkeley: University of California Press, 2008).

72. GA Arts6512, Folder: Mills College—Music (Chamber Music Ensemble) 1965–1966, Box 378, Series 200R, Subgroup 2, RG1, RF, RAC.

73. GIA RF64090, Folder: San Francisco Tape Music Center 1965, Box 413, Series 200R, Subgroup 2, RG1, RF, RAC.

74. RF 66010, ibid.

75. From Nathan Rubin to Norman Lloyd, 10 05 1967, Folder: Mills College—Music (Chamber Music Ensemble) 1967–1971, Box 378, Series 200R, Subgroup 2, RG1, RF, RAC.

76. From Norman Lloyd to Nathan Rubin, 19 05 1967, ibid.

77. Norman Lloyd interview with Robert Wert, 18 04 1969, ibid.

78. RF64041, Folder: University of Chicago—Music 1963–1965, Box 99, Series 200R, Subgroup 3, RG1, RF, RAC.

79. Of the $250,000, Rockefeller allocated $150,000 to the costs of renovating the old music building. Instead, the university decided to build an entirely new music building as part of a $2 million arts complex, which the officers agreed was a suitable revision of plans.

80. RF67036, Folder: University of Chicago—Music 1965–1969, Box 100, Series 200R, Subgroup 3, RG1, RF, RAC.

81. From Martin Bookspan to Gerald Freund, 26 03 1964, ibid. Foss cautioned the foundation against "paying for costs that the university normally undertakes." From Lukas Foss to Gerald Freund, 23 04 1964. Bookspan noted that Leonard Meyer "certainly sounds solid and intelligent" and had received positive reviews from Foss and Copland.

82. Babbitt also received two Fromm commissions: *Vision and Prayer* (1961) and *Canonical Form* (1963).

83. Gable and Wolff, *A Life for New Music*, 10.

84. Also see Rachel Vandagriff, "An Old Story in a New World: Paul Fromm, the Fromm Music Foundation, and Elliott Carter," *Journal of Musicology* 35, no. 4 (2018): 535–66.

85. From Salvatore Martirano to Norman Lloyd, 21 01 1967, Folder: University of Illinois—Contemporary Music Workshop 1967–1968, Box 427, Series 200R, Subgroup 2, RG1, RF, RAC. Martirano's letter to Lloyd did not list the performers' names.

86. Norman Lloyd interview with Salvatore Martirano, University of Illinois Urbana, 30 03 1967, ibid.

87. Packer, *This Life of Sounds*, 84

88. Interview Norman Lloyd and Gerald Freund with Ralph Shapey, 06 10 1965, Folder: University of Illinois—Contemporary Music Workshop 1967–1968, Box 427, Series 200R, Subgroup 2, RG1, RF, RAC.

89. From Salvatore Martirano to Norman Lloyd, 21 01 1967, ibid.

90. From Salvatore Martirano to Norman Lloyd, 26 10 1967, ibid.

91. Also see Catherine M. Cameron, *Dialectics in the Arts: The Rise of Experimentalism in American Music* (Westport, CT: Praeger, 1996).

92. It became coed in 1968.

93. RF66035, Folder: Sarah Lawrence College—Aeolian Chamber Players 1965–1970, Box 414, Series 200R, Subgroup 2, RG1, RF, RAC.

94. From Gerald Freund to Norman Lloyd and Martin Bookspan, 09 02 1966, ibid.

95. From Martin Bookspan, 15 02 1966, ibid.

96. From Julius Bloom to Martin Bookspan, 28 02 1966, ibid.

97. From Martin Bookspan to Gerald Freund, 16 03 1966, ibid.

98. Note from Esther Raushenbush to Gerald Freund, 17 03 1966, ibid.

99. From George Rochberg, 11 03 1966, ibid.

100. From Ralph Shapey, 14 03 1966, ibid.

101. Norman Lloyd Interview with Aeolian Chamber Players Concert of Electronic Music and Mixed Media, 24 10 1968, ibid.

102. From Esther Raushenbush to Norman Lloyd, 04 11 1968, ibid.

103. In 1994, Davidovsky joined Harvard University's Department of Music. He won many major fellowships and prizes, including the Koussevitzky fellowship, two Guggenheim fellowships, and the Pulitzer prize.

104. "Liner Notes: George Rochberg: Volume One," New World Composers Recordings (NWCR) 768, 1997.

105. George Crumb, "Peter Westergaard: Variations for Six Players," *Perspectives of New Music* 3, no. 2 (1965): 152–59.

106. Richard Taruskin, "The Third Revolution," *Oxford History of Western Music: Music in the Late Twentieth Century*, http://www.oxfordwesternmusic.com/view/Volume5/actrade-9780195384857-div1-004008.xml?rskey=tyFBrS&result=76 (Accessed 13 07 2019).

107. Lukas Foss, director of the Buffalo program, also had numerous performances of his works, like *Time Cycle* (the Ford Foundation and Adele Addison commission) at Buffalo (May 1965), Mills College (October 1965; January 24 and 31, 1967), and Rutgers (November 1965).

108. Also see William Robin, "Balance Problems: Neoliberalism and New Music in the American University and Ensemble," *Journal of the American Musicological Society* 71, no. 3 (2018): 749–93, for the current state of neoliberal, market branding for new music ensembles. And see Ian Power, "The New Musical Imaginary: Description as Distraction in New Music," *Tempo* 73, no. 289 (2019): 6–20 for the role of program notes for "insiders" and "outsiders," and the role they play signaling status in grant applications.

109. Rockefeller Foundation, "Annual Report 1971," 72–73.

110. In the mid-1980s Columbia and Princeton ceased formal affiliation: the center in New York became the Computer Music Center and Princeton founded its own Princeton Sound Lab.

111. Broyles, *Mavericks and Other Traditions in American Music*, 279.

112. Straus, "The Myth of Serial 'Tyranny' in the 1950s and 1960s," 303. Italics my emphasis.

CHAPTER 5

1. Charles Clotfelter, ed., *Who Benefits from the Nonprofit Sector?* (Chicago: University of Chicago Press, 1992), 2.

2. Ford Foundation, *The Finances of the Performing Arts: A Survey of 166 Professional Nonprofit Resident Theaters, Operas, Symphonies, Ballets, and Modern Dance Companies*, vol. I (New York: Ford Foundation, 1974), 50.

3. The average salary in 2003 for a musician performing in a fifty-two-week-schedule orchestra was $100,480. Robert J. Flanagan, *The Perilous Life of Symphony Orchestras: Artistic Triumphs and Economic Challenges* (New Haven, CT: Yale University Press, 2012), 162.

4. Ford Foundation, *The Finances of the Performing Arts*, preface.

5. In the 1970–71 season, across the 166 organizations, the earnings gap was $66.1 million ($400 million in 2017): they spent $157.4 million to perform, but only earned $91.3 million from ticket sales and other sources of revenue. Over time, with inflation and other increasing costs, economists forecasted the $66.1 million per year to skyrocket.

6. Ford Foundation, *The Finances of the Performing Arts*, 14.

7. Richard Magat, *The Ford Foundation at Work: Philanthropic Choices, Methods, and Styles* (New York: Plenum Press, 1979), 76–77.

8. Mary Anna Culleton Colwell, "The Foundation Connection: Links Among Foundations and Recipient Organizations," in *Philanthropy and Cultural Imperialism: The Foundations at Home and Abroad*, ed. Robert F. Arnove (Boston: G. K. Hall, 1980), 413–52. Internal Revenue Code Section 4945.

9. Colwell, "The Foundation Connection," 416–17.

10. Merrimon Cuninggim, *Private Money and Public Service: The Role of Foundations in American Society* (New York: McGraw-Hill Book Company, 1972), 215.

11. Junius Eddy, "Cultivation of Other Sources of Support," Division of Humanities and the Arts, Grants Awarded Between March 1957 and April 1970, Folder: Strengthening Institutional Resources in Humanities and the Arts, Box 62, FA640 Ford Foundation Records, Education and Public Policy Program (EPP), Office of the Arts, Program Files, Ford Foundation (FF), Rockefeller Archive Center, Tarrytown, New York (RAC).

12. Ibid.

13. Letters to Victor Babin, Efrem Zimbalist, John Brownlee, Leopold Mannes, Chester W. Williams, and Peter Mennin, 16 04 1962, Folder: Independent Schools—Background 1962–1973, Box 52, FA640, FF, RAC.

14. Trustee Docket: Scholarships for Training in the Creative Arts, Folder: Independent Schools—Background 1962–1973, ibid.

15. From Oleg Lobanov to Files, 12 01 1970, Folder: Evaluation of 1969–1972, ibid.

16. From W. McNeil Lowry to Charles Kent, 23 01 1963, Folder: Consultants 1962–1974, ibid.

17. Trustee Docket: Scholarships for Training in the Creative Arts, Folder: Independent Schools—Background 1962–1973, ibid.

18. Ibid.

19. Ibid.

20. "The General Situation Today" and "Evaluation of Independent Schools of Music," 18 12 1969, Folder: Evaluation of 1969–1972, ibid. On the other hand, the NEC argued that they tied their fundraising success in scholarship money to funds received from the Ford Foundation.

21. Ford Foundation Oral History Project, 14 01 1972, Folder: Lowry, W. McNeil, Box 2, Series IV, FA618, FF, RAC.

22. "Humanities and the Arts Program Discussion Paper: Program for Symphony Orchestras," 24-25 09 1964, Report 02853, Catalogued Reports, FF, RAC.

23. The original budget was even larger, totaling $110 million, using approximately $77 to $85 million in Ford Motor Company stock then held by the foundation. Ibid. Also see Ben Negley, "The Ford Foundation Symphony Orchestra Program," *Journal of Musicological Research* 36, no. 2 (2017): 1–28.

24. "The Major Orchestra classification was defined in June 1962 by the Major Symphony Managers' Conference as those orchestras operating on annual budgets of $500,000 and over, and which pay their musicians on a weekly basis under a season contract." By contrast, "the Metropolitan Orchestra classification referred originally to orchestras operating on annual budgets of between $100,000 and $250,000." Folder: Misc. Grant Programs—Fact Sheets, Etc. 1963–1965, Box 10, Series VI, FA640, FF, RAC.

25. "Activities in the Creative and Performing Arts Support in the Musical Arts (1957–1969)," 30 09 1969, Report 06721, Catalogued Reports, FF, RAC.

26. Ford Foundation, "The Ford Foundation: Millions for Music—Music for Millions," *Music Educators Journal* 53, no. 1 (1966): 85.

27. Ford Foundation, "Annual Report 1972."

28. See also Negley, "The Ford Foundation Symphony Orchestra Program."

29. Sigmund Koch Notes: Symphony Orchestra Program Negotiation—1965/66, Folder: Background (1964 to 10/22/65), Box 42, Series VI, FA640, FF, RAC.

30. Symphony Orchestra Program: Trust Committee Meeting, 20 04 1972, Folder: Background/Trust Agreement (2/2) 1964–1972, ibid.

31. Community Foundation for Southeast Michigan, "Robert H. Tannahill Foundation," https://cfsem.org/organization/robert-h-tannahill-foundation/ (Accessed 21 01 2019) and George Bulanda, "Portrait of a Collector," *Hour Detroit*, August 27, 2014.

32. Audit by Tamblyn & Brown, Inc. "Analysis of the Fundraising Potentialities of the Baltimore Symphony Orchestra," 01 1966, Reel 2936, FA732A, FF, RAC.

33. "Baltimore Symphony Orchestra," Reel 2936, FA732A, FF, RAC.

34. "Honolulu Symphony Society," Reel 2940, 2941, FA732D, FF, RAC.

35. "Kalamazoo Orchestra," Reel 2978, FA732D, FF, RAC.

36. "Minnesota Orchestral Association," Reel 3078, FA732H, FF, RAC.

37. Negley, "The Ford Foundation Symphony Orchestra Program," 21.

38. "K. N. Dayton, Chief Executive of Retailer, 80," *New York Times*, July 22, 2003.

39. I thank Susan Paine and archivists Alison Fulmer and Bridget Carr for their assistance at the Boston Symphony Orchestra Archives. TRUS Series 244, Trustee Meeting Minutes, Vol. 4, 2/5/19–1/17/68, Box 1, Folder: Trustees Meeting Minutes 3/16/66–01/17/68.

40. Request for Grant Authorization, Support of Professional Training in Conservatories, Folder: Independent Schools—Background 1962–1973, Box 52, FA640, FF, RAC.

41. From Oleg Lobanov to Files, 18 12 1969, Folder: Evaluation of 1969–1972, ibid.

42. Request for Grant Authorization Cleveland and Juilliard, Reel 1726, FA732G, FF, RAC.

43. From Oleg Lobanov to Files, 18 12 1969, Folder: Evaluation of 1969–1972, Box 52, FA640, FF, RAC.

44. From the Secretary of the Ford Foundation to Mrs. Frank E. Joseph, 27 08 1971, "Cleveland Institute of Music," Reel 1726, FA732G, FF, RAC.

45. For example, in a letter from Lowry to president McGeorge Bundy on 07 04 1971, Lowry wrote that "our use of stock for gifts would free the Foundation from capital gains on that amount of stock so used," ibid.

46. From Mrs. Frank E. Joseph to Oleg Lobanov, 24 05 1974, ibid.

47. Three other conservatories were beneficiaries of the Mellon Foundation's eleemosynary activities: the Peabody Institute ($500,000 in 1972 and $400,000 in 1978), the Manhattan School of Music (also $500,000 in 1972 and $400,000 in 1978), and the Mannes School of Music ($100,000 in 1972).

48. Cuninggim, *Private Money and Public Service*, 215, and Colwell, "The Foundation Connection," 416–17.

49. "Cleveland Institute of Music," Reel 1726, FA732G, FF, RAC.

50. Case Western Reserve University, "Smith, Albert Kelvin," *Encyclopedia of Cleveland History*, https://case.edu/ech/articles/s/smith-albert-kelvin (Accessed 21 01 2019).

51. Case Western Reserve University, "Schubert, Leland," *Encyclopedia of Cleveland History*, https://case.edu/ech/articles/s/schubert-leland (Accessed 21 01 2019).

52. Case Western Reserve University, "Schmitt, Ralph S.," *Encyclopedia of Cleveland History*, https://case.edu/ech/articles/s/schmitt-ralph-s (Accessed 21 01 2019) and "Schmitt, Dorothy Prentiss," https://case.edu/ech/articles/s/schmitt-dorothy-prentiss (Accessed 21 01 2019).

53. From Oleg Lobanov to Files, 19 06 1970, Folder: Evaluation of 1969–1972, Box 52, FA640, FF, RAC.

54. "Juilliard School," Reel 2287, FA732G, FF, RAC.

55. The foundation had already pegged down Juilliard's initial requests for $15 million, and failing that, $10 million, both of which Ford decided were too high.

56. I thank Jeni Dahmus Farah, director, Archives, The Juilliard School, and Tiffany Kuo for sharing this information with me. Email correspondence 09 01 2019.

57. "Juilliard School," Reel 2287, FA732G, FF, RAC.

58. "David Keiser of Philharmonic Dead," *New York Times*, November 27, 1975.

59. From W. McNeil Lowry to McGeorge Bundy, 24 04 1974, Reel 2427, FA732G, FF, RAC.

60. Ibid.

61. From Richard Sheldon to Files, 09 05 1969, "New England Conservatory," Reel 1871, FA732H, FF, RAC.

62. "New England Conservatory," Reel 3632, FA732H, FF, RAC.

63. Rockefeller Archive Center, "Martha Baird Rockefeller, 1895–1971," http://rockarch.org/bio/marthabaird.php (Accessed 21 01 2019).

64. Howard Taubman, "Mrs. Rockefeller's Bequests Spread Hope in Arts," *New York Times*, February 14, 1971.

65. Report of the President, Gunther Schuller, 08 12 1975, "New England Conservatory," Reel 3633, FA732H, FF, RAC.

66. From J. Stanley Ballinger, President to Marcia Thompson, 01 05 1980, ibid.

67. Request for Grant Authorization, 18 04 1972, "San Francisco Conservatory of Music," Reel 1370, FA732H, FF, RAC.

68. Ibid.

69. Ford Foundation Oral History Project, 28 08 1973, Folder: Thompson, Box 3, Series IV, FA618, FF, RAC.

70. "Government Policy in the Arts," 08 1968, Folder 9, Box 7, Series IV, FA582, FF, RAC.

71. According to the Ford data, overall, symphony orchestras had spent $82.8 million during the season but only took in $41.9 million through ticket sales and other services. Even the $37.5 million raised from individuals, corporations, foundations, and government did not cover the shortfall. Ford Foundation, *The Finances of the Performing Arts*, 40.

72. Earned income grew from $324,000 to $461,000 and unearned income from $178,000 to $412,000. Ibid., 90.

73. Negley, "The Ford Foundation Symphony Orchestra Program," 19. As Negley also distinguishes, chapter 11 bankruptcy is a means of reorganizing existing contractual obligations versus a more permanent chapter 7 liquidation filing.

74. Flanagan, *The Perilous Life of Symphony Orchestras*, 129. In addition to Philadelphia and Minnesota, the cost disease has consumed and bankrupted a greater number of smaller and medium-sized orchestras, including Birmingham, Denver, Honolulu, New Orleans, Oakland, San Jose, and Sacramento. Some have reopened under new operating structures and new names.

75. Gerald Freund, "Concerning a Philosophy of the Arts Program," Folder: Program and Policy 1964–1968, Box 1, Series 925, Subgroup 3, Record Group 2, Rockefeller Foundation, RAC.

76. Paul DiMaggio and Michael Useem, "Social Class and Arts Consumption: The Origins and Consequences of Class Differences in Exposure to the Arts in America," *Theory and Society* 5, no. 2 (1978): 141–61, 142.

77. Paul DiMaggio and Francie Ostrower, "Participation in the Arts by Black and White Americans," *Social Forces* 68, no. 3 (1990): 753–78.

78. Ibid., 774.

79. Tom Bethell, "Welfare Arts," *The Public Interest* 53 (1978): 134–38. Cited in Charles T. Clotfelter, ed., *Who Benefits from the Nonprofit Sector?*

CHAPTER 6

1. From Lawrence H. Horwitz to Nancy Hanks, 02 06 1971, Folder: Council Members Miscellaneous, Box 11, A1 Entry 2, Record Group (RG) 288, The National Archives at College Park, Maryland (Archives II).

2. National Endowment for the Arts, "Annual Report 1971," 1. A third goal was to assist major arts institutions in their "cultural resources development."

3. Profile of Current Council, Folder: Council Members Miscellaneous, Box 11, A1 Entry 2, RG288, Archives II.

4. By "vernacular," I refer to a variety of folk, popular, dance, and ethnic musics along the lines of H. Wiley Hitchcock's famous distinction between "vernacular" and "cultivated" (art, classical) music. H. Wiley Hitchcock, *Music in the United States: A Historical Introduction* (Englewood Cliffs, NJ: Prentice-Hall, 1969).

5. Research Division National Endowment for the Arts, "Minorities and Women in the Arts: 1970" (1978), 1.

6. Ibid., 3.

7. From Walter Anderson to Nancy Hanks, 07 11 1969, Subject: Awards to Ethnic Groups, Folder: A, Box 1, A1 Entry 3, RG288, Archives II.

8. From Carolyn Kizer to Nancy Hanks, 10 11 1969, Subject: Walter Anderson's memo on ethnic groups, ibid.

9. Sidford argues further that arts funders cannot only consider quality in terms of "imagination, talent, and skill," but also *relevance* and *local context* must be elements in assessing quality." Holly Sidford, "Fusing Arts, Culture, and Social Change: High Impact Strategies for Philanthropy," National Committee for Responsive Philanthropy (2011), 20. Emphasis in original.

10. Ethnomusicologist Ingrid Monson argues that the mythology of separatism was a useful cultural tool that permitted a greater sense of social and racial identity in an otherwise hostile world. Ingrid Monson, *Freedom Sounds: Civil Rights Call Out to Jazz and Africa* (Oxford: Oxford University Press, 2007).

11. A. B. Spellman, *Four Jazz Lives* (Ann Arbor: University of Michigan Press, 2004), 16.

12. Ibid., 46.

13. Ibid., 48.

14. The NEA also supported the Cecil Taylor residency at Antioch College, the same institution at which NEA music director Walter Anderson had taught.

15. See also Iain Anderson, "Jazz Outside the Marketplace: Free Improvisation and Nonprofit Sponsorship of the Arts, 1965–1980," *American Music* 20, no. 2 (2002): 154.

16. Norman Lloyd interview with Julius Bloom, 23 08 1966, Box 266, Series F-L, RG12, Rockefeller Foundation (RF), Rockefeller Archive Center, Tarrytown, New York (RAC).

17. One interesting exception was officer Lloyd's unique support for the first performance of African American composer Scott Joplin's opera, *Treemonisha*, staged and performed by T. J. Anderson, Katherine Dunham, Morehouse College, and the Atlanta Symphony Orchestra.

18. Junius Eddy, "Government, the Arts, and Ghetto Youth," *Public Administration Review* 30, no. 4 (1970): 399–408.

19. Iain Anderson, *This Is Our Music: Free Jazz, the Sixties, and American Culture* (Philadelphia: University of Pennsylvania Press, 2007), 93.

20. Ibid., 98. As many jazz scholars and historians have written, "free jazz" also went by the terms "free improvisation," the "new thing," and "avant-garde jazz," among others. Ornette Coleman's album *Free Jazz* came out in 1961.

21. As trumpeter Bill Dixon said, "my music *wasn't* for everyone, and neither was [Arnold] Schoenberg's music for everyone, and neither was [Anton] Webern's music for everyone, and neither was [Béla] Bartók's." Quoted in Anderson, *This Is Our Music*, 86. Emphasis in original. Amiri

Baraka (at the time, LeRoi Jones) also wrote in *Blues People* that "Ornette Coleman has had to live with the attitudes responsible for Anton Webern's music whether he knows that music or not." LeRoi Jones, *Blues People: Negro Music in White America* (New York: William Morrow and Company, 1963), 82.

22. Anderson, *This Is Our Music*, 171.

23. Anderson, "Jazz Outside the Marketplace," 150.

24. From Marjory Hanson to Nancy Hanks, 17 11 1969, Subject: Willis Conover, Folder: A, Box 1, A1 Entry 3, RG288, Archives II.

25. Folder: FY-70 Jazz Program General, Box 2, A1 Entry 35, RG288, Archives II.

26. National Endowment for the Arts, "Annual Report 1971." The NEA's Composer-Performer Commissioning Program was a useful point of comparison, however, in the differential funds it gave jazz and classical music. It awarded nearly the same amount ($48,568) that year to just three individuals and five organizations, enabling them to defray the costs of completing and copying orchestral scores and parts, and for the groups to commission new works. As another example, its support of "Contemporary Performing Ensembles" for workshops and performing new works demonstrated much larger grants to these experimental groups compared to similarly sized jazz groups. The Bennington Composers Conference and Chamber Music Center, for example, received $5,000, and New Dimensions in Music in Seattle obtained $12,700. By contrast, the average-sized grant to jazz organizations was $1,274 ($31,855 split among twenty-five organizations). It gave its largest grant of $2,500 to the Jazz Composer's Orchestra Association in New York City, and the smallest grant of $250 to East Texas State University.

27. Folder: 28th Meeting (Dec. 1972), Box 9, A1 Entry 18, RG288, Archives II.

28. Anderson, *This Is Our Music*, 170.

29. Eddy, "Government, the Arts, and Ghetto Youth."

30. National Endowment for the Arts, "Annual Report 1971," 33, quoted from Eddy, "Government, the Arts, and Ghetto Youth."

31. From John Hoare Kerr to For the Record, 14 09 1970, Folder: Developing Arts, Box 13, A1 Entry 2, RG288, Archives II.

32. Transcript of Conclusions of Meeting of "Developing Arts" Consultants with Nancy Hanks, 22 01 1971, ibid.

33. When pressed by Junius Eddy to define what he meant by "minorities," Carew replied "Blacks, American Indians, Puerto Ricans, Mexican groups." While "Orientals" were included in the minutes, Carew did not specify them nor "Appalachian Whites." Ibid.

34. From John Hoare Kerr to Nancy Hanks, Michael Straight, and Charles Kerr, 02 02 1971, Subject: "Developing Arts"—Vantile Whitfield, ibid.

35. Guidelines for National Endowment for the Arts Grants Developing Arts Program, Fiscal Year 1972 (Draft #1, January 6, 1971), ibid.

36. From Robert Wise to Nancy Hanks, 08 09 1973, Folder: Council Members—Correspondence 1973 and 1974, Box 11, A1 Entry 2, RG288, Archives II.

37. Folder: NCA Minutes of the 37th Meeting (Nov. 22–24, 1974), Box 13, A1 Entry 18, RG288, Archives II.

38. Ibid.

39. From Stephen Benedict to Anthony S. Keller, Executive Director State of Connecticut, 19 08 1971, Folder: Expansion Arts, Box 4, A1 Entry 1, RG288, Archives II.

40. From Michael Straight to Vantile Whitfield, 22 03 1974, Folder: Expansion Arts 1974 Straight, Box 9, A1 Entry 26, RG288, Archives II.

41. From Vantile Whitfield to Nancy Hanks via Michael Straight, 12 08 1975, Re: Approval requested for FY76 Panelists, Folder: FY76 Expansion Arts Straight, Box 9, A1 Entry 26, RG288, Archives II.

42. Ibid.

43. Minutes of the 27th Meeting, Folder: 28th Meeting (Dec. 1972), Box 9, A1 Entry 18, RG288, Archives II.

44. Folder: 31st Meeting (July 1973), Box 10, A1 Entry 18, RG288, Archives II.

45. Folder: 33rd Meeting (Nov. 1973), Box 11, A1 Entry 18, RG288, Archives II.

46. Folder: 35th Meeting (May 1974), Box 12, A1 Entry 18, RG288, Archives II.

47. From Walter Anderson to Nancy Hanks via Diane Lansing, 31 01 1972, Subject: "Requested Administrative Projections for Fiscal Year 1974 and Fiscal Year 1975," Folder: Harlow Heneman— Chairman of Task Force, Box 5, A1 Entry 1, RG288, Archives II.

48. National Endowment for the Arts, "Annual Report 1974," 4.

49. Folder: Bicentennial, Box 9, A1 Entry 2, RG288, Archives II. The first, August 14, 1972, "Bicentennial Commissions: Deeply Involved in Politics"; the second, August 15, 1972, "Red, White, Blue—and Green"; the third, August 16, 1972, "Diluting the Spirit of '76: Bicentennial Plans Avoid the Controversial."

50. Folder: Endowment Awards $470,000 to Composers and Librettists '77, Box 1, A1 Entry 37, RG288, Archives II.

51. Folder: Bicentennial, Box 8, A1 Entry 2, RG288, Archives II.

52. Jazz/Folk/Ethnic Guidelines, May 1975 for FY1976 and 77, Folder: Minutes of the 39th Meeting (May 1–4, 1975), Box 13, A1 Entry 18, RG288, Archives II.

53. Ibid.

54. Folder: 35th Meeting (May 1974), Box 12, A1 Entry 18, RG288, Archives II.

55. Folder: NCA Minutes of the 38th Meeting (Feb. 7–9, 1975), Box 13, A1 Entry 18, RG288, Archives II.

56. Folder: 36th Meeting (Sep. 3–5, 1974), Box 12, A1 Entry 18, RG288, Archives II.

57. Folder: NCA Minutes of the 39th Meeting (May 1–4, 1975), Box 13, A1 Entry 18, RG288, Archives II.

58. Folder: NCA 38th Meeting (Feb. 1975) 2 of 2, Box 13, A1 Entry 18, RG288, Archives II.

59. Folder: 34th Meeting (Feb. 1974), Box 11, A1 Entry 18, RG288, Archives II.

60. Jazz/Folk/Ethnic Program: An Overview, June 14, 1977, Folder: Budget—Jazz/Folk/Ethnic—1976 Statistics on 1976 J/F/E Prog., Box 1, A1 Entry 35, RG288, Archives II.

61. The American Folklife Center and The Folk Programs of the Arts Endowment, January 1975, with Michael Straight, Alan Jabbour, and Archie Green, Folder: Folk Life, Box 7, A1 Entry 26, RG288, Archives II.

62. Folder: 34th Meeting (Supp.) (Feb 74), Box 11, A1 Entry 18, RG288, Archives II.

63. Report to the National Council on the Arts on Program Planning for Folk Arts, February 1974, ibid.

64. From Robert Wade to Nancy Hanks, 06 09 1973, Subject: H.R. 8770, A Bill to Establish an American Folklife Center in the Library of Congress, Folder: Folk Life, Box 7, A1 Entry 26, RG288, Archives II.

65. Ibid.

66. Folder: 36th Meeting (Sep. 3–5, 1974), Box 12, A1 Entry 18, RG288, Archives II.

67. Donna Binkiewicz, *Federalizing the Muse: United States Art Policy and the National Endowment for the Arts, 1965–1980* (Chapel Hill: University of North Carolina Press, 2004), 212.

68. Ibid., 213.

69. "Jazz and Folk/Ethnic Appropriations Materials," Folder: Budget—Jazz/Folk/Ethnic—1976, Box 1, A1 Entry 35, RG288, Archives II.

70. Jazz/Folk Music (formerly Jazz/Folk/Ethnic Music) Guidelines FY1979, November 1977, Folder: FY-79 Jazz Program-General, Box 2, A1 Entry 35, RG288, Archives II.

71. Ibid. Emphasis in original.

72. Baker also received the NEA Jazz Masters Award in 2000. David N. Baker, ed., *New Perspectives on Jazz* (Washington, DC: Smithsonian Institution Press, 1990).

73. Mark Bauerlein and Ellen Grantham, eds., *National Endowment for the Arts: A History, 1965–2008* (Washington, DC: National Endowment for the Arts), 49.

74. Ibid., 48.

75. Expansion Arts Program, Fiscal Year 1975 Guidelines, Folder: 30th Meeting (May 1973), Box 10, A1 Entry 18, RG288, Archives II.

EPILOGUE

1. Darren Walker, "The Art of Democracy: Creative Expression and American Greatness," March 20, 2017, https://www.fordfoundation.org/about/library/speeches/the-art-of-democracy-creative-expression-and-american-greatness/ (Accessed 02 07 2019).

2. Thomas Piketty, *Capital in the Twenty-First Century*, trans. Arthur Goldhammer (Cambridge, MA: Belknap Press of Harvard University, 2014).

3. Robert Putnam, *Bowling Alone: The Collapse and Revival of American Community* (New York: Simon and Schuster, 2000).

4. Theda Skocpol, *Diminished Democracy: From Membership to Management in American Civic Life* (Norman: University of Oklahoma Press, 2003).

5. Larissa MacFarquhar, "What Money Can Buy: Darren Walker and the Ford Foundation Set Out to Conquer Inequality," *New Yorker*, December 27, 2015.

6. Darren Walker, "Toward a New Gospel of Wealth," October 1, 2015, https://www.fordfoundation.org/ideas/equals-change-blog/posts/toward-a-new-gospel-of-wealth/ (Accessed 02 07 2019). Walker expanded his argument in his book *From Generosity to Justice: A New Gospel of Wealth* (New York: Disruption Books, 2019). In the book, he argues that philanthropy should be targeted at addressing issues of justice, more than the short-term deliverance of charity. In his words, justice is "investing your money, time, resources, knowledge, and networks to change the root causes that create the need for charity in the first place," 8.

7. Darren Walker, "Introducing the Ford Foundation Center for Social Justice," October 3, 2018, https://www.fordfoundation.org/ideas/equals-change-blog/posts/introducing-the-ford-foundation-center-for-social-justice/ (Accessed 02 07 2019).

8. Holly Sidford, "Fusing Arts, Culture and Social Change: High Impact Strategies for Philanthropy," National Committee for Responsive Philanthropy (2011), 1.

9. Ibid.

10. The latest data from 2015, "Foundation Stats," Foundation Center, https://data.foundationcenter.org/ (Accessed 02 07 2019).

11. Anand Giridharadas, *Winner Takes All: The Elite Charade of Changing the World* (New York: Alfred A. Knopf, 2018), 30.

12. Also see William Robin, *Industry: Bang on a Can and New Music in the Marketplace* (Oxford: Oxford University Press, forthcoming).

13. Pam Breaux, "Better Together: Public and Private Funding for the Arts," June 2017, https://mellon.org/resources/shared-experiences-blog/better-together-public-and-private-funding-arts/ (Accessed 02 07 2019).

14. Lawrence W. Levine, *Highbrow/Lowbrow: The Emergence of Cultural Hierarchy in America* (Cambridge, MA: Harvard University Press, 1988), 222.

15. Richard Peterson, "The Rise and Fall of Highbrow Snobbery as a Status Marker," *Poetics* 25 (1997): 75–92.

16. Folder: Fourth Meeting (Feb. 11, 1966), Box 1, A1 Entry 18, Record Group 288 (RG288), The National Archives at College Park, Maryland (Archives II).

17. Gloria Origgi, *Reputation: What It Is and Why It Matters* (Princeton, NJ: Princeton University Press, 2017), and Edge, "What Is Reputation? A Conversation with Gloria Origgi," May 11, 2015, http://edge.org/conversation/gloria_origgi-what-is-reputation (Accessed 01 10 2015).

18. For example, Christopher Small's *Musicking* is a main reference source regarding the idea of music as "process" and "practice," turning "music" from noun to verb. Christopher Small, *Musicking: The Meanings of Performing and Listening* (Middletown, CT: Wesleyan University Press, 1998). The fact that musicking is so well cited—according to Google Scholar, 3,635 citations as of the year 2019, which is more than a 50% increase of the 2,190 citations it had in 2016—stands in contrast to Small's nonconventional academic pedigree and career path. Despite his lack of institutionalized credentials from elite universities, scholars continue to reference his idea.

19. Robert Merton, "The Matthew Effect in Science," *Science* 159, no. 3810 (1968): 56–63.

20. James F. English, *The Economy of Prestige: Prizes, Awards, and the Circulation of Cultural Value* (Cambridge, MA: Harvard University Press, 2005).

21. Cheng Gao et al., "Overcoming Institutional Voids: A Reputation-Based View of Long-Run Survival," *Strategic Management Journal* 38, no. 11 (2017), 2147–67.

22. *National Endowment for the Arts v. Finley*.

23. The Independent Commission's first meeting occurred right before the NEA Four lawsuit.

24. Mark Bauerlein and Ellen Grantham, eds., *National Endowment for the Arts: A History 1965–2008* (Washington, DC: National Endowment for the Arts, 2009), 107.

25. Samuel Gilmore, "Minorities and Distributional Equity at the National Endowment for the Arts," *Journal of Arts Management, Law & Society* 23, no. 2 (1993): 137–73. Congress and the NEA have also defined "underserved" communities as rural populations and inner-city minority populations.

26. Ibid.

27. Also see Robin, *Industry: Bang on a Can and New Music in the Marketplace*.

28. Gilmore, "Minorities and Distributional Equity at the National Endowment for the Arts."

29. Lauren A. Rivera, *Pedigree: How Elite Students Get Elite Jobs* (Princeton, NJ: Princeton University Press, 2015), 29.

30. Ralph H. Turner, "Sponsored and Contest Mobility and the School System," *American Sociological Review* 25, no. 6 (1960): 855–67.

31. In 2019, the Foundation Center merged with GuideStar to become Candid. Through paid subscription, users can search the Foundation Directory Online at http://www.fconline.foundationcenter.org (Accessed 11 12 2019). Previously, data could be searched at regional centers such as the Boston Public Library.

32. The largest of these grants were made by the MacArthur, Pritzker, and Polk Bros. Foundations to the Old Town School of Folk Music in Chicago ($6.3 million total); the Milken Family Foundations to its own Milken Archive of American Jewish Music in Santa Monica, California ($4.5 million); and the Barr Foundation to World Music Inc. in Cambridge, Massachusetts ($2.7 million). The Hewlett Foundation made two grants to Bay area groups: the Berkeley Society for the Preservation of Traditional Music ($2.1 million) and the San Jose Taiko ($1.3 million). The James Irvine Foundation embarked on a significant arts-for-Californians program in 2011 but concluded its work in 2016. The Kresge Foundation supports arts and culture exclusively through creative placemaking grants, which have historically not included many music-based projects.

33. Officially, Jazz at Lincoln Center is located in the Time Warner Center at Columbus Circle, a few blocks away from Lincoln Center.

34. Breaux, "Better Together."

35. Ibid., 9.

36. *Giving USA: The Annual Report on Philanthropy for the Year 2016* (Chicago: Giving USA Foundation, 2017).

37. Cited in David Callahan, *The Givers: Wealth, Power, and Philanthropy in a New Gilded Age* (New York: Vintage Books, 2017), 32. The survey is from 2016.

38. Rob Reich, *Just Giving: Why Philanthropy Is Failing Democracy and How It Can Do Better* (Princeton, NJ: Princeton University Press, 2018). Reich cites data from the Center on Philanthropy at Indiana University, "Patterns of Household Charitable Giving." Wealthier Americans also give more to health (25% versus 5% overall) and education (25% versus 4%) and less toward basic needs (4% versus 10%) and significantly less for religion (17% versus 61%).

39. Reich, *Just Giving*, 71.

40. Ibid., 78.

41. Ibid., 123.

42. Ibid., 79.

43. Ibid., 81.

44. The Giving Pledge, https://givingpledge.org/About.aspx (Accessed 02 07 2019).

45. Callahan, *The Givers*, 27. On the other hand, moral philosophers like Peter Singer have questioned whether these billionaires have the ethical right to donate their money wherever they wish. Singer and others have espoused the idea of "effective altruism," arguing that there is a moral obligation to give to the neediest first. As a poignant example, Singer contends that there should be no choice between donating $100 million to Lincoln Center and saving the vision of millions of African children afflicted with trachoma—the latter wins out. Peter Singer, *The Most Good You Can Do: How Effective Altruism is Changing Ideas About Living Ethically* (New Haven, CT: Yale University Press, 2015) and William MacAskill, *Doing Good Better: How Effective Altruism Can Help You Make a Difference* (New York: Gotham Books, 2015). Additionally, philosopher Chiara Cordelli states that affluent donors "should regard their donations as a way of returning to others what is rightfully their own," and so "exercise no *personal* discretion." The wealthy "benefit from public cuts to public services" and so "have a duty to repair the injustice." Chiara Cordelli, "Reparative Justice and the Moral Limits of Discretionary Philanthropy," in *Philanthropy in*

Democratic Societies, ed. Rob Reich, Chiara Cordelli, and Lucy Bernholz (Chicago: University of Chicago Press, 2016), 247.

46. Ray D. Madoff, "When Is Philanthropy?: How the Tax Code's Answer to This Question Has Given Rise to the Growth of Donor-Advised Funds and Why It's a Problem," in *Philanthropy in Democratic Societies*, ed. Rob Reich, Chiara Cordelli, and Lucy Bernholz (Chicago: University of Chicago Press, 2016), 159.

47. Ibid., 160.

48. Callahan, *The Givers*, 293.

49. Ibid., 6.

50. Ibid., 7

51. For example, see Jerry Muller, *The Tyranny of Metrics* (Princeton, NJ: Princeton University Press, 2018) and William Easterly, *The Tyranny of Experts: Economists, Dictators, and the Forgotten Rights of the Poor* (New York: Basic Books, 2015).

52. Callahan, *The Givers*, 44.

53. Ibid., 9.

54. Han van Meegeren, for instance, famously sold $60 million worth of fake Vermeer paintings, including to the Dutch government. Julie Zeveloff and Liz Weiss, "Eight of the Biggest Art Forgeries of All Time," *Business Insider*, July 5, 2011, https://www.businessinsider.com/art-forgeries-2011-6 (Accessed 02 07 2019).

55. Admittedly, the NEA has only had to make two payments totaling $4,700 since the program began in 1975 because museums are generally good at protecting artwork; however, the issue is not just the cost to the U.S. taxpayer, but its symbolic safeguarding of the system. Deborah Vankin, "L.A. Without the NEA: How One Little-Known Program Saves Museums Millions," *Los Angeles Times*, March 24, 2017.

56. Gund sold it to Steven Cohen, a hedge fund investor, for $165 million. Ford Foundation, "Art for Justice Fund Established with $100 Million Gift from Philanthropist Agnes Gund," June 12, 2017, https://www.fordfoundation.org/the-latest/news/art-for-justice-fund-established-with-100-million-gift-from-philanthropist-agnes-gund/ (Accessed 02 07 2019).

57. One could make the case that attending a performance at the Met is also a form of conspicuous consumption with the possibility of intoxication. I am also specific in reference to "champagne" as the sparkling wine grown in the French region of Champagne, and protected as a "controlled designation of origin" (*appellation d'origine contrôlée)*, made in accordance with the *Comité Interprofessionnel du vin de Champagne*.

58. "French Wine Regions Champagne, Burgundy, Win World Heritage Status," *Reuters*, July 5, 2015 https://www.reuters.com/article/us-france-unesco/french-wine-regions-champagne-burgundy-win-world-heritage-status-idUSKCN0PF0FE20150705 (Accessed 29 08 2019).

59. The DuBois Orchestra, http://www.duboisorchestra.org (Accessed 02 07 2019). The Sphinx Organization is another good example, http://www.sphinxmusic.org (Accessed 02 08 2019).

60. Malcolm Gay, "Area Musicians Call on BSO to Diversify Programming," *Boston Globe*, December 20, 2017.

61. Amy Watson, "U.S. Music Industry—Statistics & Facts," January 17, 2019, https://www.statista.com/topics/4948/music-industry/ (Accessed 02 07 2019).

62. He also argues, though, that the turn to the "market" has not necessarily led to a richer cultural environment. Nevertheless, it does represent a reaction to changing conditions. William

Robin, "Balance Problems: Neoliberalism and New Music in the American University and Ensemble," *Journal of the American Musicological Society* 71, no. 3 (2018): 749–93.

63. Daniel Drezner would argue that there is a distinct difference between "public intellectuals" who "point out when an emperor has no clothes" and "thought leaders" who are not skeptics, but "true believers." Daniel Drezner, *The Ideas Industry: How Pessimists, Partisans, and Plutocrats Are Transforming the Marketplace of Ideas* (Oxford: Oxford University Press, 2017).

64. Tom Nichols, *The Death of Expertise: The Campaign Against Established Knowledge and Why It Matters* (Oxford: Oxford University Press, 2017).

65. Michael Bhaskar, *Curation: The Power of Selection in a World of Excess* (London: Piatkus, 2016), 109.

66. Ibid., 114.

67. For example, see Michael Sy Uy, "Venezuela's National Music Education Program *El Sistema*: Its Interactions with Society and Its Participants' Engagement in Praxis," *Music and Arts in Action* 4, no. 1 (2012): 5–21.

Bibliography

American Music Center. *The National Endowment for the Arts Composer/Librettist Program Collection at the American Music Center*. New York: AMC, 1979.

Anderson, Iain. "Jazz Outside the Marketplace: Free Improvisation and Nonprofit Sponsorship of the Arts, 1965–1980." *American Music* 20, no. 2 (2002): 131–67.

———. *This Is Our Music: Free Jazz, the Sixties, and American Culture*. Philadelphia: University of Philadelphia Press, 2007.

Ansari, Emily Abrams. "Shaping the Politics of Cold War Musical Diplomacy: An Epistemic Community of American Composers." *Diplomatic History* 36, no. 1 (2012): 41–52.

———. *The Sound of a Superpower: Musical Americanism and the Cold War*. New York: Oxford University Press, 2018.

Appiah, Kwame Anthony. *The Lies That Bind: Rethinking Identity*. New York: Liveright Publishing Corporation, 2018.

Arian, Edward. *The Unfulfilled Promise: Public Subsidy of the Arts in America*. Philadelphia: Temple University Press, 1989.

Arnove, Robert F., ed. "Introduction." In *Philanthropy and Cultural Imperialism: The Foundations at Home and Abroad*, 1–18. Boston: G. K. Hall & Co., 1980.

Babbitt, Milton. "Who Cares If You Listen?" *High Fidelity* 8, no. 2 (1958): 38–40, 126–27.

Baker, David, ed. *New Perspectives on Jazz*. Washington, DC: Smithsonian Institution Press, 1990.

Banaji, Mahzarin R., and Anthony G. Greenwald. *Blindspot: Hidden Biases of Good People*. New York: Delacorte Press, 2013.

Bauerlein, Mark, and Ellen Grantham, eds. *National Endowment for the Arts: A History 1965–2008*. Washington, DC: National Endowment for the Arts, 2009.

Baumol, William J. *Performing Arts: The Economic Dilemma: A Study of Problems Common to Theater, Opera, Music, and Dance*. New York: Twentieth Century Fund, 1966.

Baumol, William J., and William G. Bowen. "On the Performing Arts: The Anatomy of Their Economic Problems." *American Economic Review* 55, no. 1/2 (1965): 495–502.

Beal, Amy. *New Music, New Allies: American Experimental Music in West Germany from the Zero Hour to Reunification.* Berkeley: University of California Press, 2006.

Becker, Howard S. *Art Worlds.* Berkeley: University of California Press, 1982.

Belfy, Jeanne Marie. *The Commissioning Project of the Louisville Orchestra, 1948–1958: A Study of the History and Music.* Louisville: UMI Publishers, 1986.

Benedict, Stephen, ed. *Public Money and the Muse: Essays on Government Funding for the Arts.* New York: Norton, 1991.

Berman, Edward. *The Ideology of Philanthropy: The Influence of the Carnegie, Ford, and Rockefeller Foundations on American Foreign Policy.* Albany: State University of New York Press, 1983.

Bernstein, David, ed. *The San Francisco Tape Music Center: 1960s Counterculture and the Avant-Garde.* Berkeley: University of California Press, 2008.

Bhaskar, Michael. *Curation: The Power of Selection in a World of Excess.* London: Piatkus, 2016.

Binkiewicz, Donna. *Federalizing the Muse: United States Art Policy and the National Endowment for the Arts, 1965–1980.* Chapel Hill: University of North Carolina Press, 2004.

Bohlman, Andrea. *Musical Solidarities: Political Action and Music in Late Twentieth-Century Poland.* Oxford: Oxford University Press, 2019.

Born, Georgina. *Rationalizing Culture: IRCAM, Boulez, and the Institutionalization of the Musical Avant-Garde.* Berkeley: University of California Press, 1995

Bourdieu, Pierre. *Distinction: A Social Critique of the Judgement of Taste.* London: Routledge & Kegan Paul, 1986.

———. "The Forms of Capital." In *Handbook of Theory and Research for the Sociology of Education,* edited by John Richardson, 241–58. New York: Greenwood, 1986.

———. *The Logic of Practice.* Translated by Richard Nice. Palo Alto: Stanford University Press, 1990.

Bourdieu, Pierre, and Randal Johnson. *The Field of Cultural Production: Essays on Art and Literature.* European Perspectives. New York: Columbia University Press, 1993.

Bourdieu, Pierre, and Loïc J. D. Wacquant. *An Invitation to Reflexive Sociology.* Chicago: University of Chicago Press, 1992.

Brackett, David. *Categorizing Sound: Genre and Twentieth-Century Popular Music.* Oakland: University of California Press, 2016.

Bremner, Robert H. *American Philanthropy.* 2nd ed. Chicago: University of Chicago Press, 1988.

Brody, Martin. "Class of '54: Friendship and Ideology at the American Academy in Rome." In *Music and Musical Composition at the American Academy in Rome,* edited by Martin Brody, 222–56. Rochester: University of Rochester Press, 2014.

———. "Review: Joseph Straus, Twelve-Tone Music in America." *Journal of the American Musicological Society* 65, no. 1 (2012): 291–97.

Broyles, Michael. *Mavericks and Other Traditions in American Music.* New Haven, CT: Yale University Press, 2004.

Callahan, David. *The Givers: Wealth, Power, and Philanthropy in a New Gilded Age.* New York: Vintage Books, 2017.

Cameron, Catherine M. *Dialectics in the Arts: The Rise of Experimentalism in American Music.* Westport, CT: Praeger, 1996.

Carroll, Mark. *Music and Ideology in Cold War Europe.* Cambridge: Cambridge University Press, 2003.

Cheng, William. "Staging Overcoming: Narratives of Disability and Meritocracy in Reality Singing Competitions." *Journal of the Society for American Music* 11, no. 2 (2017): 184–214.

Clotfelter, Charles T., ed. *Who Benefits from the Nonprofit Sector?* Chicago: University of Chicago Press, 1992.

Collins, Harry, and Robert Evans. *Rethinking Expertise.* Chicago: University of Chicago Press, 2007.

Colwell, Mary Anna Culleton. "The Foundation Connection: Links Among Foundations and Recipient Organizations." In *Philanthropy and Cultural Imperialism: The Foundations at Home and Abroad,* edited by Robert F. Arnove, 413–52. Boston: G. K. Hall & Co., 1980.

Cordelli, Chiara. "Reparative Justice and the Moral Limits of Discretionary Philanthropy." In *Philanthropy in Democratic Societies,* edited by Rob Reich, Chiara Cordelli, and Lucy Bernholz, 244–65. Chicago: University of Chicago Press, 2016.

Covey, Paul Michael. "'No Restrictions in Any Way on Style': The Ford Foundation's Composers in Public Schools Program, 1959–1969." *American Music* 33, no. 1 (Spring 2015): 89–130.

Crawford, Richard. "MUSA's Early Years: The Life and Times of a National Editing Project." *American Music* 23, no. 1 (2005): 1–38.

Cuninggim, Merrimon. *Private Money and Public Service: The Role of Foundations in American Society.* New York: McGraw-Hill Book Company, 1972.

DiMaggio, Paul. "Decentralization of Arts Funding from the Federal Government to the States." In *Public Money and the Muse: Essays on Government Funding for the Arts,* edited by Stephen Benedict, 216–56. New York: W.W. Norton, 1991.

DiMaggio, Paul, and Francie Ostrower. "Participation in the Arts by Black and White Americans." *Social Forces* 68, no. 3 (1990): 753–78.

DiMaggio, Paul, and Michael Useem. "Cultural Democracy in a Period of Cultural Expansion: The Social Composition of Arts Audiences in the United States." *Social Problems* 26, no. 2 (1978): 179–97.

———. "Social Class and Arts Consumption: The Origins and Consequences of Class Differences in Exposure to the Arts in America." *Theory and Society* 5, no. 2 (1978): 141–61.

Dorian, Frederick. *Commitment to Culture: Art Patronage in Europe, Its Significance for America.* Pittsburgh: University of Pittsburgh Press, 1964.

Drezner, Daniel. *The Ideas Industry: How Pessimists, Partisans, and Plutocrats Are Transforming the Marketplace of Ideas.* Oxford: Oxford University Press, 2017.

Easterly, William. *The Tyranny of Experts: Economists, Dictators, and the Forgotten Rights of the Poor.* New York: Basic Books, 2015.

English, James F. *The Economy of Prestige: Prizes, Awards, and the Circulation of Cultural Value.* Cambridge, MA: Harvard University Press, 2005.

Epstein, Louis K. "Toward a Theory of Patronage: Funding for Music Composition in France, 1918–1939." Harvard University, 2013.

Ericsson, K. Anders, Neil Charness, Robert R. Hoffman, and Paul J. Feltovich, eds. *The Cambridge Handbook of Expertise and Expert Performance.* Cambridge: Cambridge University Press, 2006.

Evans, Robert. "The Sociology of Expertise: The Distribution of Social Fluency." *Sociology Compass* 2, no. 1 (2008): 281–98.

Evetts, Julia, Harald Mieg, and Ulrike Felt. "Chapter 7: Professionalization, Scientific Expertise, and Elitism: A Sociological Perspective." In *The Cambridge Handbook of Expertise and Expert Performance*, 105–23. Cambridge: Cambridge University Press, 2006.

Fischer, Frank. *Democracy and Expertise*. Oxford: Oxford University Press, 2009.

Flanagan, Robert J. *The Perilous Life of Symphony Orchestras: Artistic Triumphs and Economic Challenges*. New Haven, CT: Yale University Press, 2012.

Fleishman, Joel L. *The Foundation: A Great American Secret: How Private Wealth Is Changing the World*. New York: Public Affairs, 2007.

Ford Foundation. *The Finances of the Performing Arts: A Survey of 166 Professional Nonprofit Resident Theaters, Operas, Symphonies, Ballets, and Modern Dance Companies*. Vol. 1. 2 vols. New York: Ford Foundation, 1974.

———. "The Ford Foundation: Millions for Music—Music for Millions." *Music Educators Journal* 53, no. 1 (1966): 83–86.

———. *Sharps and Flats: A Report on Ford Foundation Assistance to American Music*. New York: Ford Foundation, 1980.

Fosdick, Raymond. *The Story of the Rockefeller Foundation*. New York: Harper & Brothers, 1952.

Fosler-Lussier, Danielle. *Music in America's Cold War Diplomacy*. Berkeley: University of California Press, 2015.

Frey, Bruno. *Arts and Economics: Analysis and Cultural Policy*. Berlin: Springer Verlag, 2000.

Frith, Simon. *Performing Rites: On the Value of Popular Music*. Cambridge, MA: Harvard University Press, 1996.

Gable, David, and Christoph Wolff, eds. *A Life for New Music: Selected Papers of Paul Fromm*. Cambridge, MA: Harvard University Press, 1988.

Garafola, Lynn. "Dollars for Dance: Lincoln Kirstein, City Center, and the Rockefeller Foundation." *Dance Chronicle* 25, no. 1 (2002): 101–14.

Garrett, Charles Hiroshi. *Struggling to Define a Nation: American Music and the Twentieth Century*. Berkeley: University of California Press, 2008.

Giddens, Anthony. *The Consequences of Modernity*. Palo Alto: Stanford University Press, 1990.

Gilmore, Samuel. "Minorities and Distributional Equity at the National Endowment for the Arts." *Journal of Arts Management, Law & Society* 23, no. 2 (1993): 137–73.

Giridharadas, Anand. *Winner Takes All: The Elite Charade of Changing the World*. New York: Alfred A. Knopf, 2018.

Giving USA: The Annual Report on Philanthropy for the Year 2016. Chicago: Giving USA Foundation, 2017.

Grenfell, Michael, and Cheryl Hardy. *Art Rules: Pierre Bourdieu and the Visual Arts*. Oxford: Berg, 2007.

Hamm, Charles. *Music in the New World*. New York: Norton, 1983.

Harris, John. *Government Patronage of the Arts in Great Britain*. Chicago: University of Chicago Press, 1970.

Heckscher, August. *The Arts and the National Government: A Report to the President*. Washington, DC: U.S. Government Printing Office, 1963.

Herrera, Eduardo. *Elite Art Worlds: Philanthropy, Latin Americanism, and Avant-Garde Music*. Oxford: Oxford University Press, forthcoming.

———. "The Rockefeller Foundation and Latin American Music in the 1960s: The Creation of Indiana University's LAMC and Di Tella Institute's CLAEM." *American Music* 35, no. 1 (2017): 51–74.

Hixson, Walter. *Parting the Curtain: Propaganda, Culture, and the Cold War, 1945–1961*. Basingstoke: MacMillan, 1997.

Hobsbawm, Eric, and Terence Ranger, eds. *The Invention of Tradition*. Cambridge: Cambridge University Press, 1983.

Horowitz, Joseph. *Classical Music in America: A History of Its Rise and Fall*. New York: W.W. Norton, 2005.

Hubbs, Nadine. *The Queer Composition of America's Sound: Gay Modernists, American Music, and National Identity*. Berkeley: University of California Press, 2004.

Jakelski, Lisa. *Making New Music in Cold War Poland: The Warsaw Autumn Festival, 1956–1968*. Berkeley: University of California Press, 2016.

Jones, LeRoi. *Blues People: Negro Music in White America*. New York: William Morrow and Company, 1963.

Katz-Gerro, Tally, and Oriel Sullivan. "Voracious Cultural Consumption: The Intertwining of Gender and Social Status." *Time & Society* 19, no. 2 (2010): 193–219.

Khan, Shamus R. *Privilege: The Making of an Adolescent Elite at St. Paul's School*. Princeton, NJ: Princeton University Press, 2011.

Kingsbury, Henry. *Music, Talent, and Performance: A Conservatory Cultural System*. Philadelphia: Temple University Press, 1988.

Kurin, Richard. *Reflections of a Culture Broker: A View from the Smithsonian*. Washington, DC: Smithsonian Institution Press, 1997.

Lamont, Michèle. *How Professors Think: Inside the Curious World of Academic Judgment*. Cambridge, MA: Harvard University Press, 2010.

Larson, Gary. *The Reluctant Patron: The United States Government and the Arts, 1943–1965*. Philadelphia: University of Pennsylvania Press, 1983.

Lehmann, Andreas C., and Hans Gruber. "Chapter 26: Music." In *The Cambridge Handbook of Expertise and Expert Performance*, 457–70. Cambridge: Cambridge University Press, 2006.

Levine, Lawrence W. *Highbrow/Lowbrow: The Emergence of Cultural Hierarchy in America*. Cambridge, MA: Harvard University Press, 1988.

Lindsay, Tedrin Blair. "The Coming of Age of American Opera: New York City Opera and the Ford Foundation, 1958–1960." University of Kentucky, 2009.

Locke, Ralph, and Cyrilla Barr, eds. *Cultivating Music in America: Women Patrons and Activists Since 1860*. Berkeley: University of California Press, 1997.

MacAskill, William. *Doing Good Better: How Effective Altruism Can Help You Make a Difference*. New York: Gotham Books, 2015.

Macdonald, Dwight. "The Philanthropoids." *The New Yorker*, December 10, 1955.

Madeja, Stanley. "Kathryn Bloom and the Genesis of the Arts in Education Movement." *Art Education* 45, no. 4 (1992): 45–51.

Madoff, Ray D. "When Is Philanthropy?: How the Tax Code's Answer to This Question Has Given Rise to the Growth of Donor-Advised Funds and Why It's a Problem." In *Philanthropy in Democratic Societies*, edited by Rob Reich, Chiara Cordelli, and Lucy Bernholz, 158–76. Chicago: University of Chicago Press, 2016.

Margo, Robert. "Chapter 7: Foundations." In *Who Benefits from the Nonprofit Sector?*, edited by Charles T. Clotfelter, 207–34. Chicago: University of Chicago Press, 1992.

Mark, Charles. *Reluctant Bureaucrats: The Struggles to Establish the National Endowment for the Arts*. Dubuque, IA: Kendall/Hunt Pub. Co., 1991.

McCarthy, Kathleen. "From Cold War to Cultural Development: The International Cultural Activities of the Ford Foundation, 1950–1980." *Daedalus* 116, no. 1 Philanthropy, Patronage, Politics (1987): 93–117.

———, ed. *Women, Philanthropy, and Civil Society*. Bloomington: Indiana University Press, 2001.

Merton, Robert. "The Matthew Effect in Science." *Science* 159, no. 3810 (1968): 56–63.

———. *The Sociology of Science: Theoretical and Empirical Investigations*. Chicago: University of Chicago, 1973.

Mieg, Harald. "Chapter 41: Social and Sociological Factors in the Development of Expertise." In *The Cambridge Handbook of Expertise and Expert Performance*, 743–60. Cambridge: Cambridge University Press, 2006.

———. *The Social Psychology of Expertise*. Mahwah, NJ: Erlbaum, 2001.

Mills, Charles Wright. *The Power Elite*. New ed. Oxford: Oxford University Press, 2000.

Monson, Ingrid. *Freedom Sounds: Civil Rights Call Out to Jazz and Africa*. Oxford: Oxford University Press, 2007.

Morris, Robert. "Listening to Milton Babbitt's Electronic Music: The Medium and the Message." *Perspectives of New Music* 35, no. 2 (1997): 85–99.

Muller, Jerry. *The Tyranny of Metrics*. Princeton, NJ: Princeton University Press, 2018.

Murphy, Raymond. *Social Closure: The Theory of Monopolization and Exclusion*. Oxford: Clarendon Press, 1988.

Negley, Ben. "The Ford Foundation Symphony Orchestra Program." *Journal of Musicological Research* 36, no. 2 (2017): 1–28.

Nichols, Tom. *The Death of Expertise: The Campaign Against Established Knowledge and Why It Matters*. Oxford: Oxford University Press, 2017.

Oja, Carol. *Making Music Modern: New York in the 1920s*. Oxford: Oxford University Press, 2000.

———. "'Picked Young Men,' Facilitating Women, and Emerging Composers: Establishing an American Prix de Rome." In *Music and Musical Composition at the American Academy in Rome*, edited by Martin Brody, 159–94. Rochester: University of Rochester Press, 2014.

Origgi, Gloria. *Reputation: What It Is and Why It Matters*. Princeton, NJ: Princeton University Press, 2017.

Packer, Renee Levine. *This Life of Sounds: Evenings for New Music in Buffalo*. Oxford: Oxford University Press, 2010.

Pantoja, Antonia, Wilhemina Perry, and Barbara Blourock. "Towards the Development of Theory: Cultural Pluralism Redefined." *Journal of Sociology and Social Welfare* 4, no. 1 (1976): 125–46.

Parmar, Inderjeet. *Foundations of the American Century: The Ford, Carnegie, and Rockefeller Foundations in the Rise of American Power*. New York: Columbia University Press, 2012.

Pasler, Jann. *Composing the Citizen: Music as Public Utility in Third Republic France*. Berkeley: University of California Press, 2009.

———. *Writing Through Music: Essays on Music, Culture, and Politics*. Oxford: Oxford University Press, 2008.

Peterson, Richard. "Problems in Comparative Research: The Example of Omnivorousness." *Poetics* 33 (2005): 257–82.

———. "The Rise and Fall of Highbrow Snobbery as a Status Marker." *Poetics* 25 (1997): 75–92.

———. "Understanding Audience Segmentation: From Elite and Mass to Omnivore and Univore." *Poetics* 21 (1992): 243–58.

Peterson, Richard, and Roger M. Kern. "Changing Highbrow Taste: From Snob to Omnivore." *American Sociological Review* 61, no. 5 (1996): 900–907.

Piketty, Thomas. *Capital in the Twenty-First Century.* Translated by Arthur Goldhammer. Cambridge, MA: Belknap Press of Harvard University, 2014.

Polanyi, Michael. *Personal Knowledge: Towards a Post-Critical Philosophy.* Chicago: University of Chicago Press, 1958.

Pollack, Howard. *Aaron Copland: The Life and Work of an Uncommon Man.* New York: Henry Holt and Company, 1999.

Power, Ian. "The New Musical Imaginary: Description as Distraction in New Music." *Tempo* 73, no. 289 (2019): 6–20.

Putnam, Robert. *Bowling Alone: The Collapse and Revival of American Community.* New York: Simon and Schuster, 2000.

Reich, Rob. *Just Giving: Why Philanthropy Is Failing Democracy and How It Can Do Better.* Princeton, NJ: Princeton University Press, 2018.

Reich, Rob, Chiara Cordelli, and Lucy Bernholz, eds. *Philanthropy in Democratic Societies: Histories, Institutions, Values.* Chicago: University of Chicago Press, 2016.

Rivera, Lauren A. *Pedigree: How Elite Students Get Elite Jobs.* Princeton, NJ: Princeton University Press, 2015.

Robin, William. "Balance Problems: Neoliberalism and New Music in the American University and Ensemble." *Journal of the American Musicological Society* 72, no. 3 (2018): 749–93.

———. *Industry: Bang on a Can and New Music in the Marketplace.* Oxford: Oxford University Press, forthcoming.

Rockefeller Brothers Fund. *The Performing Arts: Problems and Prospects: Rockefeller Panel Report on the Future of Theatre, Dance, Music in America.* New York: McGraw-Hill Book Company, 1965.

Rockefeller, Nelson. "The Value of Art Education." *Art Education* 28, no. 6 (1975): 6–25.

Roelofs, Joan. *Foundations and Public Policy: The Mask of Pluralism.* Albany: State University of New York Press, 2003.

Sargeant, Winthrop. *Listening to Music.* Westport, CT: Greenwood Press, 1958.

Schmelz, Peter. "Review: Twelve-Tone Music in America." *Notes* 67, no. 2 (2010): 320–23.

Scott, W. Richard. *Organizations: Rational, Natural, and Open Systems.* Englewood Cliffs, NJ: Prentice-Hall, 1981.

Shaplen, Robert. *Toward the Well-Being of Mankind: Fifty Years of the Rockefeller Foundation.* New York: Doubleday & Company, 1964.

Shreffler, Anne. "Ideologies of Serialism: Stravinsky's 'Threni' and the Congress for Cultural Freedom." In *Music and the Aesthetics of Modernity*, edited by Karol Berger and Anthony Newcomb, 217–45. Cambridge, MA: Harvard University Press, 2005.

———. "The Myth of Empirical Historiography: A Response to Joseph N. Straus." *Musical Quarterly* 84, no. 1 (2000): 30–39.

Sidford, Holly. "Fusing Arts, Culture, and Social Change: High Impact Strategies for Philanthropy." National Committee for Responsive Philanthropy, 2011.

Simeone, Nigel, ed. *The Leonard Bernstein Letters.* New Haven, CT: Yale University Press, 2013.

Singer, Peter. *The Most Good You Can Do: How Effective Altruism Is Changing Ideas About Living Ethically.* New Haven, CT: Yale University Press, 2015.

Skocpol, Theda. *Diminished Democracy: From Membership to Management in American Civic Life.* Norman: University of Oklahoma Press, 2003.

Small, Christopher. *Musicking: The Meanings of Performing and Listening.* Middletown, CT: Wesleyan University Press, 1998.

Spellman, A. B. *Four Jazz Lives.* Ann Arbor: University of Michigan Press, 2004.

Stead, Bette. "Corporate Giving: A Look at the Arts." *Journal of Business Ethics* 4, no. 3 (1985): 215–22.

Stern, Isaac, with Chaim Potok. *My First 79 Years.* New York: Alfred A. Knopf, 1999.

Straight, Michael. *Nancy Hanks, An Intimate Portrait: The Creation of a National Commitment to the Arts.* Durham, NC: Duke University Press, 1988.

Straus, Joseph N. "The Myth of Serial 'Tyranny' in the 1950s and 1960s." *Musical Quarterly* 83, no. 3 (1999): 301–43.

———. "A Revisionist History of Twelve-Tone Serialism in American Music." *Journal of the Society for American Music* 2, no. 3 (2008): 355–95.

———. *Twelve-Tone Music in America.* Cambridge: Cambridge University Press, 2009.

Swayne, Steve. *Orpheus in Manhattan: William Schuman and the Shaping of America's Musical Life.* New York: Oxford University Press, 2011.

Taylor, Fannie, and Anthony Barresi. *The Arts at a New Frontier: The National Endowment for the Arts.* New York: Plenum Press, 1984.

Taylor, Nick. *American-Made: The Enduring Legacy of the WPA: When FDR Put the Nation to Work.* New York: Bantam Books, 2008.

Thompson Jr., Frank. "Are the Communists Right in Calling Us Cultural Barbarians?" *Music Journal* 13, no. 6 (1955): 5.

Thompson, James D. *Organizations in Action: Social Science Bases of Administrative Theory.* New York: McGraw-Hill, 1967.

Thomson, Virgil. *The State of Music.* New York: W. Morrow and Company, 1939.

Thorndike, Edward L. "A Constant Error in Psychological Ratings." *Journal of Applied Psychology* 4, no. 1 (1920): 25–29.

Tocqueville, Alexis de. *Democracy in America.* 2nd ed. New York: Vintage Books, 1990.

Turner, Ralph H. "Sponsored and Contest Mobility and the School System." *American Sociological Review* 25, no. 6 (1960): 855–67.

Uy, Michael Sy. "Nations of Cultural Barbarians? Overcoming Cultural Inferiority and the Development of Government Patronage of the Arts in the United States and Great Britain." Oxford University, 2011.

Vandagriff, Rachel. "The History and Impact of the Fromm Music Foundation, 1952–1983." University of California, Berkeley, 2015.

———. "An Old Story in a New World: Paul Fromm, the Fromm Music Foundation, and Elliott Carter." *Journal of Musicology* 35, no. 4 (2018): 535–66.

———. "*Perspectives* and the Patron: Paul Fromm, Benjamin Boretz and *Perspectives of New Music*." *Journal of the Royal Musical Association* 142, no. 2 (2017): 327–65.

Veblen, Thorstein. *The Theory of the Leisure Class: An Economic Study in the Evaluation of Institutions*. New York: MacMillan, 1899.

von Eschen, Penny. *Satchmo Blows Up the World: Jazz Ambassadors Play the Cold War*. Cambridge, MA: Harvard University Press, 2004.

Walker, Darren. *From Generosity to Justice: A New Gospel of Wealth*. New York: Disruption Books, 2019.

Wuorinen, Charles. "The Outlook for Young Composers." *Perspectives of New Music* 1, no. 2 (1963): 54–61.

Wyszomirski, Margaret. "Congress, Presidents, and the Arts: Collaboration and Struggle." *Annals of the American Academy of Political and Social Science* 499 (1988): 124–35.

———. "The Politics of Art: Nancy Hanks and the National Endowment for the Arts." In *Leadership and Innovation: A Biographical Perspective on Entrepreneurs in Government*, edited by Jameson W. Doig and Erwin C. Hargrove, 171–209. Baltimore: Johns Hopkins University Press, 1987.

Zeigler, Joseph. *Arts in Crisis: The National Endowment for the Arts Versus America*. Chicago: A Cappella Books, 1994.

Index

For the benefit of digital users, indexed terms that span two pages (e.g., 52–53) may, on occasion, appear on only one of those pages.

Printed in the USA
CPSIA information can be obtained
at www.ICGtesting.com
CBHW052315151123
1919CB00004B/25